About The Author

Joe Pettitt is a freelance high-performance automotive journalist, photographer, and car-fi guy. He's written hundreds of articles for the performance press including *Hot Rod, Sport Compact Car, Drag Racer, Car Craft, Circle Track*, and *Motor Trend*. His adventures as a high-performance journalist include piloting IROC cars around the famous ovals of Daytona and Talladega and strapping into the world's fastest open road race record holder vehicle as a journalist/passenger. This mind-warping experience offered 27 minutes of sheer terror at over 220 mph while making the 90-mile Silver State Challenge run from Ely to Lund, Nev., with an average speed of over 194 mph. As a car audio journalist he wrote for *Autotronics* magazine, where he indulged his passion for great cars and great music.

An avid do-it-yourselfer, Pettitt modified and tuned numerous sports cars, hot rods, and street machines, installing sound systems in all of them. His favorite was a '59 XK 150 Jag. "I didn't have the most expensive gear in that car," said Pettitt, "but I installed it right and it made wonderful music as it moved swiftly through the turns and twist of the canyons of Southern California." Every time you build a car," says Pettitt, "you learn something new. You learn how to do it a little smarter and a little easier; you learn how to find the right people to answer your questions. Finding good information about installing nitrous oxide injection and super-tuning your engine isn't easy; but once you have it, it makes your high-performance projects run much smoother."

That's why SA Design had Pettitt write this book—to help you cut through all the marketing hype and get to the truth of the subject. He knows how to find the best experts in the field and get the real high-performance story.

Pettitt currently lives in his own virtual reality in Southern California with wife Patricia, stepdaughter, Vanessa, and their new baby daughter, Jordan. In addition to *How To Install Nitrous Oxide Injection*, and the *High Performance Honda Builder's Handbook*, Pettitt has written SA Design's *How to Install High-Performance Car Stereo*.

Credits

I wish to thank everyone who helped me with this book. Getting the facts, then writing them down in an intelligible way is a laborious, sometimes tedious, and frustrating yet rewarding endeavor. And while I doubt I can give an adequate account of all those deserving credit, I shall try.

Special thanks go to Louie Hammel. Though this project was originally his, a severe illness kept him from completing it. I was brought in as a hired pen, and took full advantage of his technical direction and years of nitrous experience to write a volume approximating his original concept.

I also want to express gratitude to Harold Bettes of SuperFlow, Corp. for additional guidance through the mathematical mirages of dynamometer data.

Thanks go to the crew at NOS, Mike Thermos, Karl Staggemeier, Bob Franzke, and in particular Mike Flynn. Flynn was an invaluable liaison at NOS. He help arrange photo sessions of installation procedures and product, as well as advising me on technical issues.

And I must bestow much gratitude to my family, especially my wife Patricia, for their patience as I threaded my way through this project.

By JOE PETTITT

On The Cover: The cover photo features a NOS port injection fogger system installed on a 355-cubic-inch small-block Chevy. This nitrous test engine was built with primarily off-the-shelf components available to anyone. The goal was to exceed 1000 horsepower, and while this engine had only exceeded 950 horsepower by press time, the author is confident that it will deliver the desired power level with tuning and final adjustments.

How To Install Nitrous Oxide Injection

By Joe Pettitt

EDITED BY
B. J. KILLEEN

PRODUCTION BY
JOHN BAECHTEL

OVERSEAS DISTRIBUTION BY:

BROOKLANDS BOOKS LTD.
P.O. BOX 146, Cobham, Surrey, KT11 1LG, England
Telephone 01932 865051 • FAX 01932 868803
http://www.brooklands-books.com

BROOKLANDS BOOKS LTD.
1/81 Darley Street, P.O. Box 199, Mona Vale, NSW 2103, Australia
Telephone 2 9997 8428 • FAX 2 9997 5799

ISBN 1-884089-22-4
PART No. SA50

CARTECH®, INC, 11481 KOST DAM RD., NORTH BRANCH, MN 55056
http://www.cartechbooks.com

CONTENTS

INTRODUCTION TO NITROUS OXIDE

Nitrous oxide has, for many years now, led a double life of sorts. In one life, its existence is based on myth, magic, legend, and fear. In its other life, it exists based on logic, ingenuity, imagination, and the laws of physics. Depending on who you may have talked to or what you may have read in all of your exposure to nitrous oxide, your personal opinion about nitrous could be shaped by one of either of these two lives, or somewhere in between. It's interesting to observe how different people approach something they don't immediately understand. Some people condemn anything that differs from whatever they're accustomed to in their daily routine. Some people are so "closed-minded" that they tend to be skeptical and distrust anything new or different. Remember when electronic ignition systems with their magnetic pickups and ignition modules replaced point-type ignition systems nearly overnight? I can still hear a few of the older dealership

mechanics cursing the new systems with comments like "How am I supposed to fix this thing if I can't take it apart to find out what's wrong with it?" or "How ya 'sposed 'ta fix a black box?. What they were really saying was "I don't know how this works, so I can't fix it." With today's vehicles, dealership mechanics have to learn the new systems, and quickly, or they can't do the work.

With nitrous oxide, the situation is the same. At the first sign of problems, there are always those who instantly blame the nitrous system for everything. On the other hand, there are those who are willing to spend a little extra time and effort to learn how nitrous works so that they can make an educated choice when the time comes to buy the correct type of system for their application or to track down a problem they may be dealing with right now. I'm willing to bet that you belong in the second group. This is a pretty safe bet because if you were in the first group of closed-minded people, you wouldn't even have read this far into this book. So, if you can spare a little more of your

time, I'll try to make sense of all this nitrous oxide mystery. Along the way, we'll spend time in the real world and try to get rid of those old myths and legends.—*Louie Hammel*

1.1
WHAT IS NITROUS OXIDE?

Nitrous oxide is a simple substance. It's composed of two (2) nitrogen atoms stuck to one (1) oxygen atom. The scientific abbreviation for nitrogen is N, and 0 for oxygen. The correct abbreviation for one nitrous oxide molecule is N_2O. This is where the familiar phrase "N-2-O" comes from when people talk about nitrous oxide. It's one of a family of various versions of nitrogen and oxygen that are all grouped under the name of "oxides of nitrogen." Another one of these combinations may also be familiar to you. It's routinely one of several things that are monitored by the Environmental Protection Agency (EPA) as a major component of air pollution and is commonly referred to as NO_X, which is a different combination of nitrogen and oxygen, this one poisonous to anything that depends on breathing air.

Nitrous oxide isn't poisonous and isn't harmful to the atmosphere or the ozone layer as are some refrigerants such as R-12 and R-22. The method recommended by the Compressed Gas Association (CGA) for disposing of nitrous oxide is simply to vent it slowly to atmosphere in an open area with no one close enough to breathe it in any significant concentrations. Occupational Safety and Health Administration (OSHA) lists nitrous oxide as a simple asphyxiant. This means you can't breathe it in moderate to high concentrations without the risk of being suffocated. Just like CO_2, nitrous oxide does not support life because it replaces or, more correctly, displaces the air that you should be breathing with a substance from which your lungs can't get any oxygen. The oxygen in nitrous oxide is stuck to the nitrogen, and your lungs don't have the ability to take it apart.

To set the record straight, the correct name is nitrous oxide. Common pronunciation mistakes and slang references include: Nitro Oxide, Nitric Oxide, Noss (obviously derived from NOS, which actually is the trademarked abbreviation used by Nitrous Oxide Systems, Inc.), Laughing Gas, Giggle Gas, On the Bottle, Squeeze (this one comes from the action of "squeezing" a push-button to activate a nitrous system), Juice, etc.

Nitrous oxide does not exist naturally in the atmosphere; it must be manufactured by various procedures that involve using heat and different forms of catalysts. Once produced, it's siphoned into cooling and compression vessels for storage and transfer into smaller tanks for distribution. It is available in three different grades: medical or USP, commercial, and High-Purity. The medical grade is the same as the other two except it must pass certain criteria to ensure that there are a minimum of impurities in it since this is the type the medical/dental profession uses. In the medical/ dental field it's used as a mild anesthetic by mixing it in low percentages into purified air and warmed to room temperature before being administered to a patient. This can only be obtained and used by licensed dental and medical profes-

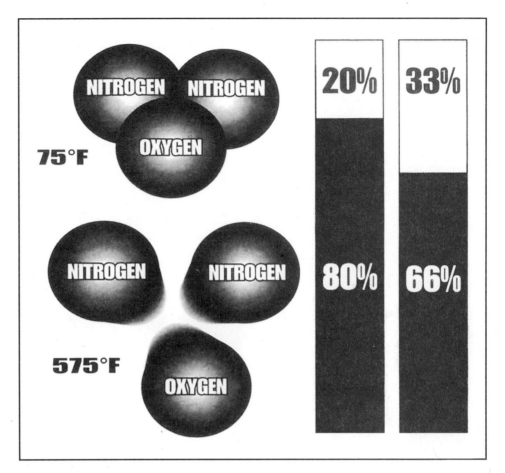

sionals. Don't waste your time trying to get this type of nitrous for your refills; there's absolutely *no* performance advantage to using this type.

High-Purity grade is used in some forms of cryosurgery and therefore must be extremely free of any impurities. This type also only can be obtained by licensed medical professionals.

The commercial grade is the type we use in our engines. The only type of nitrous oxide that you are likely to find on a wide scale across the United States is a particular version of commercial grade marketed and sold under the trademarked name, Nytrous+, by the Puritan-Bennett Corporation. This particular brand of nitrous oxide contains 99.9 percent nitrous oxide and 0.01 percent (that's one-hundredth of one percent) of sulfur dioxide. Sulfur dioxide is added as an odorizing agent and as an irritant to discourage substance abuse by ignorant people who try to achieve the laughing gas effect. Sulfur dioxide is highly irritating to the eyes, throat, and respira-

tory tract, but is virtually invisible to your engine and has no detrimental effect on the performance of your engine. Look for and use only this type when getting your nitrous tank refilled.

Nitrous oxide is stored by pumping it into a pressure vessel. The legal specifications for a nitrous oxide tank (pressure vessel) are the same as that used for carbon dioxide gas. It must have a certified working limit of 1800 pounds of pressure per square inch (psi). The tanks must have a certification date stamped into the tank near the outlet and must be current within five years. Your refill dealer will not refill your nitrous tank if it is out of date. If this happens, you'll need to pay a nominal fee for recertification. Depending on the resources of your refill dealer, they will either perform this service if they have the proper equipment or send it out to have it done.

Nitrous oxide, like many other substances is stored in its tank in a liquid form. This is only possible if the nitrous is stored at a high

The Puritan Bennett plant where nitrous oxide is manufactured in large quantities is a formidable-looking structure. Nytrous Plus with sulphurous odor added to prevent substance abuse is produced here.

enough pressure to liquify it. At room temperature and normal atmospheric pressure (14.7 psi @ sea level), nitrous oxide can only exist in a gaseous form. There are two ways to get nitrous oxide into a liquid state. You can cool it down until it liquifies or compress it with pressure until it liquifies. In order to cool it down enough, you would have to lower the temperature of the nitrous to 127 degrees Fahrenheit below zero. That's right, minus 127 degrees F. That would be difficult to do and not practical for the automotive world. The other choice is to compress it into a tank at high pressure. If the nitrous oxide was at a temperature of 70 degrees F, then you would have to compress it to 760 psi to make change to a liquid state. As the temperature of the nitrous oxide increases, the pressure required to keep it in a liquid state goes up. At 80 degrees F it takes 865 psi to keep it in a liquid state. This is far

easier to accomplish than the cooling method. Pressure tanks commonly are available for this type of pressure. This is how the automotive industry has handled this problem from the first use of nitrous oxide in the mid '60s. The main advantage of storing nitrous oxide under pressure in a liquid state is that it occupies much less space. This also makes things easier because no pump is needed for the nitrous oxide—the pressure supplies all the force necessary to make the nitrous oxide flow.

To control the flow of nitrous and the additional fuel are simple electrical valves called solenoids. A solenoid opens a passage by creating a strong magnetic field that moves a small plunger away from a hole and allows the nitrous or fuel to flow. When the electrical current is shut off, the plunger closes the hole and seals to stop the flow. In a modern nitrous system there are quite a few different ways to control

when the solenoids open and close. In the first years of automotive uses of nitrous oxide, the solenoids were controlled with a simple momentary push-button that the driver operated manually whenever he wanted the system to come on. Today, there are components available that will do this for the driver at a predetermined rpm point or time. There are even systems that will start the operation of the nitrous system at a low power level and smoothly reach full power according to the time for which it is preset. This works best with high-power systems that would otherwise have traction problems when the vehicle is just beginning to move.

Once the system is on and flowing, the nitrous oxide and additional fuel are introduced into the intake system of the engine and carried to the individual cylinders along with the normal air/fuel mixture. All nitrous systems should only be activated at wide-open-throttle. You normally control the engine's power by throttling it. This means that you are controlling how much air and fuel is entering the engine by varying the position of the accelerator pedal. As you drive the vehicle, you open the throttle more and more until you reach the necessary power level. If you get to the point of maximum throttle opening and that isn't enough, then you activate the nitrous system. Since there is a limited amount of nitrous in the nitrous tank, you would just be wasting it if you used during part-throttle.

There are many different ways to get the nitrous and additional fuel into the engine. Form a simple spacer-type plate and install it between the carburetor base and the intake manifold, to individual mixer-type nozzles the are installed into each intake runner passage. Nearly all the types allow calibration changes for various power levels by implementing removable jets of various sizes. The individual pod nozzle arrangement allows for tuning any one cylinder differently than the others. This can be a valuable tuning tool for serious racing setups.

Work Safely: Always wear eye protection and gloves when working with lines or hoses that contain pressurized nitrous oxide or fuel. Never transport nitrous cylinders loose in a trunk or the back of a pick-up truck and especially not within a vehicle's interior, whether the cylinder is full or empty. Always disconnect the ground side of the battery when working on any electrical components.

Be Realistic About the Amount of Additional Power Your Engine Reliably Can Handle: If you're in doubt, it's always better to guess less than more. The various nitrous companies can lend some very valuable information concerning particular engine and component strength and durability. They don't want you to reach the point of damage any more than you do.

Consistency is Everything: Fluctuating fuel pressure, different nitrous cylinder temperatures, worn or sticky mechanical advance mechanisms, intermittent wiring problems, etc., can all lead to erratic system performance and possibly engine damage.

Nitrous Oxide Won't Fix Problems You Already Have: Before you install your nitrous system, be sure your engine is in good mechanical condition. Ignition or carburetor calibration problems become bigger when combined with nitrous oxide.

Install as Many Safety Devices as You Can: Power relays, oil pressure safety switches, wide-open-throttle switches, rpm-activated switches, and low fuel pressure safety switches are just a few examples of things you can install to ensure that your system can only be activated when the engine is running and is at wide-open-throttle.

Never Defeat the Operation of the Safety Relief Disc in the Nitrous Cylinder's Valve Stem: It's required by law and is there for your safety. Don't be stupid.

Never Drill, Machine, Weld, Deform, Scratch, Drop, or Modify a Nitrous Oxide Tank: Although some people have polished their tanks to a chrome-like appearance, even this isn't recommended because it removes a non-uniform layer of the tank's material that may or may not affect its integrity. Never attempt to subject a nitrous tank to any type of plating process because this often affects the strength of the tank's material.

Never Overfill Nitrous Cylinders: That tiny little bit extra will put you and others at great risk for injury. More often than not, when the cylinder warms up, the pressure goes above the limit of the safety relief disc and you lose all the nitrous you just paid for. If you are a retail dealer and you overfill a cylinder beyond its rated capacity in weight, whether intentional or not, you could be held liable for the consequences of any damages or injury. If your customer specifically requests an overfill, don't do it.

All the Power Comes From the Fuel, Not the Nitrous: Nitrous oxide is simply a tool that allows you to adjust how much and how quickly the engine burns the fuel. If the fuel isn't there, the power won't be either.

Avoid Detonation at All Times: Nitrous-enhanced detonation is much more damaging than detonation that occurs when naturally aspirated due to the increased amount of fuel available for releasing energy and the fact that more oxygen is present.

When You Check the Spark Plugs, Check Every Plug: Don't just spot check the easiest plug you can reach. Due to the wide possibility of air/fuel mixture variations, you need to check every plug for signs of detonation or other problems.

Always Start With the Recommended Calibration That Came With Your System: If your system is an adjustable type, begin with the lowest supplied level of calibration. Calibration is the combination or nitrous and fuel jets that determine how much nitrous and fuel will flow when the system is activated.

At the First Sign of Detonation, Backfire, or Misfire, Always Reduce the Nitrous Jet First: Don't think that you'll "cool things down" by adding more fuel. Since nitrous oxide is an oxidizer, the safest approach is to reduce the nitrous first, identify the problem, and go from there.

Check the Fuel and Nitrous Filter Screens on a Regular Basis: This rates right up there with the most common problems that can lead you in circles for days. It doesn't take much to alter the calibration. Even a small scrap of pipe sealing tape can cause big problems.

When Your System is Activated, If Something Doesn't Feel or Sound Right, Back Off: If you hear any detonation or feel anything unusual, get off the throttle. It's a lot less costly to check everything over than it is to just try to drive through it and break a lot of expensive parts.

Nitrous oxide does not make any power. In fact, engines in general don't make power. All of the power comes from the fuel that you put in the fuel tank. An engine isn't capable of making power. An engine can only release the potential energy contained in the fuel. The engine provides the proper environment to convert the potential energy of the fuel into motion. If there is little potential energy in the fuel, there will be little power available. Nitrous oxide supplies an additional amount of oxygen to the engine that allows the engine to burn the fuel at a faster rate. This additional oxygen also allows more fuel to be burned in the same time period as the engine would without the additional oxygen that comes from the nitrous oxide. And as we just stated, the power is released from the fuel, not the nitrous oxide. The nitrous oxide provides you with a tool to control how much and how quickly the fuel is burned. When fuel burns, it expands. This expansion is the pressure that pushes the piston down. The greater the force of the expansion, the greater the available power placed on the top of the piston—to a point, which brings us to the last portion of your introduction to this stuff we call nitrous oxide: the limitations of the engine.

The issue of nitrous breaking engines isn't really an issue about nitrous as much as it is an issue about making mistakes and misapplications. Anything can be broken with the correct amount of force. Since most adjustable nitrous systems can be calibrated for some high-potential power levels, the user must be acutely aware of the point at which the engine's components are going to fail. It can be much like an addiction. Once you are used to a certain power level, you begin to want more. If you ignore the maximum capabilities of the engine's strength then you would have only yourself to blame. The nitrous system did what it was supposed to do, which was to release more power. If that power level exceeded the strength of the engine's components, damage will occur. This, probably more than any other reason, is where nitrous gets a reputation for tearing up engines. Overestimating the power level the engine can adequately and reliably handle is what breaks engines, not nitrous oxide. The nitrous companies are responsible for delivering to you the amount of additional power you request. The container you provide to capture and transform this power is your responsibility, so it just makes good sense to learn as much as you can about your particular engine and its realistic limitations. Only then can you make an intelligent choice about which type of nitrous system best serves your purpose. With that said, let's get on to the matter of all the individual components of a nitrous oxide system and how they work. Welcome to the world of nitrous oxide!

1.3
STREETABLE 12-SECOND CIVIC
GARY KUDOS' TURBOCHARGED, 1.7 VTEC-POWERED CIVIC HYBRID

Yo!—Gary Kudos' super-clean Civic may look and drive mild mannered, but once he spools up the turbo and squeezes it, he's gone—through the quarter-mile in 12 seconds. And that's a fact, Jack.

He's driven his sleeping beast from his SoCal home to Sacramento, Calif., bolted on a set of slicks, laid down a couple of 12 second blasts, then drove it home. No problem. He's got his full interior, a sound system, windshield wipers, and heaters; this is a legit street car man, running in the 12s—dig?

How he does it is a simple matter of designing a good combination and tuning, though he's walking a razor's edge on the tuning.

The combination is straight-forward. After he and Eric Valdez, then working at Pro-Motion, swapped in the 1.7-liter GS-R drivetrain, Kudos had Dan Paramore Racing massage the head to work with a turbo and nitrous. Kudos knew the stock rods wouldn't hang with the cylinder pressures he'd be running so he installed Arias forged pistons and Cunningham rods, but otherwise left the bottomed alone. Then he proceeded, with the help of the crew at Pro Turbo, to pump up the engine with an HKS wastegated, intercooled, and EVC-controlled turbo system. Russ Collins advised on the injector sizing, which included the calculations for the nitrous and the use of an HKS Additional Injector Controller. The crew at NOS gave

Gary Kudos and Eric Valdez built this radical streeter. It turns consistent 12-second ETs and drives to and from the track.

This turbocharged 1.7-liter GS-R powered Civic hybrid posted about 370 horsepower at the wheels, or close to 400 horsepower at the flywheel.

When you're stuffing the engine with air from a turbo and injecting nitrous, you have to have a big wastegate to handle the exhaust flow. Valdez and Kudos use an HKS unit.

Valdez and Kudos tech support while chasing this wild combination.

Wild's the right word for this motor. On K&N's DynoJet dyno we saw close to 400 horsepower at the wheels. Running nitrous with a turbocharger is one of those hard-to-control combinations. But when it works, it works big. And when it doesn't...well you know the weak links on Honda engines. The cylinder sleeves rupture, which usually leads to hydro-lock and bends the rods or hangs one out of the block. But for now, Kudos' running strong. As long as he controls timing, fuel ratio, nitrous, and boost, he'll probably keep running strong, and maybe even stronger.

The transplanted 1.7-liter GS-R engine is almost a direct bolt in to the Civic's engine bay. The turbo hangs on a log-style exhaust manifold. Notice the NOS nitrous and fuel solenoids mounted on the firewall.

When it all comes together at the strip, man this little Civic flies. It'll slam the timing lights in 12 seconds.

FIVE POINT OH...YEAH

HOW KEN DUTTWEILER TURNS FIVE BOTTLE-FED LITERS INTO 8-SECOND ETS

For those unaware, Ken Duttweiler is one of the premier west coast engine builders. Though he's best known for his brutally powerful Turbocharged Buick V-6 engines, Duttweiler brings out the best of any engine on which he lays his wrench.

Take this happy, gassed Ford Mustang as an example. Under Duttweiler's guidance, the machine routinely posts eight-second blasts with its bottle fed Blue Oval small block. Nothing really fancy, it's just really fast. And since you've got a whole book of how to do it in your hands, we'll spare the words and let the images do the talking.

Duttweiler uses a time-based controlled-pl NOS system on this carbureted Ford sm block.

The plumbing is textbook perfect. This is ho your installation should look.

Scotty Canon's Pro Mod on the leave.

Wildest show in drag ra The variety of body s and the flamboyant char of the drivers and c make Pro Mods the entertaining form of drag ing. Cavernous cubic ca ty and huge doses of nitr 'Nuf

PRO MOD ACTION

The ultimate nitrous users are the IHRA Pro Modified machines. Affectionately known as doorslammers because, well, they have doors, these machines push the limit of nitrous technology to the edge and beyond. While not as powerful as Top Fuel cars, these cars still run production-based big blocks and lots of nitrous—three and more stages of it—to produce thousands of horsepower at the touch of a button.

The Pro Mod purge. Exhausting gaseous nitrous from the lines before a run is just part of the allure of the wildest drag cars in the world. Racers purge the line to get liquid nitrous up the solenoid. When the nitrous hits, its quicker, colder, and more powerful.

The extra nitrous solenoid is used with the time-based system controller, which flutters the nitrous injection to let the driver tune how quickly the nitrous system reaches full flow and power enhancement.

The purge valve line splices off the nltrous feed line just before the nitrous solenoid. Nitrous racers use purge valves to clear the feed line of boiled or gaseous nitrous so they get super-cooled liquid nitrous to the solenoid valve, thus delivering the most nitrous in the least amount of time.

... course, Duttweiler's crew ...unted the bottle so the liquid ...trous sloshes back toward the ...ckup tube during an acceleration ...n.

The fuel pump moves fuel through one line until it splits—one line for the carburetor, one line for the nitrous system. Both lines have fuel pressure gauges because fuel pressure is a critical tuning variable.

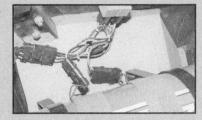

Detail of bottle heater wiring. Controlling bottle temperature is the nitrous racer's primary means of controlling bottle pressure. This is extremely important as you soon shall see.

A top-notch nitrous system depends on accurate fuel delivery. Duttweiler used a Weldon pump on this machine to deliver the fuel he calculated the engine needs, no matter how hard the car hooks.

Bottle pressure is of such importance that the gauge is displayed prominently on the dash. If it's not right, abort the run or you may be sweeping up your engine.

Some of the keys to quick and consistent ETs with nitrous.

Probably the best nitrous tuner in the business, ...agle Racing Engine's Mike Hedgecock is on hand at most Pro Mod races help-ing racers find the tune to put them in the winner's circle.

SOURCES

COMPUCAR
509 Old Edgefield Rd.
North Augusta, SC 29841
803/442-9206

NITROUS OXIDE SYSTEMS, INC.
2970 Airway Avenue
Costa Mesa, CA 92626
714/545-0580 (Tech line)
714/545-8319 (Fax line)

THE NITROUS WORKS
Rte. 1, Box 1900
Dahlonega, GA 30533
706/864-7009

10,000 RPM
SPEED EQUIPMENT
42541 6th St. E.
Lancaster, CA 93535
805/942-1312

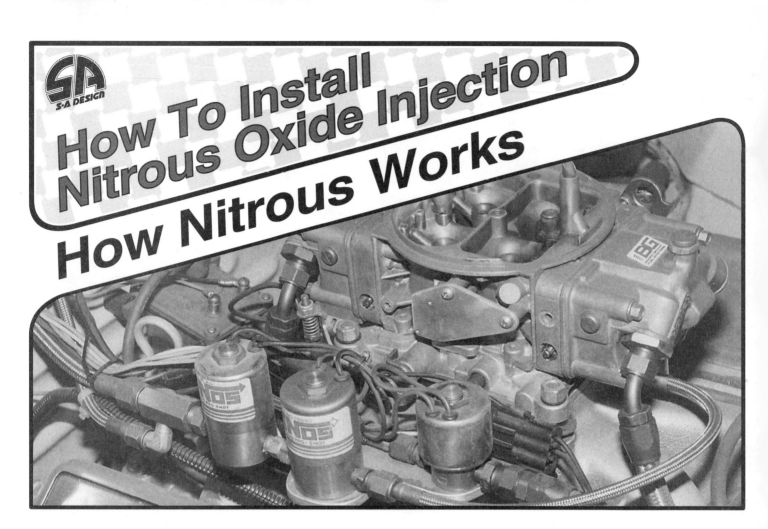

How To Install Nitrous Oxide Injection
How Nitrous Works

NITROUS FUNDAMENTALS

The fundamentals of nitrous begin with this concept: An engine is a mechanical device that releases heat energy from fuel and captures some of that energy in the form of torque. Torque is the twisting force we put to work in our race cars through spinning gears and wheels. The important fact to remember is that, without fuel, an engine creates no power or force.

Fuel, in so far as this discussion is concerned, is gasoline. Gasoline is a volatile liquid petroleum distillation that when atomized and heated to a high temperature wants to rapidly combine its atoms with oxygen atoms. A huge amount of heat is released during such a chemical reaction. The heat causes the gases in the combustion chamber to expand, thereby forcing the piston down the cylinder. This linear force of the piston is turned to a rotational force by the piston rods connected to the crankshaft.

2.1.1
FUEL BURNS FASTER
WITH MORE OXYGEN

The second concept is that fuel burns faster when more oxygen is present and slower with less oxygen. It is through the mechanism of this observed behavior of gasoline that, superchargers, turbochargers, and nitrous oxide make power. All three of these techniques put more oxygen and more fuel in the combustion chamber. The first two work by mechanically forcing more fuel and atmosphere and therefore more oxygen into the chambers.

Nitrous, in contrast, uses chemistry and stored mechanical energy to insert more oxygen and fuel into an engine's combustion chambers. The stored mechanical energy I'm referring to is the fact that nitrous gas is so highly compressed that it takes a liquid form. When released from the bottle it expands and is able to absorb heat, thus super-cooling the intake charge. By super-cooling the intake charge, the expanding nitrous gas increases the density, and therefore the oxygen content, of the intake charge.

The bottom line is that Nitrous works with an engine's fuel. It isn't a fuel unto itself. In fact, nitrous is similar to air. Earth's atmosphere is basically 80 percent nitrogen and 20 percent oxygen. (We're not going to break it down to all its components, which includes carbon dioxide, carbon monoxide, and a number of other politically active ingredients.) Nitrous oxide by comparison is 33 percent oxygen and 66 percent nitrogen. In other words it is two thirds nitrogen and one third oxygen. This is expressed by its chemical name N2O, which translates to one oxygen atom bound to two nitrogen atoms.

You might think if oxygen is so chock full of power potential, why not inject pure oxygen into an engine?

Dumping pure oxygen into your engine's combustion chambers without controlling the ratio then lighting it off would just burn a hole through the pistons. Pure oxygen can react with just about anything, but it's really fond of aluminum. You know about the solid rocket boosters on the space shuttle? The solid part is powered aluminum to which oxygen is added to create an intense hot fire. More oxygen in an engine's combustion chambers means a hotter as well as faster burn. You must add more fuel to control the rate and temperature. For maximum performance, you have to control the burn rate and the temperature precisely. Here's why.

It has to do with two things. First is the optimum timing, in crankshaft degrees, of peak cylinder pressure. Second is detonation. Detonation occurs when the fuel in the chamber develops one or more flame fronts and burns in an uncontrolled fashion. The rattling you sometime hear during severe detonation is the flame fronts colliding and the resulting pressure spikes.

2.1.2
THE IMPORTANCE OF TIMING MAX CYLINDER PRESSURE

The timing and control of peak pressure during the power stroke is the holy grail of engine tuners. Get the timing and burn rate right and the pressure builds gradually to force the piston down the cylinder with great intensity for a long time. It's beneficial to have the pressure build gradually. A long controlled burn, by definition, inhibits detonation and lengthens the amount of time the expanding charge exerts the most force against the piston without destroying it. The longer and more intense you can make cylinder pressure at the right time, the more power an engine will produce.

Detonation destroys engines and while it is doing so does not create much power. A four-cycle gasoline-fueled engine cannot capture much energy from detonation-generated pressure spikes. All the energy of the intake charge is released too quickly, focusing the force on the top of the piston. It's like the difference between driving a stake into the ground with a sledgehammer and shooting the end of the stake with a hunting rifle. There is so much force generated so quickly during detonation that it can crush the top of the piston, collapse the upper ring lands, punch holes through the pistons, destroy rod and main bearings...the list of bad things detonation can do to an engine just goes on and on. So it's important to control how the fuel burns.

2.2.0
FOUR TECHNIQUES TO CONTROL MAX CYLINDER PRESSURE TIMING

You have four techniques at your disposal to control burn rate (to avoid detonation) and peak pressure timing. One is the compression ratio of the engine. Two is the octane rating and chemistry of the fuel you choose. Three is the amount and ratio of oxygen to fuel present in the combustion chamber. Four is ignition timing. Balancing these four factors is really the essence of tuning an engine.

2.2.1
COMPRESSION RATIO

Decide on a compression ratio before you build your engine. If you're installing a nitrous system on a stock engine, or one that's already screwed together, you have to at least know its compression ratio. An engine's compression ratio is equal to the cylinder and combustion chamber volume divided by the combustion chamber volume. For example, an engine with a combined cylinder and chamber volume of 100 cc's at Bottom Dead Center (BDC) and only 10 cc's at Top Dead Center (TDC) has a compression ratio of 10 to 1.

2.2.1.1
STATIC VS. DYNAMIC COMPRESSION

We need to discriminate between static compression and dynamic compression ratios. Static is just that, the volumes of the cylinder and combustion chambers mentioned above. Dynamic compression ratio is the real compression ratio achieved in the chambers with the engine running and making power. Once you get air moving in columns as it is in an intake manifold and in the exhaust headers, the air's inertia forces more air in the cylinder than the physical volume of the cylinder. In other words charge air density is increased. If there's more air in the cylinder at the start of the compression stroke, all other things being equal, you'll get a slightly higher compression ratio. Factors affecting volumetric efficiency and therefore the dynamic compression ratio of an engine include but are not

limited to the intake runner design, head porting, and camshaft profile.

You might as well consider the dynamic compression ratio as the real comp torque.

While we can't give a recommendation for every combination, we can give a general baseline for a street-driven engine combination using pump gas. Assuming 92 octane premium, 10:1 static compression ratio is about as high a compression ratio as you should run. This should put the dynamic compression ratio, assuming a real world street cam, right around 9.5:1 at the best VE point, which we'll guesstimate as 85 percent.

2.2.1.2
CAM CONSCIOUSNESS

Nitrous engines respond to different cam profiles than naturally aspirated engines Choosing the right cam is one of your more important decisions in order to get the most from your engine combination.

Nitrous engines are sensitive to dynamic compression ratio changes, so be aware how certain cam grind affect this parameter. In general, a cam with a shorter duration will yield a higher compression ratio than a cam with a longer duration. For an engine with a static compression ratio of 12:1, using a cam with less than about 240 degrees of duration measured at 0.050 lift can get you into detonation rather quickly.

Another consideration is exhaust duration. Nitrous engines receive a lot of fuel and oxygen due to the super-cooled, high-density charge. Once it's burned and expanded, it needs to come out of the engine. Because of this, a cam with ample exhaust duration consistently makes more horsepower. Bear in mind, however, that simply increasing exhaust duration, i.e., opening the valve earlier and closing it later, will change the overlap and therefore the dynamic compression ratio as well as the amount of time the intake and exhaust tracts communicate. Most engine tuners agree that nitrous engines respond better if the increased exhaust duration is gained by opening the valve earlier in the cycle.

As with all things engine related, it's the exact combination of components and tuning that make power. So you should check with your engine builder or the component manufacturer for specific information regarding your combination.

2.2.2
OCTANE RATING

The reason we're concerned with compression ratio is because the charge (fuel mixed with air) can only be compressed so much before the mixture ignites prematurely, or detonates. Fuels are rated by their resistance to compression caused ignition or detonation. That's what an octane rating is. A higher octane number corresponds to a fuel's greater resistance to reacting with oxygen from compression induced heat. High-octane fuels are more resistant to detonation than lower octane fuels. As we discussed, detonation is detrimental to your engine's health and horsepower. Choosing an appropriate compression ratio and fuel octane is a way to avoid detonation.

2.2.3
AIR/FUEL RATIO

Assuming that you understand the effects of compression ratio and fuel octane on burn rate, lets move on. The next item is controlling the oxygen to fuel ratio. With a normally aspirated engine, the way you control the oxygen-to-fuel ratio is by mixing more or less fuel with the atmosphere as it travels down the intake manifold. Carburetor jetting, or changing the pulse duration for fuel injection motors, is the usual channel for such adjustments. The key here is that fuel is added or subtracted from the mixture since the oxygen content of the atmosphere is pretty much stable at 20 percent.

When you're tuning your carburetor, the idea is to find the right amount of fuel that—depending on atmospheric conditions—will use the available oxygen to produce the most power. On most carbureted engines, 12.5 to 13:1 air to fuel ratios are where they make the most power. Any leaner (less fuel/higher oxygen ratio) and the mixture burns hotter and quicker and it's hard to ignite. That means peak pressure is difficult to control and usually is displayed as a loss of power.

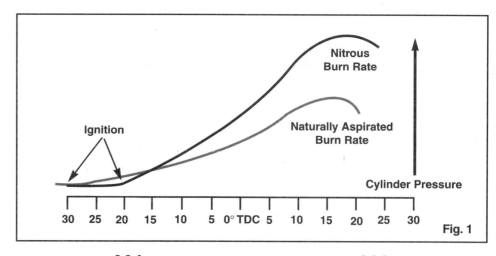

Fig. 1

2.2.4
CONTROLLING IGNITION TIMING

Controlling the timing and duration of cylinder pressure is where all your engine's power is generated. Timing peak pressure correctly is a function of ignition timing and burn rate. Since it takes time for fuel to burn and the piston is traveling at a high speed, you have to ignite the fuel before you want peak pressure. Look at Figure 1 and you can see why you typically have advanced ignition curves. Notice the accelerated burn rate of of fuel with additional oxygen supplied by injecting nitrous. With the burn rate accelerated, you have to retard the ignition timing to keep peak pressure in the engine's "sweet spot" around the 12 to 14 crankshaft degree mark.

We have explained the accelerated burn rate of the fuel as a consequent of adding oxygen. But merely accelerating the burn rate does not account for the increased power output of a nitrous-injected engine combination. Referring again to Figure 10-1, notice the cylinder pressure associated with a nitrous system. From where does the increase come? The only way to do that is to add more fuel. Since there's more oxygen, you can add more fuel. Mixed in the proper ratios, you get a desired burn rate plus more heat to raise cylinder pressure. The additional cylinder pressure results in more horsepower. It's as simple as that. No magic, just physics.

That's essentially how nitrous creates power in an engine. Now let's look at how better nitrous system components can help your engine make even more horsepower.

2.3.0
THE DELIVERY SYSTEM

The nozzle is the device that mixes the nitrous with additional fuel. This is a critical phase in making horsepower with nitrous injection. How the nitrous is mixed with fuel has an impact on how much of the new mixture is available to burn in the combustion chamber. Remembering the basics tells you that this will affect the power generated by your engine.

2.3.1
FUEL HAS TO BE ATOMIZED TO BURN

Fuel has to be suspended in the charge air to burn. Technically, this is known as atomization or vaporization. Vaporization occurs when liquid fuel turns to a vaporous or gaseous state. If the fuel is still in a liquid form in the combustion chamber, all it does is take up space and raise the dynamic compression ratio. If you get enough fuel remaining in liquid form in your engine, you can raise the dynamic compression ratio enough to force detonation. This is an extreme case and is given purely to drive home the point that liquid fuel does not burn.

In addition to all the fundamentals we've covered, the trick of making horsepower with an internal combustion engine is getting the fuel vaporized. That's the job of the carburetor, the fuel injectors ,and the chemistry of the fuel. These devices take liquid fuel and disperse it into the intake air in small droplets. Droplet size is critical to the rate at which fuel will then vaporize. Fuel can only vaporize from the surface area of the droplet.

The rate fuel vaporizes is key to how much power you can create. The intake charge is moving quickly and is in the engine a short time before it's ignited. For a carbureted engine, all you have is the distance from the venturi to the chamber and the time it takes for the charge to travel that distance. On a port-injected engine there's even less time for vaporization. So increasing the vaporization rate of the fuel is important even when you're not using nitrous.

Looking for more efficient ways to vaporize fuel and keeping it suspended in the charge air keeps engine tuners up late at night. Manifold, carburetor, and fuel-injector designs are all the product of this pursuit. So as simple a process as vaporization can become a serious challenge when you have only a few fractions of a seconds to work with. And of course, with nitrous the problem is compounded.

Getting fuel to vaporize into a super-cold nitrous stream is excruciatingly difficult. It's just one of those things about air. When it's warm, it likes to sponge up other molecules. When it's cold, it likes to drop them. That's why moisture condenses on a cold surface. Imagine then the difficulty of keeping fuel suspended in a stream of air that's colder than 100 degrees below zero Fahrenheit. Obviously, you need to do something besides just squirting a bunch of fuel into the intake charge.

NOS has taken the approach of creating what it refers to as a fog. The crew at NOS calls it that because well, that's what it is. The NOS Fogger® nozzles and plates are designed to turn a nitrous stream and a fuel stream into a fog. What is a fog? Well Webster's Dictionary defines it as "a vapor condensed to fine particles of water suspended in the lower atmosphere…." Substitute fuel in place of water and we've still got a fog.

Why does NOS go to the trouble of Fogging™ nitrous and fuel? Quite simply because it helps make more power. How? We were just discussing the fact that fuel will not burn unless it is vaporized. It takes time to vaporize fuel, and this process is restricted by the exposed surface area. What the Fogger® systems does is mix the nitrous and fuel in such as way as to create fine particles of fuel suspended in the charge air. As the droplets become finer, or smaller, more

surface area is created. More surface area, quicker vaporization. Quicker vaporization, more fuel to burn. More fuel to burn, more power. Simple. At least in concept.

NOS has a new Fogger® nozzle design that atomizes the fuel much better than the old nozzle. The old style deflected parallel streams of fuel and nitrous. This technique atomized the mix with turbulence created from changing directions of the gas and the liquid fuel. The new nozzle directs the high pressure, high velocity stream of nitrous gas across the stream of fuel. The shearing force of the velocity of the gas just rips the liquid fuel into tiny pieces. The mist created with this method is much finer and vaporizes more quickly.

The primary advantage of a more homogeneous cone of mixture is that it tends to keep more fuel in suspension. Air can only hold so much fuel. If the fuel distribution is uneven, then some of the air is being asked to carry more of the fuel. But it can only carry so much before it becomes saturated, so some will fall out of suspension onto the intake runner floor just because the air cannot hold it. The new nozzle distributes the fuel evenly so all the air in the cone is being asked to hold the same amount of fuel, so more of it stays in suspension to vaporize and burn, thereby creating more power.

In addition to generating a more homogeneous nitrous/fuel flow, the new nozzles offer a variety of cone flow patterns. These give you the ability to tune various combos more precisely. For example, four-valve heads generally respond better to a broader pattern, whereas a two-valve-head engine may make more power with a narrow spray pattern. This is one more tuning technique designed to keep fuel in suspension so it can vaporize and burn. Directing the nitrous/fuel mixture sometimes can reduce the area of the cone that hits runner and port walls, causing the intake charge to change directions. When a fuel/air mix is forced to turn much of the fuel in suspension (since it has more inertia than air) more will end up on the wall.

Now that we've mentioned inertia, that brings up another advantage of Fogging™ the mix. Since the particles of fuel are so finely distributed in the nitrous stream, they tend not to disturb the regular airflow in the intake as much as sim-

ply squirting in some fuel. Much of this advantage comes from aiming the nozzle output with the airflow, but some of it is due to even distribution of the fuel's mass in the air.

The new nozzles from NOS deliver more usable fuel to your combustion chambers and make fine-tuning the air/fuel ratios more accurate. In other words, the fuel ratio you choose with orifice size and system pressure is closer to that actually received by the combustion chamber. The new nozzle makes this possible by creating a finer atomized mist in combination with a well defined spray pattern.

We just mentioned "system pressure," and need to talk about that a little so you can see how NOS' new Super Hi-Flo bottle valve works to keep fuel ratios stabilized on big systems. Fuel flow through a line depends on the inner diameter of the line and the pressure pushing it. The pressure at the nitrous bottle is typically 850 psi, depending on the temperature of the bottle. (Because pressure in the bottle is dependent on temperature, heating elements are used to stabilize bottle temperatures on high-power racing systems.) So there's no problem pushing lots of nitrous through a particular line size or even orifice size. The line and orifice sizes on small- to medium-powered nitrous system are intended to restrict the flow at the desired level. That's how nitrous is calibrated.

However, when you start making really big power figures, you have to flow lots of nitrous and at some point the restriction becomes the bottle valve instead of the tuning orifices and nozzles. When that occurs, it causes a pressure drop of sufficient magnitude, which allows the liquid nitrous to turn to a gas or boil in the line. When nitrous boils in the line it loses pressure and density. You can surmise what happens to the fuel ratio. With less pressure and density on the nitrous side you get less oxygen in the chamber. Less oxygen means a richer, slower-burning fuel mix. That means peak cylinder pressure occurs way too late and you're competition blows by you halfway down the track.

Controlling the combustion process is really what tuning an engine is all about. That's how you make more power. Making power and putting it to the ground is how you win races. Nothing less will do.

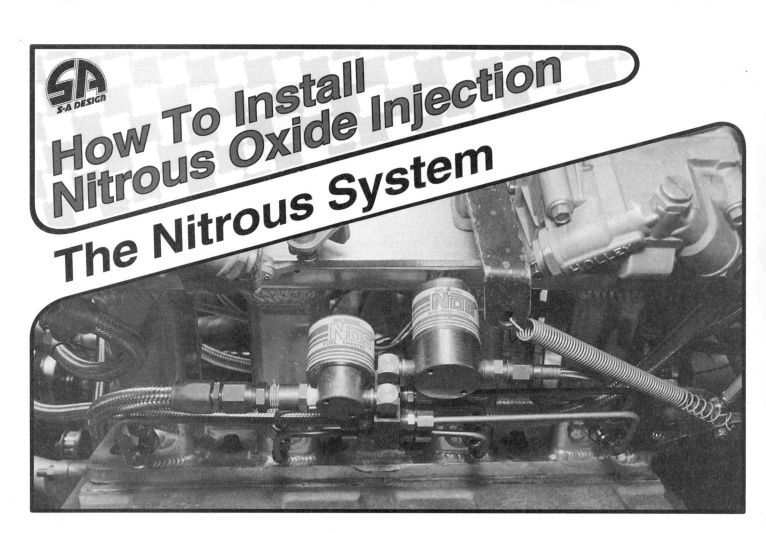

3.1.0
A BASIC NITROUS SYSTEM

In its most basic form, a nitrous-oxide system is a simple device. (Figure 3.1-A shows a typical plate system.) A nitrous-oxide system begins with a bottle of nitrous. The most common bottle is an aluminum tank capable of containing 10 pounds of nitrous oxide. A bottle's weight is how you determine how much nitrous it contains. The bottle will have a label on it that tells you the weight of the bottle when empty and when full. The bottle has a safety pressure-relief disc mounted in the valve. This disc is required by law to relieve the pressure in the bottle if it gets too high. At room temperature, the pressure of a typical nitrous bottle is about 850 psi. The safety disc will rupture at somewhere around 1200 psi. Each bottle also carries a certification date stamped into it. When you get your bottle refilled, the refill vendor cannot legally refill your bottle if it's out of date. An out-of-date bottle has to pass a pressure test and get recertified before being refilled.

Inside each bottle is a tube that's attached to the bottle valve and extends to the bottom of the inside of the bottle. More nitrous can be transferred in liquid than in gaseous form. This fact permits small hoses and lines to carry the nitrous toward the engine. The tube inside the bottle is called a siphon tube. It sucks up liquid nitrous until there is little left. Each manufacturer supplies instructions for mounting the bottle. The instructions show how to properly position the siphon tube so the liquid nitrous flows during acceleration.

The bottle is usually mounted in the trunk for convenience—and also because it doesn't fit well anywhere else. A high pressure hose gets the nitrous from the bottle to the rest of the system under the hood. This is a special hose that has a Teflon inner liner and a braided-steel outer covering. The ends are power-crimped. Don't replace this hose with a standard neoprene-rubber-lined braided-steel hose, especially one that has screw-together-type ends. These hoses cannot take the high pressures

of nitrous and will become brittle at the extremely low temperatures of nitrous.

The solenoids are the next step along the way. There's one for nitrous and one for fuel in most typical carburetor-style systems. There are some systems designed for factory fuel-injection systems that don't use a fuel solenoid. These systems supply the additional fuel during nitrous-assisted operation by raising the fuel pressure to the fuel injectors. The solenoids are the valves that control the on/off operation of the system. These electro-mechanical valves use 12 volts to create a strong magnetic field, which in turn pulls open a small plunger (see photo 3.1-1). The solenoids are designed so that the supply pressure assists in keeping the valve closed. The arrangement works similar to a ball covering the drain in a bathtub. As the water gets deeper, the pressure on the ball increases, thereby increasing the sealing action. In a solenoid, the magnetism created by the wire windings of the coil must be strong enough to pull open the plunger. A

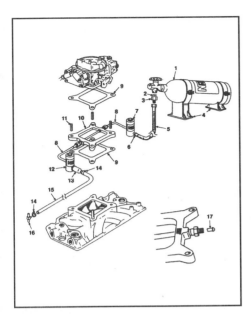

This layout of a basic plate system shows the component breakdown and basic design if a NOS system.

solenoid is simply an electrically operated valve.

From the solenoids, the nitrous and the fuel—which are still completely separated from each other—travel to the small jets that set the calibration of the system. These jets are typically small brass inserts that are easily changed for tuning purposes. After passing through the jets, the nitrous and the fuel then can be introduced into the engine.

There are various schemes for introducing these substances to the engine. The most common method for carbureted applications involves a thin plate, which mounts below the carburetor and has thin brass tubes that are paired together. One tube is positioned over the other. The upper tube is usually nitrous and the lower tube is usually fuel. The high velocity of the nitrous as it comes out of the upper tube helps to atomize the fuel.

Another method of getting nitrous and fuel into the engine involves a mixer nozzle). This type of nozzle combines the nitrous and the fuel as they are injected into the engine. It can be used as a single nozzle for the entire engine or as individual nozzles per cylinder. The individual nozzles allow you to tune each cylinder differently if necessary.

The fuel supply from the fuel side of the system must be reliable and stable. The calibration accuracy of any nitrous system depends on the ability of the fuel side to deliver a consistent flow of fuel at a consistent pressure. Most carbureted systems tap the fuel line into the carburetor to supply fuel to the fuel solenoid. This method is adequate up to a certain power level. At higher power levels a separate fuel pump, usually electric, supplies an adequate amount of fuel. A fuel-pressure regulator, which keeps the fuel pressure at a constant level, may be required to maintain the calibration accuracy. A majority of the problems encountered with nitrous systems can be traced to the fuel supply.

3.1.1
ACTIVATION SCHEMES

The most basic, bare-bones nitrous systems have only two switches between the battery and the solenoids (see figure 3.1-B). One, called the "arming switch," makes 12 volts from the battery available to the second switch. The second switch is a momentary, spring-loaded switch that's operated by hand. With the arming switch on and the momentary switch depressed, or squeezed (hence the slang terminology "on the squeeze"), the solenoids open and the system is activated. This style of actuation circuitry was used years ago when nitrous systems were in their infancy.

The next addition in the evolution was a switch mounted on the throttle linkage to sense wide-open throttle (WOT). This switch helps prevent the system from coming on at part throttle, but it's susceptible to activation without the engine running. Filling the engine with nitrous and fuel when it isn't running will cause amazing tech-

nicolor carburetor and hood removals if the engine is started within the next 15 minutes. If you accidentally activate the system without the engine running, remove the coil wire at the distributor end and ground it securely; open the throttle nearly wide open and crank the engine for 10 seconds to clear out the nitrous.

A good way to avoid activating the system without the engine running is to wire the activation circuit through an oil-pressure switch. This setup assumes that if there's oil pressure the engine is running and vice versa. All of this still leaves the ultimate timing of the system to the coordination of the driver, whose hand is holding the activation button. Accidental activation at too low an rpm or when the clutch is in could cause bad things to happen. Unless you have the driving skills of Bob Glidden, don't push a button while shifting a manual-transmission car.

The smoothest, no-thought-just-drive way of activating any nitrous system is to use an electronic rpm-activated on/off switch (see figure 3.1-C). When used in conjunction with WOT switches, an rpm switch is the easiest and safest way to wire up your nitrous. The system can only come on when it is running at WOT and somewhere between a low- and high-rpm point. You can select the rpm at which the system comes on, as well as the rpm at which it turns off. This setup prevents backfires caused by activating the system at too low an rpm and over-revving the engine while shifting gears. You just put your foot down and drive.

You should be aware that the electrical current draw, measured in amps, is a concern when wiring your

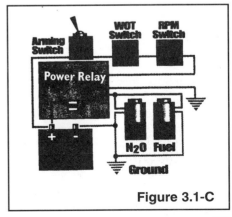

Figure 3.1-B

Figure 3.1-C

nitrous system. Remember that the nitrous solenoid must generate a magnetic field strong enough to open the plunger against 850 psi. As a result, the nitrous-solenoid coil windings require four to six amps in the smaller solenoids and upward of 16 to 18 amps in the largest solenoids currently available. Therefore, it's always a good practice to use a power relay for the high-amperage circuit that feeds the voltage from the battery to the solenoids. The switches, the micro switches, the electronic boxes, and the connections easily could be damaged by the high-amperage draw of the solenoids. A power relay isolates the switch circuitry from the high-amperage circuits.

There are lots of goodies and extra add-ons for nitrous systems these days. Of all the parts available, the most important is a bottle heater. For example, NOS' fully automatic, thermostatically controlled strap-type heater maintains the bottle temperature at a toasty 75 degrees, even if the temperature outside is below zero. The bottle temperature is important because as the temperature of the bottle falls, so does the pressure. If the pressure in the bottle falls too low, the calibration of the system will be way off, and most likely the system will run poorly.

There are no other power-enhancing devices on the market that make it as easy to increase the power output of an engine so dramatically as a nitrous system. It's easy to change those two tiny brass jets and get another 50 horsepower, so remember to exercise some discipline as well as common sense. This lack of restraint is exactly what has given nitrous oxide the reputation of destroying engines. The truth is, nitrous doesn't destroy engines; the fuel that was put in there and burned destroyed the engine. Nitrous doesn't make power, fuel does. Engines don't make power, they only release the potential energy in the fuel given to them. Nitrous oxide is simply a tool that allows you to adjust how much or how quickly the engine burns the fuel. If the fuel is there and a sufficient amount of oxygen is available to it, it will release its energy. It won't care if it's in an engine or a

tin can, which leads us to our final point: the limitations of your engine.

Every engine has limitations. An engine will only take a certain amount of heat, stress, and abuse before it breaks. It's just a device. Before you bust out your cell phone for an emergency call to NOS to get your mega horsepower system, check out the chapter on engine-building tactics. It'll give you a dose of reality, fiscally and otherwise. In the meantime, feel free to peruse the Buyer's Guide section immediately following this introduction. We've compiled just about every nitrous system concocted to satisfy your need for speed.

SYSTEM ARMING AND ACTIVATION TACTICS

3.3.1
Arming, Activation, and Control Fundamentals

The most basic of bare-bones nitrous systems have only two switches between the battery and the solenoids. One, called the arming switch, makes 12 volts from the battery available to the second switch. The second switch is a momentary, spring-loaded switch that's manually operated. With the arming switch on and the momentary switch depressed (or squeezed), the solenoids open and the system is activated. This style of activation circuitry was used when nitrous systems were in their infancy years ago.

The next evolutionary variation used a switch mounted on the throttle linkage to sense WOT. This switch helps prevent the system from coming on at part throttle, but it's susceptible to activation without the engine running. Filling the engine with nitrous and fuel when it isn't running will cause spectacular intake and hood removals if the engine is started within the next 15 minutes. If the system is accidentally activated without the engine running, remove the coil wire at the distributor end and ground it securely. Now open the throttle nearly wide-open and crank the engine for 10 seconds to clear out the nitrous.

3.3.2
FAIL-SAFE CONTROL TACTICS

A common way to avoid activating your system without the engine running is to wire the activation circuit through an oil pressure switch. This setup assumes that if there is oil pressure the engine is running, and vice versa. You can also use a fuel pressure switch in concert with the oil pressure switch. Using a fuel pressure switch gives you an extra measure of security since, theoretically, the nitrous system won't discharge unless the engine has oil and fuel pressure.

For turbo motors, NOS offers several adjustable pressure switches, to disengage the nitrous system at a particular manifold pressures. If you're running nitrous on a turbo motor, these switches are a must. When the nitrous hits, the engine revs up so quick you can over-rev it easily. Because nitrous lets an engine rev so quick, it's almost a reflex among nitrous cognoscenti to install a rev limiter.

Designing a fail-safe control scheme doesn't only involve an intricate mix of electronic devices. It can be as simple as an appropriate toggle switch. For example, a covered toggle switch will keep you from accidentally arming your nitrous system. Or a keyed arming switch may be a better choice. (If others drive your car, you shouldn't even think about it; just buy it and install it.) All of this still leaves the ultimate timing of the system to the coordination of the driver, whose hand is holding the activation button. Accidental activation at too low an rpm or when the clutch is in could cause bad things to happen. So, unless you have the driving skills of Bob Glidden, don't try pushing a button while shifting a manual-transmission car.

3.3.3
ELECTRONIC ACTIVATION AND CONTROL

Several strategies to remove driver error from the activation loop also have evolved. A simple and popular method is to use an electronic rpm-activated on/off switch. When used in conjunction with WOT switches and pressure switches, they are the easiest and safest way to activate your nitrous system. The system can only come on when it's running at WOT and somewhere between a low- and high-rpm point. You can select the rpm at which the system comes on as well as the rpm at which it turns off. This setup prevents backfires caused by activating the system at too low an rpm and over-revving the engine while shifting gears. You just put your foot down and drive. With nitrous systems, it's sometimes far too easy to have a heavier foot. When the power comes, it comes with a vengeance. It can, and usually does, turn slicks into smoke as soon as you hit the button. Enter the Nitrous Oxide Systems progressive controls. NOS makes two versions of this device. The first is a stand-alone progressive nitrous controller; the second allows you to adjust the timing of how the power is applied.

The NOS Time Based Progressive Nitrous Oxide Injection Controller is designed to allow you to tune the rate at which power from your nitrous oxide injection kit is applied. Initial power is adjustable from zero to 100 percent. The rate at which the remainder of the power is applied is adjustable from zero to five seconds. Maximum power is adjusted through jetting changes, similar to a conventional nitrous oxide injection kit.

A secondary feature of this unit is its ability to function as a delay device. Length of delay is adjustable between zero to 20 percent of the time setting selected on the "Time to Full Power" knob.

The time-based progressive nitrous controller is applicable to a variety of vehicles using NOS nitrous oxide injection kits. The basic controller and operating principle is the same for your vehicle regardless of whether it's carbureted or equipped with electronic fuel injection. However, the mounting hardware necessary for a safe installation varies with application.

NOS makes three types of nitrous oxide injection kits. 1) Dry Manifold EFI Kits. These are characterized by their use of two nitrous solenoids and no fuel solenoids. Vehicles that use this type of system typically are late-model fuel-injected vehicles with return-style fuel systems. No application kit is necessary to install

NITROUS OXIDE INJECTION Tips & Tricks

FUEL SYSTEM ALERT

1) Carbureted Engines

When used correctly, NOS nitrous oxide injection elevates cylinder pressures and temperatures while increasing the combustion rate. These characteristics make the engine more sensitive to detonation. Maintenance of adequate fuel pressure and delivery is an absolute must to ensure proper performance and engine life. Most carburetors are designed to operate at five to 10 psi. When designing your fuel system, plan on your pumps and lines flowing at least 0.1 gallons of gasoline per hour per horsepower at five psi. For example, an engine that makes 350 horsepower when the Power Shot System is activated will require a fuel pump that flows at least 35 gallons per hour at five psi. Most fuel pumps are rated at free flowing conditions; at five psi fuel pressure, their flow rates may be reduced greatly.

2) Fuel-Injected Engines

Stock fuel-injection systems typically operate at 35 to 40 psi. Several Kits for fuel-injected engines increase fuel pressure to 80 psi. Always use quality high-pressure fuel hose when installing this kit.

NITROUS OXIDE INJECTION Tips & Tricks

TYPES OF NITROUS OXIDE SYSTEMS

Nitrous Oxide Systems come in several configurations. The primary difference between them is how the nitrous is delivered to the engine and mixed with the fuel.

The first and most common is a Carburetor Plate. This application involves a thin plate that mounts below the carburetor and has thin brass tubes that are paired together. One tube is positioned over the other. The upper tube is usually nitrous and the lower tube is usually fuel. The high velocity of the nitrous as it comes out of the upper tube helps to atomize the fuel.

Carbureted direct-port systems use a series of mixer nozzles. This type of nozzle combines the nitrous and the fuel as they are injected into the engine. Direct-port systems use individual nozzles per cylinder, allowing you to tune each cylinder differently, if necessary.

A carbureted hybrid system uses a plate and direct-port mixing schemes usually staged, i.e., the plate system is active off the start, then as the chassis settles, it's switched off and the second stage, in this case the direct -port system, is activated.

Fuel-injected plate systems are virtually the same as carbureted plate systems except the plate mounts between a throttle body; in some designs the plate is spliced into the intake runners in some fashion.

Fuel-injected nozzle system types use a mixer nozzle to deliver nitrous oxide and fuel to the engine. An example of this system type is the Turbo Nitrous system for the 3.8-liter Buick V-6 turbo.

The fuel-injected direct-port system is essentially the same as the carburetor direct port system discussed above.

A fuel-injected dry manifold system uses a spray nozzle to deliver nitrous oxide only to the intake. The additional fuel is supplied by increasing fuel pressure when the nitrous system is activated. It's called a dry manifold system because there isn't any fuel present in the intake manifold. A dry manifold is safer than a wet manifold because nitrous by itself is not explosive. It's when you mix nitrous with fuel in the manifold that you get spectacular manifold and hood removals.

Electronic progressive controls in these vehicles. 2) Wet Manifold Power Shot/Super Power Shot Cheater/Big Shot Kits. These systems use one fuel and one nitrous Super Power Shot or Cheater solenoid. One installation kit (Part # 00050) is required. 3) Wet Manifold Sportman Fogger/Pro Shot Fogger Kits. These systems use two fuel and two nitrous Super Power Shot/ Cheater/Big Shot solenoids. Two installation kits (Part # 00050) are required.

Here's how these devices work:

On Dry Manifold Style NOS Systems, the flow of nitrous oxide into your engine is controlled using the technique known as "pulse width modulation." This is the same principle employed on all factory fuel-injection systems. In simple terms, this means that the second (or downstream) solenoid is opened and shut 25 times per second. In dry manifold-style NOS nitrous oxide injection kits, the number one, or upstream, solenoid works as a safety solenoid, preventing accidental leakage of nitrous oxide into the engine if the second solenoid (the unit being modulated) were to experience premature degradation of the solenoid plunger seat.

In Wet Manifold Carbureted and EFI Fogger Nozzle Style NOS Systems, the flow of nitrous oxide and supplemental fuel into your engine is also controlled by a microprocessor using the technique known as "Pulse Width Modulation." Again, a secondary or redundant solenoid must be used on the nitrous side of the system as a safety feature. When the timer is activated, the secondary solenoid opens 100 percent and stays open until the throttle switch is deactivated. Once the throttle switch is deactivated, this secondary solenoid also closes, preventing accidental leakage of nitrous oxide into the engine.

The advantage of these devices is twofold. First, they add power, gradually letting you tune to the limits of traction of your tires. Second, they let you tune consistently when the power is applied. Basically the driver is out of the loop except he has to launch and drive the car and of course enjoy the ride.

3.3.4
ELECTRICAL REQUIREMENTS

To operate a nitrous system, your vehicle has to have some sort of electrical system. It can be as simple as a dry cell battery with no alternator or generator to recharge it. As long as it has the appropriate voltage and amperage capacity, it will work.

Of course, the next question you must answer is what the current demands of a nitrous system are. The nitrous solenoids are the most current-hungry devices in a basic nitrous system. For example, the Cheater and Pro Shot nitrous solenoids pull between 12 and 16 amps each; the Power Shot and Super Power Shot pull about four or five amps each. The fuel solenoids demand far less, somewhere on the order of one to 1.5 amps each, because they don't have to overcome the high pressures of the nitrous line. That doesn't mean you can ignore their amperage draw; you have to design the system to provide power to all components. Because, if you have a bottle warmer, remote valve controller, and/or other electronic components added to a staged nitrous system, the total current draw can be substantial.

Determining the power draw for your nitrous system can be an exact science, but we don't really need to go to those lengths, an approximation should do fine. As we said, the nitrous solenoids are the most power-hungry components in the system, so we've provided a chart with the peak current draw of several popular solenoid sizes. You'll have to measure the other components current demand with a multi-meter.

Fundamentally, you need to add up the amperage values of all the components on a circuit. For example, if you have a pair of Pro Shot solenoids on a circuit, you have to have a system that will deliver 32 amps. By breaking down your system in such a way and adding up the amperage draw, you can arrive at the total current your power system will have to deliver.

If you're connecting your fuel pump to the accessory power supply, make sure that circuit will support the additional 7-amp draw required by the fuel pump.

Remember, with an automotive electrical system, although a portion is lost in heat, what goes in has to be returned to the battery. So it is best to err on the high side and build in reserve current capacity. It's not only safer, but your system will be more reliable and perform as designed.

3.4.1
FUEL TO HP REQUIREMENTS

At the risk of being redundant, we'll say this one more time: fuel is the source of engine performance, in that it mixes with air so combustion can occur in the cylinders. The air to fuel ratio (a/f ratio) that's accepted as safe and will produce the most acceleration from a high-performance, naturally aspirated gasoline-fueled internal combustion four-stroke engine is 12.8:1, or a brake specific fuel consumption (BSFC) of 0.50. Advanced engine tuners can run a/f ratios of 13:1 or 0.45 BSFC to get the most steady-state power from an engine. Keep in mind you're getting closer to the lean side of the fuel curve, and if you're not completely dialed in, you can get into detonation. By the way, these ratios are for full-throttle, high-load situations. When you're cruising under low load conditions, you can run right at 14.7:1 or stoichiometric and lower depending on the engine load.

The above is for naturally aspirated gasoline fueled engines. When you add nitrous to the mix, the ratios change because of the high oxygen content of nitrous and the super-cooled state in which it arrives at the combustion chamber. If you look at the fuel flow to horsepower chart, you'll see the relationship between fuel flow and horsepower requirements for a particular power level at a BSFC of 0.50. (See advanced section for more info BSFC.) The crew at NOS suggest a 5:1 nitrous-to-fuel ratio as a base line tune. This is on the rich side, but it's pretty safe while making pretty good power. From this ratio a racer tunes toward a 6:1 nitrous to fuel ratio.

When used correctly, NOS nitrous oxide injection elevates cylinder pressures and temperatures while increasing the combustion rate. These char-

Figure 3.3.3.1 Fuel/horsepower					
Horsepower	Gas lbs./hr @BSFC=.50	Gas Gals./hr @BSFC=.50	Gas Gals./min. @BSFC=.50	Mins. to flow 1-gal @BSFC .50	Secs. to flow 1-gal @BSFC .50
1000.00	500.00	75.87	1.26	0.79	47.45
980.00	490.00	74.36	1.24	0.81	48.42
960.00	480.00	72.84	1.21	0.82	49.42
940.00	470.00	71.32	1.19	0.84	50.48
920.00	460.00	69.80	1.16	0.86	51.57
900.00	450.00	68.29	1.14	0.88	52.72
880.00	440.00	66.77	1.11	0.90	53.92
860.00	430.00	65.25	1.09	0.92	55.17
840.00	420.00	63.73	1.06	0.94	56.49
820.00	410.00	62.22	1.04	0.96	57.86
800.00	400.00	60.70	1.01	0.99	59.31
780.00	390.00	59.18	0.99	1.01	60.83
760.00	380.00	57.66	0.96	1.04	62.43
740.00	370.00	56.15	0.94	1.07	64.12
720.00	360.00	54.63	0.91	1.10	65.90
700.00	350.00	53.11	0.89	1.13	67.78
680.00	340.00	51.59	0.86	1.16	69.78
660.00	330.00	50.08	0.83	1.20	71.89
640.00	320.00	48.56	0.81	1.24	74.14
620.00	310.00	47.04	0.78	1.28	76.53
600.00	300.00	45.52	0.76	1.32	79.08
580.00	290.00	44.01	0.73	1.36	81.81
560.00	280.00	42.49	0.71	1.41	84.73
540.00	270.00	40.97	0.68	1.46	87.87
520.00	260.00	39.45	0.66	1.52	91.25
500.00	250.00	37.94	0.63	1.58	94.90
480.00	240.00	36.42	0.61	1.65	98.85
460.00	230.00	34.90	0.58	1.72	103.15
440.00	220.00	33.38	0.56	1.80	107.84
420.00	210.00	31.87	0.53	1.88	112.97
400.00	200.00	30.35	0.51	1.98	118.62
380.00	190.00	28.83	0.48	2.08	124.86
360.00	180.00	27.31	0.46	2.20	131.80
340.00	170.00	25.80	0.43	2.33	139.55
320.00	160.00	24.28	0.40	2.47	148.28
300.00	150.00	22.76	0.38	2.64	158.16
280.00	140.00	21.24	0.35	2.82	169.46
260.00	130.00	19.73	0.33	3.04	182.49
240.00	120.00	18.21	0.30	3.29	197.70
220.00	110.00	16.69	0.28	3.59	215.67
200.00	100.00	15.17	0.25	3.95	237.24
180.00	90.00	13.66	0.23	4.39	263.60
160.00	80.00	12.14	0.20	4.94	296.55
140.00	70.00	10.62	0.18	5.65	338.91
120.00	60.00	9.10	0.15	6.59	395.40
100.00	50.00	7.59	0.13	7.91	474.48

acteristics make the engine more sensitive to detonation. Maintenance of adequate fuel pressure and delivery is an absolute must to ensure proper performance and engine life. Most carburetors are designed to operate at five to 10 psi. When designing your fuel system, plan on your pumps and lines flowing at least 0.1 gallons of gasoline per hour per horsepower at five psi. For example, an engine that makes 350 horsepower when the Power Shot System is activated will require a fuel pump that flows at least 35 gallons per hour at five psi. Most fuel pumps are rated at free-flowing conditions; at five psi fuel pressure, their flow rates greatly may be reduced.

We'll get far too involved with fuel to nitrous ratios in the advance engine tech section. We present it here to show you just how demanding is the job of your fuel system. It has to move fairly large amounts of fluid and do so precisely and reliably at specific pressure. We assume you're now suitably impressed and won't wimp out when it comes to your fuel system.

3.5.1
Nitrous Bottles and Accessories

Nitrous oxide is stored by pumping it into a pressure vessel. The legal specifications for a nitrous oxide tank (pressure vessel) are the same as that used for carbon dioxide gas. It must have a certified working limit of 1800 pounds of pressure psi. The tanks must have a certification date stamped into the tank near the outlet and must be current within five years. Your dealer will not refill your nitrous tank if it is out of date. If this happens, you will need to pay a small fee for recertification. Depending on the resources of your refill dealer, he will either perform this himself if he has the proper equipment or send it out to have it done.

Nitrous oxide, like many other substances is stored in its tank in a liquid form. This is only possible if the nitrous is stored at a high enough pressure to liquefy it. At room temperature and normal atmospheric pressure (14.7 psi @ sea level), nitrous oxide can only exist in a gaseous form. There are two ways to get nitrous oxide into a liquid state. You can cool it down until it liquifies or compress it with pressure until it liquifies. In order to cool it down enough, you would have to lower the temperature of the nitrous to 127 degrees F below zero. That's right, minus 127 degrees F. That would be difficult to do and not practical for the automotive world. The other choice is to compress it into a tank at high pressure. If the nitrous oxide was at a temperature of 70 degrees F, then you'd have to compress it to 760 psi to make change to a liquid state. As the temperature of the nitrous oxide increases, the pressure required to keep it in a liquid state goes up. At 80 degrees F it takes 865 psi to keep it in a liquid state. This is far easier to accomplish than the cooling method. Pressure tanks commonly are available for this type of pressure. This is how the automotive industry has handled this problem from the first use of nitrous oxide in the mid '60s.

Nitrous oxide follows a temperature/pressure curve, which means that when it's captured in a closed container, it will be at a certain pressure for a given temperature. At 70 degrees F it's 760 psi; at 85 degrees it's at 925 psi. Raise the temperature and you raise the pressure; lower the temperature and you lower the pressure. Because of this property, it's extremely important that the temperature of the bottle is kept the same just prior to using the system. If you ignore this simple rule, you will be changing the calibration of your nitrous system just as you would the jets in a carburetor, except you won't have any idea of what to expect of the system when it's activated.

There are lots of goodies and extra add ons for nitrous systems these days. Of all the products available, there's one item that can be worth its weight in gold if you live where it gets cold during the winter—which means everywhere except Hawaii. It's a bottle heater. NOS sells a fully automatic, thermostatically controlled, strap-type heater that maintains the bottle temperature at a toasty 75 degrees F, even if the temperature outside is below zero. The bottle temperature is important because as the temperature of the bottle falls, so does the pressure. If the pressure in the bottle falls too low, the calibration of the system will be way off and most likely the system will run poorly.

There's not much else to talk about, at least concerning the physical pressure vessel. We'll talk more about the temperature/pressure relationship of compressed nitrous, positioning the bottle for a correct install, and several other intricacies in the installation and tuning sections. There are a few things you should know about nitrous bottles, before we go on.

Never drill, machine, weld, deform, scratch, drop, relabel, or modify a nitrous oxide tank or the valve in *any* way whatsoever! As we've said before, although some people have polished their tanks to a chrome-like appearance, this isn't recommended because it removes a non-uniform layer of the tank's material that may or may not affect its integrity. Certainly, never attempt to subject a nitrous tank to any type of plating process because this often affects the strength of the tank's material.

Never overfill nitrous cylinders! That tiny little bit extra will put you and others at great risk for injury. More often than not, when the cylinder warms up, the pressure goes above the limit of the safety relief disc and you lose all the nitrous you just paid for. If you are a retail dealer and you overfill a cylinder beyond it's rated capacity in weight, whether intentional or not, you could be held liable for the conse-

quences of any damages or injury. Don't do it.

3.5.4
TECH TIPS TO HELP YOU RUN LINES AND INSTALL FITTINGS RIGHT

Running nitrous lines, and fuel lines for that matter, is pretty simple in concept. There isn't a lot that can go wrong; still, there's a right way and a wrong way to install and layout your fluid transport system, be it nitrous, fuel or whatever. For nitrous systems, it's important to avoid running these lines near the exhaust system. Heating the nitrous line can boil it, reducing the amount of nitrous delivered to the engine. If you look at the drawing from Aeroquip, you can see the most common mistakes and how to correct them. To these we should add several more conditions to be aware of and avoid.

The most important of these tips is not to install a line so that it gets hit or tangled up in some dynamic situation. Remember, the suspension is usually at full droop on the jacks, and what looks like a handy avenue for the nitrous lines may not be so free-flowing once the suspension begins working in its normal space. This is just one of many scenarios you need to anticipate when you route your nitrous and fuel hoses.

Carrol Smith, in the *Nuts, Bolts, fasteners and Plumbing Handbook,* lists several situations to avoid. First is leaving insufficient clearance between each hose end and anything that it might contact or vibrate against. While the hose is flexible, the hose ends are not.

Second, never allow a hose to come in contact with a sharp corner, a nut, a bolt, a rivet stem, or anything else that isn't perfectly smooth. This one includes failure to install a grommet at each point where a hose passes through a panel.

Third, never let a hose rub against anything—even when the surface against which it will rub is flat and smooth. The stainless braid makes an efficient file and will abrade through anything with which it comes in contact. This is particularly true in those instances where brake and clutch lines pass through the fuel cell com-

partment. In this case, encase the hoses in a thin-walled aluminum tube. Spiral wrap is a neat and convenient way to prevent chafe damage under normal conditions.

Fourth, don't kink the hose—either by bending it too tightly (both Earl's and Aeroquip include minimum-bend radii tables in their catalogs) or by placing the hose in a torsional bind.

Fifth, don't over-tighten the hose ends onto their adapter fittings or into their ports. Both the seal and the self-locking feature are provided by the design, not by force. It helps a lot to use the wrenches made for the job. Their handles are short enough to make over-tightening difficult.

Sixth, don't stretch the hose or not allow enough room for flex. There's a right way and a wrong way to run hoses. The right way mainly calls for common sense.

Finally, flex hose and hard lines are not designed to carry weight; they're designed to transport fluids. As such, they need to be supported. Current design practices suggest a clamp or tie wrap at 18-in. intervals.

Keep in mind the above are general rules. You'll find out more as you get into your own installation, and indeed we have more to show you as we install several systems. For now, this introduction should start you thinking

Fig3.5.1-B-Temp/Press Chart	
Bottle Temp. °F	Bottle Pressure (psi)
-30	67
-20	203
-10	240
0	283
10	335
20	387
32	460
40	520
50	590
60	675
70	760
80	865
97	1069

Tech note: As ambient temperature drops, so will bottle pressure which can cause a potentially fuel rich condition. Although usually not harmful to the engine, loss of optimal power can occur. On the other hand, very high ambient temperatures can lead to leaner buring conditions and possible engine damage.

about where you'll put the lines and how to connect them to make a safe reliable, and powerful nitrous system.

3.5.4.1
EARL'S PERFORMANCE PRODUCTS ON AN AND NPT SIZING

AN (Army-Navy) Sizes—were established by the Aerospace industry years ago and were designated outside diameters (O.D.) of the rigid metal tube with which each size fitting is used.

The numbers assigned equate to the O.D. of the tubing in 1/16-in.increments that's considered equal in flow to the hard line it replaces. Since tubing and hoses have assorted wall thicknesses, we now can understand that the designated size number does not necessarily tell you how large the inside diameter will be. (For example, the inside diameter of an Earl's size 6 hose end is nearly as large as the inside diameter of some other manufacturers' -8 hose ends.)

Each AN size number has its own standard thread size that can be seen in column three of the chart. Again, these are the same thread sizes that have been used in aircraft and industrial applications for many years.

AN and MS (Military Spec) specify a 37-degree cone angle. Industrial hose ends and adapters are designed to JIC (Joint Industrial Council) specs with a 45° cone angle. The two do not mix—be careful.

AN Size	Metal Tube O.D.	Thread Size
- 2	1/8	5/16-24 SAE
- 3	3/16	3/8-24 SAE
- 4	1/4	7/16-20 SAE
- 5	5/16	1/2-20 SAE
- 6	3/8	9/16-18 SAE
- 8	1/2	3/4-16 SAE
-10	5/8	7/8-14 SAE
-12	3/4	1 1/16-12 SAE
-24	1 1/2	1 7/8-12 SAE
-28	1 3/4	2 1/4-12 SAE
-32	2	2 1/2-12 SAE

National Pipe Threads (NP) are the next most popular thread size used in "Competition Plumbing." We actually can find a resemblance between the size callouts and the inside diameter (I.D.) of the fitting as shown in the chart. Some of the most popular adapter fittings shown in Earl's catalog are AN to NPT adapters. While many variations are offered, the last column in the chart above shows which AN size corresponds to each NPT size when inside diameters (flow dimensions) are considered.

All Earl's Swivel-Seal™ hose ends are designed to provide little or no restriction when used with the corresponding AN fitting size. The company also offer a number of Metric and British Standard Pipe threads to AN fitting adapters.

Pipe Threads

Pipe Thread	Threads Per Inch	Theoretical I.D. of Ftg.	Closest AN Ftg. Size
1/16-in.	27	1/16-in.	
1/8-in.	27	1/8-in.	4
1/4-in.	18	1/4-in.	6
3/8-in.	18	3/8-in.	8
1/2-in.	14	1/2-in.	10
3/4-in.	14	3/4-in.	12
1-in.	11 1/2	1-in.	16
1 1/4-in.	11 1/2	1 1/4-in.	20
1 1/2-in.	11 1/2	1 1/2-in.	24
2-in.	11 1/2	2-in.	32

3.5.5
SOLENOID BASIC TECH

3.5.5.1
SOLENOID CHARACTERISTICS

NOS offers ten unique solenoids. Each is designed for a specific set of operating conditions, liquid medium, i.e., nitrous, gasoline, alcohol, nitromethane, etc.; flow rate and operating pressure. When installed with the correct components and used as intended, they are effective and reliable. If used incorrectly or in the wrong application, the solenoid may fail to work, or have a drastically reduced life expectancy. To correctly select a solenoid for an application, adhere to the following tips.

3.5.5.2
SEAL COMPOSITION

The seals in NOS solenoids are made of materials compatible with their intended operating environments. Flowing fluids other than those for which a solenoid was designed may result in seal failure. So don't try to run methanol through your Cheater gasoline solenoid.

When a solenoid is cycled, a large amount of force can be placed on the solenoid seal. The durometer, or "toughness," of the seal is varied depending upon the pressure at which the solenoid is intended to operate. Use of a soft seal in a high-pressure application will result in the seal being cut. If a hard seal is used in a low-temperature environment (such as with nitrous oxide), the seal may chip or shatter. Use of an excessively hard seal in a low-pressure environment may result in solenoid leakage.

3.5.5.3
MAXIMUM OPENING PRESSURE

NOS solenoids use electronic coils for opening and closing the solenoid orifices. The strength of the coil is determined by the size of the solenoid orifice and the pressure at which it will

Solenoid Specs						
NOS #	ORIFICE	AMPS	OHMS	SEAL TYPE	FLOWING MEDIA	MAX OPENING
16000	0.09	10	1.2	RTM	N20	1400
16004	0.09	10	1.2	RTM	N20	1400
16020	0.078	8.6	1.4	RTM	N20	2000
16024	0.078	8.6	1.4	RTM	N20	2000
16040	0.11	10	1.2	RTM	N20	1100
16044	0.11	10	1.2	RTM	N20	1100
16050	0.156	1.6	7.5	VITON	GASOLINE	400
16054	0.156	1.6	7.5	VITON	GASOLINE	400
16055	0.11	1.1	10.2	TEFLON	ALCOHOL/NITRO	600
16057	0.143	1.0	11.2	TEFLON	ALCOHOL	850
	0.143	2.0	6.0	TEFLON	NITRO	850
16058	0.068 top	1	11.2	RTM	N20	900+
	.250 bottom	2.0	6.0	RTM	N20	900+
16080	0.125	0.6	20.8	VITON	GASOLINE	200
16084	0.125	0.6	20.8	VITON	GASOLINE	200
16060	0.218	0.6	20.5	TEFLON	ALCOHOL/NITRO	125

operate. When selecting a solenoid, the maximum pressure capability of the unit should exceed the operating pressure it will experience by 20 percent.

3.5.5.4
MAXIMUM OPERATING TIME

NOS solenoids are intended for momentary usage. High-pressure solenoids should not be held open for over 60 seconds with a 33-percent duty cycle. Low-pressure solenoids should not be operated for over five minutes continuously, with a 50-percent duty cycle.

3.5.5.5
AMPERAGE DRAW

The current draw required by an NOS solenoid is determined by the strength of the opening and closing coil. All wiring switches and relays must be rated for the amperage draw of the solenoids they are to operate. *Note: If solenoids are left on for extended periods, the coil will heat up. As a coil gets hot, the amperage required to operate it increases dramatically.*

3.5.5.6
ORIFICE SIZE

Orifice size dictates solenoid flow capability. The solenoid orifice should always be bigger than the combined area of all downstream metering jets. Solenoid efficiency is significantly degraded if this condition is violated.

NOS solenoid orifices should never be enlarged. Increasing the solenoid orifice will result in premature failure of the solenoid coil and plunger seal.

3.5.5.7
SOLENOID TROUBLESHOOTING

If an NOS solenoid fails to operate correctly, the problem usually stems from chemical incompatibility, contamination from debris, or coil failure due to overheating.

Chemical or debris contamination can result in flow reduction or flow stoppage. Coil failure will cause flow stoppage. Occasionally, plunger seals chip or crack from contamination, resulting in solenoid leakage.

An engine that suddenly is running lean may indicate a problem in the NOS fuel solenoid. Suddenly running rich is characteristic of a trouble in the NOS nitrous solenoid.

Disassembly and inspection of NOS solenoids is easy. Examine figures one and two for views of the components inside NOS solenoids. If a solenoid needs rebuilding, NOS has rebuild kits available for all NOS solenoids.

3.5.5.7.1
PLUNGER

Examine the plunger seal surface; it should be flat except for a small, circular indentation in the center of the seal. A chemically contaminated seal will protrude from the plunger and be dome shaped. A chemically contaminated seal will return to its original shape if left in the fresh air for several days. It may then be returned to service. Seals that are damaged should be replaced.

Note: A persistent seal swelling problem will require corrective action.

Some fuel additives are not compatible with NOS gasoline solenoids. Changing brands of fuel may cure this condition. NOS nitrous plunger seals will swell when exposed to fuel. A swollen nitrous seal is indicative of fuel collecting in the NOS nitrous solenoid. This problem can be cured by moving the NOS nitrous solenoid higher and/or further from the injection orifice.

3.5.5.7.2
COIL

Coil failure can occur if an NOS solenoid is held open too long or if it's forced to operate at pressures above which it's rated. Coils may be easily checked using a voltage-ohm meter. Proper resistance values are listed in the solenoid characteristics chart below.

3.5.5.7.3
STEM

The solenoid stem will not fail if it's not abused during disassembly/assembly. The solenoid stem is frequently crushed by mechanics who grip the stem with pliers or clamp it in a vise. If

there are scratches visible on the stem, check the inside bore of the stem for damage. Slide the plunger inside the stem and check for binding. Components that bind should be discarded.

3.5.6.1
THE ART OF MIXING FUEL WITH NITROUS

One of the tricks of making horsepower with an internal combustion engine is getting the fuel vaporized. That's the job of the carburetor, the fuel injectors, and the chemistry of the fuel. These devices take liquid fuel and disperse it into the intake air in small droplets. Droplet size is critical to the rate at which fuel will then vaporize. Fuel can only vaporize from the surface area of the droplet.

The rate fuel vaporizes is key to how much power you can create. The intake charge is moving quickly and is in the engine only a short time before it's ignited. For a carbureted engine, all you have is the distance from the venturi to the chamber and the time it takes for the charge to travel that distance. On a port-injected engine, there's even less time for vaporization. Increasing the vaporization rate of the fuel is important even when you're not using nitrous.

Looking for more efficient ways to vaporize fuel and keeping it suspended in the charge air keeps engine tuners up late at night. Manifold, carburetor, and fuel-injector designs are all the product of this pursuit. As simple a process as evaporation can become a serious challenge when you have only a scant few fractions of a seconds to work with. And, of course, with nitrous, the problem is compounded.

Getting fuel to vaporize into a super-cold nitrous stream is extremely difficult. It's just one of those things about air. When it's warm, it likes to sponge up other molecules. When it's cold, it likes to drop them. That's why moisture condenses on a cold surface. Imagine, then, the difficulty of keeping fuel suspended in a stream of air that's colder than 100 degrees below zero F. Obviously, you need to do something besides just squirting a bunch of fuel into the intake charge.

NOS has taken the approach of creating what they refer to as a fog. The crew at NOS calls it that because, well, that's what it is. The NOS Fogger nozzles and plates are designed to turn a nitrous stream and a fuel stream into a fog. What is a fog? *Webster's Dictionary* defines it as "a vapor condensed to fine particles of water suspended in the lower atmosphere...." Substitute fuel in place of water, and you still have a fog.

Why does NOS go to the trouble of fogging nitrous and fuel? Quite simply because it helps make more power. How? We were just discussing the fact that fuel will not burn unless it's vaporized. It takes time to vaporize fuel, and this process is restricted by the exposed surface area. What the Fogger systems do is mix the nitrous and fuel in such as way as to create fine particles of fuel suspended in the charge air. As the droplets become finer, or smaller, more surface area is created. More surface area, quicker vaporization. Quicker vaporization, more fuel to burn. More fuel to burn, more power. Simple. At least in concept.

NOS has a new Fogger nozzle design that atomizes the fuel much better than the old nozzle. The old style deflected parallel streams of fuel and nitrous. This technique atomized the mix with turbulence created from changing directions of the gas and the liquid fuel. The new nozzle works entirely different. What it does is direct the high-pressure, high-velocity stream of nitrous gas across the stream of fuel. The shearing force of the velocity of the gas just rips the liquid fuel into tiny pieces. The mist created with this method is much finer and so will vaporize much quicker.

The primary advantage of a finer, more homogeneous cone of mixture is that it tends to keep more fuel in suspension. Air can only hold so much fuel. If the fuel distribution is uneven, then some of the air is being asked to carry more of the fuel. But it can only carry so much before it's saturated, so some will fall out of suspension on to the intake runner floor just because the air cannot hold it. The new nozzle distributes the fuel evenly so all the air in the cone is being asked to hold the same amount of fuel, so more of it stays in suspension to vaporize and burn, creating more power.

In addition to generating a more homogeneous cone of nitrous, the new nozzles form a tighter cone as well. This has the advantage of more precise aiming of the fuel/air mix. This is one more tuning technique designed to keep fuel in suspension so it can vaporize and burn. Directing the nitrous/fuel mixture sometimes can reduce the area of the cone that hits runner and port walls causing the intake charge to change directions. When a fuel/air mix is forced to turn much of the fuel in suspension—since it has more inertia than air—it will end up on the wall, causing a lean air/fuel ratio, and we know what that can do, right?

Now that we've mentioned inertia, that brings up another advantage of fogging the mix. Since the particles of fuel are so finely distributed in the nitrous stream, they tend not to disturb the regular airflow in the intake as much as, say, simply squirting in some fuel. Much of this advantage comes from aiming the nozzle output with the airflow, but some of it is due to even distribution of the fuels mass in the air.

The new nozzles from NOS deliver more useable fuel to your combustion chambers and make fine-tuning the air/fuel ratios much more accurate. In other words, the fuel ratio you choose with orifice size and system pressure is closer to that actually received by the combustion chamber. The new nozzle makes this possible by creating a finer atomized mist in combination

of a well defined spray pattern.

Before we forget, it's not enough to vaporize the fuel and nitrous. It has to be in precise proportions. That's the job of the jets. NOS has taken the lead and produced a sapphire jet with a laser-sized orifice. This is about the most consistent and accurate piece on the market, and is discussed at length below. If you're tuning to the ragged edge, you need these jets. For most other applications, the standard jets are perfectly matched to your tuning needs.

3.5.6-1
THE RADICAL NEW
NOS SAPPHIRE JETS

NOS has just introduced the radically new Sapphire Flare Jets for use in all NOS systems that use flare jets. This unique advancement in jet technology offers you the most precise jets possible in the world today for critical tuning requirements. After machining the raw jet blanks, a sapphire stone is permanently embedded in the metering end of the jet. A powerful beam of laser light then cuts the metering passage through the sapphire with a precision that can never be matched with conventional machining methods or jet material. This guarantees you that the number stamped on the jet matches the actual metering passage size. And since the sapphire stones are much harder than conventional brass jet material, the new NOS Sapphire Flare Jets are not subject to erosion wear like conventional jets. You can be sure that your new Jewel Jets will precisely meter nitrous race after race, year after year. Jewel Flare Jets are available in the most popular sizes for your power and tuning requirements. Please contact the NOS Technical Support Department if you aren't sure as to the correct and safe ranges for your application.

To order individual jets, simply add the jet size desired to the end of the part number. For example, 13740-20 (20 = jet size in thousandths).

FUEL SYSTEM ALERT
1-CARBURETED ENGINES

When used correctly, NOS nitrous oxide injection elevates cylinder pressures and temperatures while increasing the combustion rate. These characteristics make the engine more sensitive to detonation. Maintenance of adequate fuel pressure and delivery is an absolute must to ensure proper performance and engine life. Most carburetors are designed to operate at 5 - 10 psi. When designing your fuel system, plan on your pumps and lines flowing at least O.1 gallons of gasoline per hour per horsepower at 5 psi. For example, an engine that makes 350 HP when the Powershot System is activated will require a fuel pump that flows at least 35 gallons per hour at 5 psi. Most fuel pumps are rated at free flowing conditions; at 5 psi fuel pressure, their flow rates may be greatly reduced.

2-FUEL INJECTED ENGINES

Stock fuel injection systems typically operate at 35-40 psi. Several Kits for fuel injected engines increase fuel pressure to 80 psi. Always use quality high-pressure fuel hose when installing this kit.

Types of Nitrous Oxide Systems

Nitrous Oxide Systems come in several configurations. The primary difference between them is how the nitrous is delivered to the engine and mixed with the fuel.

The first and most common is a Carburetor Plate. This application involves a thin plate, which mounts below the carburetor and has thin brass tubes that are paired together. One tube is positioned over the other. The upper tube is usually nitrous and the lower tube is usually fuel. The high velocity of the nitrous as it comes out of the upper tube helps to atomize the fuel.

Carbureted Direct Port systems use a series of mixer nozzles. This type of nozzle combines the nitrous and the fuel as they are injected into the engine. Direct Port systems use individual nozzles per cylinder

allowing you to tune each cylinder differently if necessary.

A Carbureted hybrid system uses a plate and Direct Port mixing schemes usually staged, i.e., the plate system is active off the start, then as the chassis settles, it is switch off and the second stage, in this case the direct port system is activated.

Fuel Injected plate systems are virtually the same as the plate systems used with carburetors. The differences being the plate mounts between a throttle body; or in some designs the plate is spliced into the intake runners in some fashion.

Fuel Injected nozzle systems types use a mixer nozzle to deliver nitrous oxide and fuel to the engine. An example of this system type is the Turbo Nitrous system for the 3.8 liter Buick V6 turbo.

The Fuel Injected Direct Port system is essentially the same as the Carburetor Direct Port system discussed above.

A Fuel Injected Dry Manifold system uses a spray nozzle to deliver nitrous oxide only to the intake. The additional fuel is supplied by increasing fuel pressure when the nitrous system is activated. It is called a dry manifold system because there isn't any fuel present in the intake manifold. A dry manifold is safer than a wet manifold because nitrous by itself is not explosive. It's when you mix nitrous with fuel in the manifold that you get spectacular manifold and hood removals.

PowerShot Applications

System #   Application
5000 Basic system without injector plate for building custom installations.
  5001 V8 Holley 4bbl. (125 HP)
  5004 V8 Quadrajet (125 HP)
  5009 V6 Quadrajet 4bbl. (90 HP)
  5005 V8 Holley 2bbl. (125 HP)
  5008 V6 Holley 4bbl. (90 HP)
  5011 4 cyl. 2.2L Chrysler-2bbl. (50 HP adjustable)

The NOS Powershot Kit is intended for use on domestic V-6 and V-8 engines using single 4V Holley or Quadrajet carburation. Horsepower and torque increases will vary with engine displacement

and modifications however approximate power increase estimates can be made, based on the mass flow of nitrous oxide into the engine. From a typical stock small block V8 you can expect an additional 125 horsepower; from a typical stock V6 you can expect an additional 90 horsepower; from a stock 2.2 liter four-cylinder an additional 50 horsepower.

The NOS Powershot is a non-adjustable system preset at the factory to flow enough nitrous oxide for a 120 to 130 HP increase, in most cases. The Power Shot system utilizes a thin (1/2") injector plate design which simply fits between your carburetor and intake manifold. The Powershot is ideally suited for engines which have not been modified internally.

Typical performances of the "Power Shot" kit:

1968 Chevelle, 327 CID
before: 14.3 @ 98.1
After: 12.5 @ 109.6
1977 Nova, 305 CID
Before: 14.9 @ 91.4
After: 13.4 @ 102.5
1985 Mustang GT, 302 CID
before: 15.0 @ 92.7
After 13.7 @ 105.2

BIG SHOT SYSTEMS

NOS Big Shot Kits (2101 & 2102) are intended for use on heavily modified domestic V-8 engines of at least 450 cubic inch displacement. Horsepower and torque increases will vary with engine displacement and modification. Kit Number 2115 is intended for use on modified 1986 - 1994 5.0 and 5.8 Ford engines equipped with stock Ford intake manifolds Kit Number 2117 is intended for use on modified 1986 - 1994 5.0 and 5.8 Ford engines equipped with Edelbrock Performer 5.0 intake manifolds. Horsepower and torque increases will vary with engine displacement and modification.

NOS Multiple-Carburetor Big Shot System (Kits 211 O, 2110-9 & 2111) and Two-Stage Big Shot System (Kits 2401 & 2402) are intended for use on modified domestic V-8 engines of at least 450 cubic inch displacement.

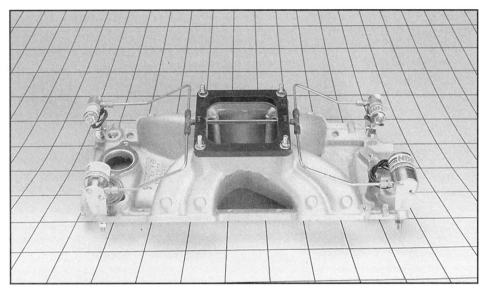

Dual Shot Cheater System for Holley Dominator offers maximum performance with two stages of nitrous for maximum power and optimized performance via two stages of nitrous activation.

PRO RACING TWO-STAGE SYSTEM

Pro-Racing Competition Plate Systems highly modified V8 applications.

The Pro Two-stage System was designed with the professional racer in mind. These injector plate systems offer up to 400 extra HP or more and are completely adjustable for maximizing performance from the starting line all the way "through the lights". Two stage performance offers the advantage of jetting the primary stage for optimum traction off the line and for all out performance during the second stage. Four NOS state-of-the-art "Cheater" solenoids are utilized for reliable and consistent power delivery for the demands of the true racing professional. These systems offer the advantage of relatively easy installation over direct port type systems with simple plate mounting under the carburetor(s). Exclusive NOS Dual-Stage Injector Plates are 1" thick and feature four Big Shot spray bars. Comes complete with 10 lb. capacity nitrous bottle and all necessary components for a complete installation.

Part #	Description
02301	V-8 w/Holley 4 bbl.
02302	V-8 w/ Dominator 4 bbl.
02310	V-8 w/Dual Holleys front to back 4 bbl.
02311	V-8 w/Dual Holley Dominators, 4bbl.

PRO SHOT FOGGER SYSTEMS

Pro Shot Fogger

Direct-port nitrous oxide injection kits are intended to provide maximum performance and tunability in a nitrous oxide injection system. Kits 2462 and 2462-A (Alcohol fuel) are intended for highly modified domestic V-8 engines using carburetors.

Kits 2462D, 2462DD, 2462H and 2462HH are two-stage (Cheater plates and direct port injection) systems designed to work with highly modified domestic V-8 engines of at least 450 cubic-inch displacement.

Kits 0062D, 0062DD, 0062H and 0062HH can be used to convert Kit 2462 into a 2462D, 2462DD, 2462H or 2462HH.

Big Shot Nitrous Injection plate system for factory injected Ford small blocks is engineered to deliver up to 300 additional horsepower on properly built, competition engines. Big Shot systems are available for standard, factory, GT40, and Edelbrock intake manifolds.

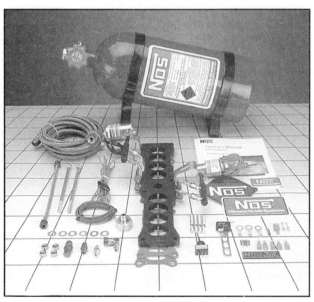

PRO SHOT FOGGER

Professional Two-Stage Perfomance Big block, highly modified V-8 applications - 150 to 500+ HP

The Pro Shot Fogger II is a two stage version of our famous record setting Pro Shot Fogger and is adjustable from 150-750+ HP. Designed primarily for highly modified big block V-8 engines, the Fogger II's dual stage feature allows an operator to jet the first stage for full traction off the line before obtaining maximum power in the second stage. In the first stage, Fogger2 nozzles inject the nitrous and supplementary fuel for a perfect launch. Then, in the second stage, special spray bar plates, which mount under the carburetors, add maximum mid-range and top end power. Fogger2 nozzle technology incorporates both fuel and nitrous injection into one nozzle for the ultimate in combustion, distribution and adjustability. Each cylinder is injected with a cool, dense fuel laden nitrous "fog" mixture, This is the system which is responsible for the original record setting six second quarter mile runs in IHRA Pro-Modified.

The Pro Shot Fogger System includes a 10lb. capacity nitrous bottle, Pro Shot nitrous and fuel solenoids, patented Fogger nozzles (including tap # 15990 for plumbing Fogger nozzles), special spray bar plates, filters, fittings, tubing, distribution blocks, jets, switches, larger 6an aircraft quality steel braided hose, and all other necessary hardware for a complete installation. Some of the hottest names in racing yesterday and today have stayed on top by utilizing NOS Pro-Fogger technology: Shannon jenkins • Larry Nance • Robbie Vandergriff • Pat Moore • Dave Riolo • Wally Stroupe * Charles Carpenter • Gordie Foust • Ron Erwin • Scott Shafiroff • Ronnie Sox • Animal Jim • Wally Bell • Tommy Mauney • Donnie Little • Dave Price • Tim McAmis • Gary Bingham • Ted May • Scotty Cannon, Pat Musi, Tony Christian and many more front runners.

System #	Application (Competition use)
02462D	2 stage, Single Dominator
02462DD	2 stage, Dual Dominator
02462H	2 stage, Single Holley
02462HH	2 stage, Dual Holley Carbs, front to back (Does not fit sideways carbs)

NITROUS BOTTLES

NOS offers D.O.T. approved aluminum nitrous bottles in a variety of sizes to suit your needs. There's no mistaking an NOS system with the famous blue bottle. Comes with the NOS. CGA approved Hi-Flo Valve and built-in siphon tube*. For extra safety, NOS has designed an exclusive blow-off venting system if your bottle is overfilled or if pressure increases beyond the maximum safety level. All bottles are shipped full and ready to use. '10 oz. bottles do not utilize siphon tubes.

Note: Bottles must be .shipped empty for air freight. For Super HiFlo valve on 5 lb. and larger bottles, add "SHF" to the bottle part number.

Part #	Capacity	length	Diameter
14700	10 oz.	14 1/4"	2"
14705	I lb.	9"	31/8"
14710	2 lb.	10 1/4"	4 3/8"
14720	2 1/2 lb.	11 112"	4 3/8"
14730	5 lb.	16 1/2"	51/4"
14745	10 lb.(std)	19"	7"
14750	15 lb.	25 1/2"	7"
14760	20 lb.	25 3/4"	8"
14770	35 lb.	40 1/8"	8"
14780	50 lb.	48 5/8"	8 5/8"

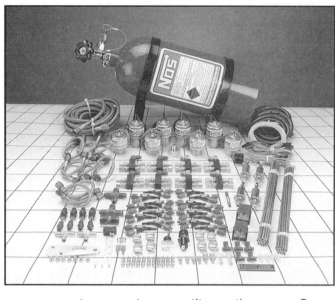

Pro Shot Twin Fogger systems offers 150 to 1000 horsepower of direct port nitrous oxide injection. This two stage system incorporates two complete fogger systems with Fogger nozzles and maximum tunability.

Note: All bottle measurements include the bottle valve.

Note: Liquid contents may cause severe burns (frostbite) on contact with skin. Use caution when handling bottle in the valve area. Safety disc on valve may relieve contents at any time. Do not ever overfill bottle, do not puncture, incenerate, use near heat, or store above 120° F (49° C). For racing use only, do not breathe. May cause damage to respiratory tract. Refill only, with Nytrous plus (100 ppm sulfur oxide added).

3.5.1-2
SUPER HIFLO VALVE

NOS has done it again! With an orifice that flows 249% more than the standard industrial valve used by most competitors, the new Super HiFlo valve provides better flow for more consistency and power in today's monster engines. The Super HiFlo valve features specially designed passages to maximize flow rate and velocity, twin gauge ports for the attachment of a nitrous pressure gauge or other performance accessories, the exclusive NOS safety venting system with -8AN fitting for professional in-car blow down tube, and a standard 660 automotive connection. A must for the serious professional.

Valves may be custom ordered to fit any bottle 5 pounds or larger.

Part #16139 - for 10 lb., 7" dia., 19" tall NOS Bottle only

3.5.1-4
HI-FLO™ BOTTLE VALVE

The NOS Hi-Flo™ Valve is the state-of-the-art in valve technology. Continuous research and development has made the Hi-Flo™ Valve a true winner on the strip. This valve comes standard on all NOS bottles. The Hi-Flo™ Valve uses a large non-restrictive orifice that eliminates pressure drop and "freezing" that causes surging and a reduction in horsepower. For extra safety, NOS has incorporated an exclusive blow-off venting system into the Hi-Flo™ Valve. In the event your bottle is overfilled or pressure in the bottle increases beyond the maximum safety level, bottle pressure is relieved.

Part #	Description
16140	All 5 lb. and larger bottles
16145	All 1 lb., 2 lb. and 2 1/2 lb. bottles
16146	10 oz. bottle only

3.5.1-5
BOTTLE BLANKET

The NOS Bottle Blanket is an excellent accessory item to 1 help stabilize nitrous bottle temperatures by keeping heat in and cold out and is an excellent companion to the NOS bottle heater. The blue Bottle Blanket is also a great cosmetic item to dress up your bottle and hide all those scrapes and scratches. Features include velcro fasteners, attractive heavy duty blue nylon material with lining for insulation and NOS logo patch.

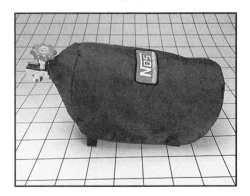

Typical dry manifold kit for factory fuel injected imports such as Acura, BMW, Honda, and Toyota engines. These kits deliver amazing performance gains when installed on small-displacement imports.

Bottle Blankets

Part #	Description
14165	New style 7" dia. 10lb. bottle
14165	Old style 6 3/4" dia. 10lb. bottle
14166	2 lb. bottle
14167	15 lb. bottle

NOS PRO44
RACING FUEL PUMP

NOS brings you the world's finest, most efficient professional racing pump. The NOS Pro 44 is engineered for the world's most powerful Pro Modified, Pro Street, and Pro Stock engines. With a higher flow rating at operating pressure than the competition, the new NOS Pro44 Racing Pump delivers enough fuel for virtually any gasoline fueled race engine and most alcohol engines. This pump provides you the reliability that other popular pumps lack. With no metal to metal contact inside the pump and a Mil-Spec motor, you get a longer lasting pump that you can depend on run after run. The new NOS Pro44 Racing Pump also runs quieter and keeps the fuel cooler than competitive pumps. Other features include an adjustable bypass that allows you to set fuel pressure out of the pump from 10 to 35 psi and CNC-machined billet construction. Fully compatible with both gasoline and alcohol, the NOS Pro44 accepts - 12AN fittings. Part #15766

RACING FUEL PRESSURE REGULATOR CARBURETED/EFI APPLICATIONS

The NOS Racing Fuel Regulator is an excellent choice where demands from a nitrous system exceed 300 HP. This state-of-the-art, by-passing type regulator has many features; adjustability from 5-50 psi with a simple spring change, can be used with either fuel injection or carburetion, 1 inlet/3 outlet ports plus a by-pass, full pressure compensating, offers steady, non-creeping fuel pressures for nitrous or other applications. Comes with 1/4" NPT inlet/outlet ports. Requires by-pass line. Part #15851.

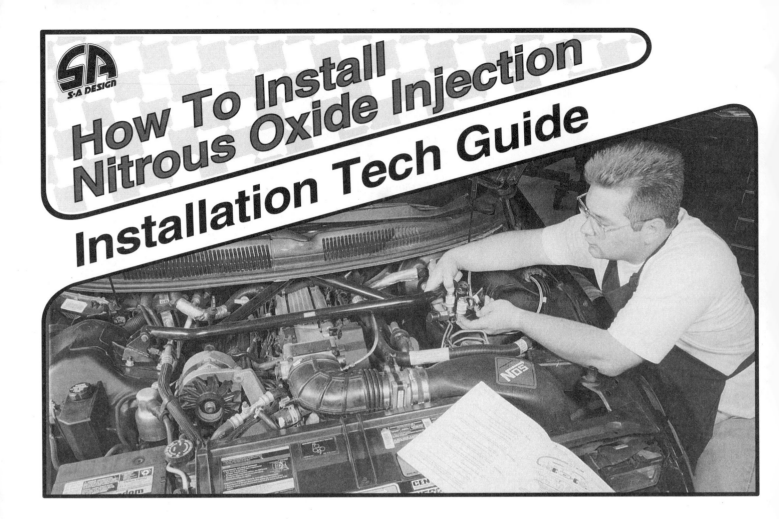

How To Install Nitrous Oxide Injection
Installation Tech Guide

INSTALLATION FUNDAMENTALS

4.1.1
INSTALLING THE BOTTLE

Accurately calibrating and tuning your NOS nitrous system depends on the bottle's temperature remaining stable. Mount the bottle away from heat sources, such as the engine compartment or exhaust system, and away from windows, where the bottle is exposed to direct sunlight. In fastback-styled vehicles such as Camaros, Firebirds, 300ZXs, etc., it's impractical to mount the bottle away from direct sunlight. For cars such as these, the bottle should be covered or insulated with an NOS bottle blanket or an equivalent.

The professionals at NOS recommend that the bottle be environmentally separated from the driver's compartment. Again, fastback vehicles do not have separate trunk compartments, so kits designed for these cars include an external blow-down tube. The safety blow-down tube should be mounted to the exterior of the vehicle (preferably under the vehicle). This procedure will prevent filling the driver's compartment with a cloud of nitrous oxide if, for any reason, the safety pressure relief cap ruptures.

4.1.1.1
BOTTLE ORIENTATION

Bottle placement is critical to the performance of your NOS nitrous system. It's important to understand how the bottle valve and siphon tube are assembled to properly orient the bottle in your vehicle and ensure that it picks up liquid nitrous while undergoing acceleration. All NOS nitrous bottles are assembled so that the bottom of the siphon tube is at the bottom of the bottle and opposite the bottle label. (Figure 4.1a)

Whenever the bottle is mounted in a horizontal position, the valve handle must be toward the front of the vehicle with the label facing up. (Figure 4.1b-1) If the bottle is mounted vertically, the valve handle and label must face toward the front of the vehicle. (Figure 4.1b-2) This orientation will position the siphon tube at the back of the bottle where the liquid N_2O will be during acceleration. *Do not* attempt to remove the siphon tube without completely emptying the bottle of all nitrous and pressure.

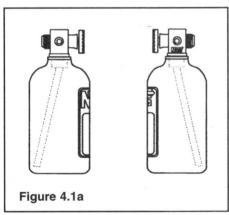

Figure 4.1a

A bottle mounted upside-down must have the siphon tube removed before use. (Figure 4.1b-3) Non-siphon bottles can be specially ordered from NOS. If the bottle must be mounted parallel to the axles of the vehicle (sideways), the valve handle and label

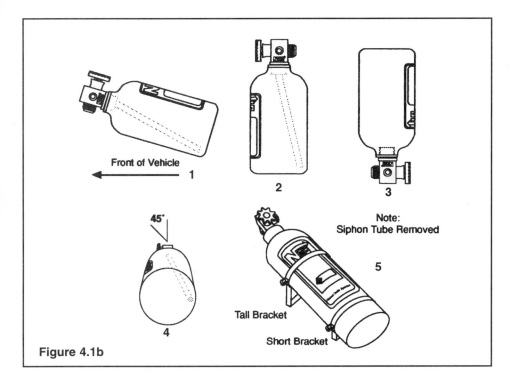

Front of Vehicle

1

2

3

45°

4

Note:
Siphon Tube Removed

5

Tall Bracket

Short Bracket

Figure 4.1b

must be angled at approximately 45° toward the front of the vehicle. (Figure 4.1b-4) This orientation will position the siphon tube toward the rear of the bottle.

When using a bottle with a siphon tube, the tall bracket should be at the valve end of the bottle and the short bracket at the bottom. (Figure 4.1b-5) The most efficient mounting is the horizontal position (Figure 4.1b-1) with the valve handle toward the front of the vehicle. This position allows the greatest amount of liquid to be used before the siphon tube begins to pick up gaseous nitrous oxide.

This Pro Mod racer mounted a pair of bottles according to the rules. They are within the confines of the safety rollcage and have the blow-down tubes routed outside the cabin.

4.1.1.2
BOTTLE PLACEMENT
IN RACING VEHICLES

Before mounting a nitrous bottle in a racing vehicle intended for use in sanctioned events, check with the sanctioning association for any rules regarding this subject. Most associations require the bottle to be mounted within the confines of the safety rollcage, with the safety pressure relief cap vented away from the driver's compartment.

Braided stainless lines coupled to AN bulkhead fittings make a nice blow-down tube system.

4.1.2
HOW TO INSTALL A
NITROUS FEED LINE

Here's a typical nitrous feed line installation on a production car. The procedure isn't what you'd call rocket science; it's more common sense. With stock street-driven cars, it's usually best to follow the stock fuel line route. One more tip: Some nitrous enthusiasts like to insulate the supply line with water heater pipe insulation, available at most hardware stores.

Following the fuel lines along the left side of the vehicle and entering the engine bay near the master cylinder works well. Determine the route for your nitrous feed line to follow. Ensure that the path is clear of exhaust system, suspension, steering, wheels, electrical lines and components, and tires.

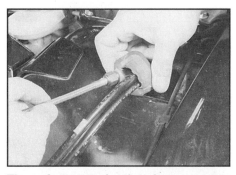

The safest route for the nitrous system fuel and nitrous lines is following the factory line. The factory has done crash studies and has determined the best route to keep the fuel line safe. We started at the front and worked our way toward the rear of the car, first working the line through the fuel line grommet.

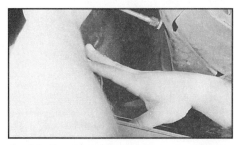

Inside the wheel house there's a channel for the nitrous line, but you have to bend back the fender liner.

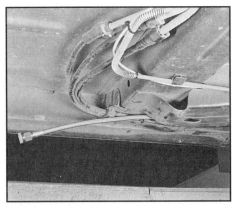

The nitrous line exiting the subframe structure. We ran the nitrous line inside the subframe rail.

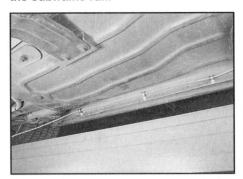

If it's necessary to support the nitrous supply line under the vehicle, use ½-inch Tinnerman clamps or nylon tie-wraps. Here we show a straight shot to the rear wheel house. Use a combination of clamps, tie-wraps, and body panels to lace the nitrous line away from the axle.

A body panel lip provided a good place to lace the line up to the point where we reentered the interior. The drain plug is an easy access point. Just punch a hole in it and run the line through it.

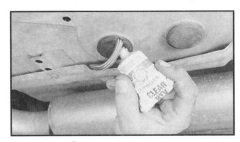

After reinstalling the drain plug and attaching it to the nitrous bottle, seal it with a liberal application of RTV. Sometimes attaching the nitrous supply line to the nitrous bottle valve adapter requires using an optional 4AN to 4AN 90° fitting.

Before you attach the nitrous supply line to the nitrous solenoid inlet port (Using the optional 4AN to 4AN 90° Fitting (21), if necessary), purge the nitrous supply line by wrapping the end of nitrous line with a rag and holding it securely. Point opening away from people and briefly open bottle valve.

4.1.3
FUEL SYSTEM DESIGN TACTICS

There are two types of fuel pumps produced for gasoline engines: low pressure (4 to 10 psi) and high pressure (30 to 90 psi).

4.1.3.1
LOW-PRESSURE PUMPS

Low pressure pumps are intended for carbureted engines, Common examples are the 110 and 140 gallon per hour (gph) units marketed by a number of manufacturers. These pumps are rated under free-flow exit conditions (no outlet restriction). When the

NITROUS OXIDE INJECTION Tips & Tricks

QUICK TECH: FULL RACE FUEL AND NITROUS LINE INSTALL

Race cars usually have shorter nitrous supply lines. The shorter the line, the more it flows, and in general the system hits harder, too. Check out how Ken Duttweiler and crew installed the supply line in this Mustang.

Racers put the bottle near the engine to shorten the nitrous feed line length. This one is in the front passenger area.

You can see how the line hangs loose a little bit then straight through the firewall. That second line spliced into the main feed line goes to the bottle pressure gauge.

Always use grommets on fuel, nitrous, or electrical lines that pass through a firewall, even if they're braided steel. The nitrous feed line takes the shortest path to the nitrous solenoid. The small line coming off the main one goes to the purge valve.

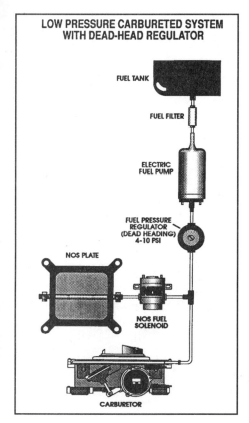

LOW PRESSURE CARBURETED SYSTEM
WITH DEAD-HEAD REGULATOR

FUEL TANK

FUEL FILTER

ELECTRIC
FUEL PUMP

FUEL PRESSURE
REGULATOR
(DEAD HEADING)
4-10 PSI

NOS PLATE

NOS FUEL
SOLENOID

CARBURETOR

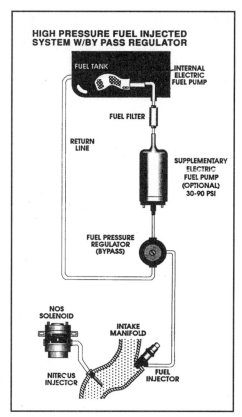

HIGH PRESSURE FUEL INJECTED
SYSTEM W/BY PASS REGULATOR

FUEL TANK

INTERNAL
ELECTRIC
FUEL PUMP

FUEL FILTER

RETURN
LINE

SUPPLEMENTARY
ELECTRIC
FUEL PUMP
(OPTIONAL)
30-90 PSI

FUEL PRESSURE
REGULATOR
(BYPASS)

NOS
SOLENOID

INTAKE
MANIFOLD

NITRCUS
INJECTOR

FUEL
INJECTOR

outlet of the pump is restricted (real-world conditions) the flow capacity is usually significantly less than the rated performance.

Low-pressure pumps are the most economical to produce. In most carbureted applications a low-pressure pump will provide adequate performance and enjoy a cost advantage.

4.1.3.2
HIGH-PRESSURE PUMPS

Flow capabilities of high-pressure pumps are specified at typical, real-world pressure levels. This results in pumps performing much closer to the manufacturer's claim than most low-pressure units.

High-pressure pumps will work well in carbureted applications when matched with the correct bypassing fuel-pressure regulator. Never attempt to use a high-pressure pump with a dead-heading fuel-pressure regulator.

Note: For more information on regulators see "Choosing the Correct Fuel Pressure Regulator."

High-pressure pumps are constructed with closer tolerances and more costly production techniques.

High-pressure pumps will tolerate more severe operating conditions and, last longer than low-pressure units.

4.1.3.3
TWO METHODS FOR CHOOSING THE CORRECT FUEL PUMP

Method #1

When purchasing a fuel pump, there are two factors to consider: performance and cost. By correctly matching a fuel pump to your requirements, you can fill your needs without spending money needlessly. Using the tips below you should be able to choose the correct pump for your vehicle.

1) Determine the horsepower the pump will have to support (be realistic—no inflated values).

2) Estimate the number of gallons of fuel per hour required to support the horsepower from 1).

Note: these figures are for gasoline; for alcohol, double them. For four-cycle engines: multiply horsepower by 0.08 to 0.095. For two-cycle engines: multiply horsepower by 0.095 to 0.11. The result is the number of gph required.

3) Determine the fuel pressure at which the pump will operate. For carbureted engines, this should be 6 to 10 psi. For fuel-injected applications, you'll have to estimate the required pressure.

4) Examine the flow versus pressure curve for the pump you're considering. Your flow requirements should be on or below the pumps plotted performance.

Note: In some instances it's impractical to use a single fuel pump. It's possible to run two pumps in parallel, resulting in an approximate doubling of flow rate if done correctly.

In high pressure applications, two pumps may be run in series. This occurs when trying to increase the fuel flow rate in a late-model fuel-injected vehicle. The resulting flow of this arrangement isn't equal to the sum of the two pump's flow rates (it will be less).

Method #2

Pressure and Flow

I like to refer to pressure and flow as night and day. How many times have you heard somebody say "it can't be a fuel problem because I had good fuel pressure." Consider this: if you put a small valve just before the carburetor and closed it down creating a restriction, wouldn't you still have good pressure before the valve? In this instance, though, you would have depreciated flow to the carburetor.

Now let's look at the other scenario. How often have you seen someone at the dragstrip run a hose from the fuel pump to a one-gallon container and measure the time to fill the can. When the calculations are all done, the rocket scientist announces, "it can't be the fuel pump because I'm pumping so many gallons per minute."

Now let's look at the proper way to check fuel flow. First, all reputable pump manufacturers rate their fuel pumps at gallons per hour (gph) @ some pressure. What you should do first is estimate the horsepower of the engine you're trying to feed. Divide the estimated horsepower by two to get a fuel flow rate required to support that maximum horsepower at a BSFC of 0.50. Once you have your theoretical fuel requirement in lb./hr., convert it to gph by dividing pounds of fuel by 6.2 to 6.8 lb./gal. Now take this number (lets use 100 gal/hr) and divide it by 60 to get the required flow in one minute. (Which, in this case, would work out to be 1.66 gal/minute). If we take the reciprocal of this (1 divided by 1.66), we would get the fraction of a minute required to flow one gallon. This would be 0.6 minutes, or 36 seconds.

Now let's get practical. Plumb a pressure gage into a fuel line just before the carburetor or injectors, followed by a small petcock or needle valve. Once you've safely attached the fuel line to a sealed, vented measuring container of at least two gallons, turn on the pump and adjust the petcock valve until the pressure reads whatever pressure at which the pump is rated. At this point, stop the pump, drain the container, then get ready to measure the time required to fill one gallon in the container with flow at rated pressure! This method will ensure accurate results and cut through all the claims and counter claims.

Note: *"If this is an electric pump, make sure that you monitor voltage to the pump and that the hot wire feeding the pump and ground wire will carry the amperage necessary to achieve full rated flow. Once you qualify your entire fuel delivery system using this method, you'll be amazed at how many 'gremlins' disappear."*
—From "Uncommon Sense In Engine Development," presented at the 1997 SuperFlow Advanced Engine Technology Conference.

4.1.3.4
CHOOSING THE CORRECT FUEL PRESSURE REGULATOR

There are two types of fuel pressure regulators available: dead-heading and bypassing. When working with a low-pressure pump, either type can be used successfully. When using a high-pressure pump, a bypassing regulator must be used.

Note: *Attempting to use a Dead-heading regulator with a high pres-*

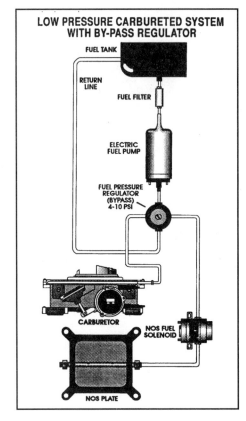

sure pump will result in premature pump failure and/or burst fuel lines.

Regardless of which type of regulator you choose, it's important that the regulator be matched to the flow capabilities of your fuel pump. Listed below are the characteristics of the two types of regulators available.

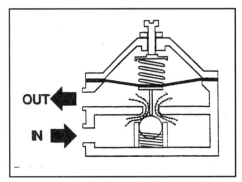

Dead-Heading

Fuel is regulated down to a set value using a diaphragm/spring arrangement. The only fuel that passes through the regulator is that which will pass into the engine.

If fuel requirement goes to zero, such as when the engine stops, fuel flow through the regulator ceases. If the fuel pump remains on, the fuel

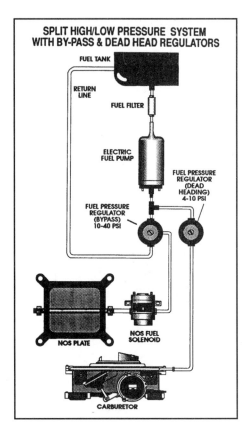

pressure in the line upstream of the regulator will climb to the value at which the pump stalls.

Dead-heading regulators are relatively inexpensive, yet provide acceptable performance in most applications.

Bypassing

A bypassing regulator controls fuel pressure by returning excess fuel to the fuel tank or the fuel line upstream of the fuel pump. This offers several advantages over the dead-heading type unit.

Stress on the fuel pump is reduced by lowering the fuel pressure at which the pump operates. (The fuel pump will not see pressures above that of the regulator setting.) Fuel pressure is

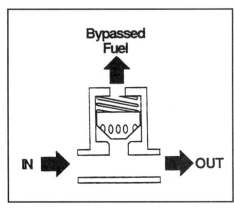

more constant with a bypassing regulator (diaphragm-type units pulse); however, in most carbureted applications this isn't critical. When using nitrous oxide injection, it's desirable to eliminate fuel pressure pulsing (nitrous/fuel ratio will fluctuate when the regulator pulses).

Designing Your Fuel System

For satisfactory performance, the entire fuel system must be matched to the fuel flow requirements. Following the guidelines listed below should provide acceptable performance.

Pump Location

When mounting a fuel pump, it's desirable to locate the pump as near the fuel tank as possible. This will minimize the chance of vapor lock on hot days.

Fuel Line Size and Length

The inner diameter of the fuel line should be as big as the inner diameter of the fuel pump fittings.

If two lines need to be split or joined in a "Y" or "T" arrangement, the cross sectional area of the two lines should be equivalent to the cross sectional area of the single line.

Fuel Lines should be kept as short and free of tight bends as practical.

Fuel Filters

Fuel filters should provide adequate filtration without being excessively restrictive. Several different types of filters are available. When choosing a filter, make sure that the flow capability is matched to your pump.

4.1.3.5
THE ADVANTAGE OF A HIGH-PRESSURE RETURN-STYLE FUEL SYSTEM

Nitrous Oxide injection systems are usually configured to operate with four to 10 psi fuel pressure. NOS kits are set up to operate at these levels to be compatible with typical carbureted fuel systems. In most low-to-moderate output applications, this works fine.

In high-output and competition environments there are performance and tuning advantages to be had from using elevated fuel pressure for the NOS injection system.

Here's how it works. The fuel injection side of an NOS injection kit is a fixed orifice/constant-flow device. When the NOS system is activated, the fuel solenoid opens fully; variations in fuel flow will only result from changes in fuel pressure.

The relationship between fuel pressure and fuel flow follows a fundamental law of fluid mechanics. This relationship can be expressed by:

Flow is proportional to the Sqrt (square root) of fuel pressure.

At carbureted fuel pressure levels, small changes in fuel pressure produce significant changes in fuel flow rate. At fuel injection-type fuel-pressure levels, the same size pressure fluctuations produce much smaller changes in flow rate. Examples one and two provide a comparison of the effects of typical fuel pressure fluctuations.

Example One:
Fuel Pressure = five psi
Fuel Pressure Fluctuation = +/- one psi

This can produce flow deviations of:

1) Sq rt of 4/5= 0.89 or 89 percent of baseline
2) Sqrt of 5/6= 1.09 or 109 percent of baseline. This means just a +/- one psi fluctuation in fuel pressure can change fuel flow up to 20 percent.

Example Two:
Fuel Pressure = 30 psi. Fuel Pressure Fluctuation -/+ one psi
This can produce flow changes of:
1) * = 0.983 or 98.3 percent of baseline
2) * = 101.6 or 101.6 percent of baseline
So a +/- one psi change In fuel pressure only changes actual fuel flow about 3.5 percent with the higher pressure.

The advantage this gives you is reducing the potential variation in fuel flow rate to the NOS injection system. This keeps the nitrous/fuel ratio

much more constant, thus minimizing lost horsepower due to overly rich conditions and preventing engine damage from excessively lean mixtures. This lets you make much finer adjustment to nitrous/fuel ratio so you can walk right to edge and not fall off.

4.1.3.6
TIPS FOR TWEAKING YOUR FUEL SYSTEM

Building and tuning a drag race car is a process that involves chasing down and correcting "weak links" in the performance chain. On the mechanical side, a race car is a collection of systems that work together to produce power and motion. If any of these systems fails to deliver a required function, the performance of the whole machine suffers.

As displacement, rpm, and nitrous flow increase, so does the engine's need for fuel. If the fuel system on your race car fails to deliver an adequate fuel supply to the carburetor, then the air-to-fuel and nitrous-to-fuel ratios will be affected, usually toward the lean side; however, it's possible to have too much pressure leading to an over rich condition. Lean air/fuel ratios tend to cause cylinder temperatures to rise and can, in extreme conditions, lead to detonation and destroy your engine; a rich condition lowers cylinder temperatures and reduces power output.

The fuel delivery system is a primary system that must function properly. If it doesn't deliver enough fuel to your carburetor and nitrous system, then no amount of tuning will achieve optimum engine performance.

There are three basic functions in the process of fuel delivery. First is the rated volume of the pump; second is the inside diameter of the fuel line; and third is the pressure, measured in pounds psi. Pressure and volume are related in that a higher pressure, for a given diameter of fuel line, will yield more volume, at least up to a point. And obviously a larger-diameter line will have a higher-volume capacity.

Delivering an adequate supply of fuel requires that the system overcome the forces of gravity (since it must be pumped up to the carburetor against Earth's gravity), the acceleration of the car, and the friction within the fuel line. As a general rule, a fuel line with a horizontal length of 13 feet between the tank and carburetor will lose 4 psi per g of acceleration. Losing pressure means you're also losing volume, thereby losing performance.

The solution to this performance problem is to design a system that has an adequate reserve of pressure to overcome the effects of gravity (both Earth's and the gs during launch) and to install a fuel line that is of adequate diameter and is as free of needless bends as possible. Bends in the fuel lines and connections are a source of turbulence and friction and reduce flow.

The trend in fuel system design has been toward high-pressure systems to overcome the obstacles stated above. In drag racing, Warren Johnson is credited with starting this move in the early '80s. His crew designed a high-torque fuel pump that revolutionized the way racers thought about fuel systems. Since then, using a high-torque, high-pressure, high-flow pump has been refined with the concept of using return lines that offer advantages in fuel pressure stability, cooling, and bleeding off air in the fuel.

The old way, with a big Holley pump and regulators near the carbs, was hard on the electric motors. With this kind of system you have a long column of fuel that would constantly stop and start as the regulator opened and closed to maintain its pressure setting. At the same time, the fuel pump's motor, being part of a hydraulic system, would stop and start with the fuel. Stopping an electric pump motor is hard on the unit. Depending on where in its cycle it stopped could create a closed circuit and burn out, which in fact was a big problem with these early systems. By using a return line, the pump is allowed to stay in constant motion, thus delivering consistent pressure in the fuel line.

If you want a state-of-the-art fuel system, the following ideas will help you achieve it. Of course, you'll still have to do the testing and tuning, preferably at the race track.

1. Delivering a consistent supply of fuel begins with choosing a proper fuel tank. A proper fuel system has a tank with baffles to keep the fuel from sloshing away from outlet during acceleration. It also should have fuel outlet bungs that are positioned such that the force of acceleration feeds fuel into the fuel line before the pump.

2. Electric fuel pumps do not pull fuel well; they're better at pushing it. So the less restriction you have before the pump the more efficient and stable your fuel supply will be. Low-pressure/high-volume systems are more sensitive to restrictions than high-pressure/low-volume systems. Since the system is gravity fed at this end by accelerating off the line, restrictions here can really impede the flow of fuel.

3. You can reduce the turbulence in the fuel line exiting the fuel tank by massaging the insides of the fitting to improve flow. It's similar to porting the heads. Drill out the I.D of the fitting, then hand blend the angles of the male and female fittings. You have to be careful not to enlarge the I.D too much or you'll compromise the integrity of the seal. If you have a fuel delivery problem, this can help somewhat.

4. You want to filter debris from the fuel before the pump. That way it can't lodge in an unknown position

CARROL SMITH ON EARL'S PERFORMANCE PRODUCTS

Earl's has the biggest supply and largest selection of parts and configurations of anyone on the planet. So no matter what you're plumbing, it probably already has the part.

As for the quality of the components, Earl's uses aircraft drawings and design specs. It doesn't keep the material source log, so it can't trace each fitting back to the shovel full of oil that came out of the ground they (FAA/AN sources) can, or at least they claim they can. The only component that we inspect 100-percent of the production is oil coolers.

Earl's batch inspects by setting up the machine, running 50 or so, then checking tolerances on one. It then lets the machine run, and at the end of the production run, checks another article for tolerance, if it is in tolerance, then you can assume the rest are.

About the only thing Earl's has to worry about is a materials defect. Particularly with aluminum bar stock. Sometimes it will get a fold in it which can be difficult to detect. If the article is being made on a lathe one at a time, the operator will notice that the drill trailings, which should be long spirals, become little chips. But on an automated machine with everything covered in sulphur oil, it's impossible to see. Sometimes, 5000 fittings have to be scrapped. Earl doesn't like that and it makes him say evil words.

When it comes to plumbing a production car versus a race car, you essentially have the same goal. The only differences are longer hoses, maybe 16-feet from the fuel tank to the engine. Since pressure is lost over distance you can use a larger-diameter line and run more pressure.

According to Earl, there's also user responsibility. If you're trying to put a nut on a bolt and the nut doesn't have any threads, you should be able to figure that out. If you make up a hose with ends and install it on an airplane and you don't pressure-test it, you ought to have your license pulled. Earl's sells a pressure tester, or you can make one for about $3. It's rather simple; use air and Formula 409; if it bubbles, it leaks; if it doesn't it's fine. Earl says he's seen guys put a hose on with one of the fittings blocked and ruin a motor.

and cause a restriction or perhaps hurt the pump. It's best to position the filter so it's easy to inspect and clean. You might want to use a filter with lots of capacity reserve so it doesn't offer much restriction to the system before the pump.

5. Pros use high-torque motors to generate reliable high pressure. A weak motor tends to stop at lower pressure, and when it does, it draws more current from the battery and wears out quickly. Pump pressures are related to the amount of voltage available. If you need more pressure run a 16-volt battery, but balance that against the heavier weight of a 16-volt battery. Another tact is to use a 12-volt because of weight and then use 10-gauge wire from the kill switch directly to the pump to deliver the max amount of voltage offered by the battery. The wiring can act as a restriction and reduce fuel pressure and flow.

6. A spring-actuated valve sets fuel pressure after the pump. The valve releases excess pressure by returning high-pressure fuel to the fuel tank. It's common to run 30 to 35 psi between the pump and a second pressure regulator just before the carburetors. This arrangement keeps the pump from stopping, which keeps the pressure and volume more consistent. Since the column of fuel isn't starting and stopping it saves the electric pump, plus it keeps the fuel cool and bleeds off air.

7. You need a second pressure regulator to reduce pressure to the carburetors. Too much pressure to the carburetor and it will blow past the needle valve and raise the level in the fuel bowl, causing a rich fuel mixture. Run a return line off the regulator block to a "T"-fitting just before the fuel pump. The amount of fuel returned is controlled by a jet, which further bleeds off air and also cools the fuel, as the fuel line is close to the engine at this point.

8. Here's another pro racer trick. Use a plug in the regulator block to install a fuel-pressure gauge. Since you can't really run it in the cockpit, why

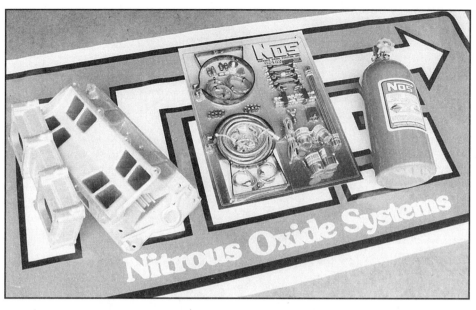

have it on the car? Check pressure between rounds to verify. Use a second plug to let you check the low pressure side (near carbs). We know a successful bracket racer that likes to run pressure to the carb at a approximately 9.5 psi—as high as he can without fuel pressure blowing off the needle valves and upsetting fuel bowl levels. Fuel pressure only varies by 0.2 to 0.3 psi when it's run this high. He used to run 8 to 8.5 psi, and pressure would fluctuate about one psi when the car left, then slowly recovered. He's not sure if dropping a pound hurts him that much, but eliminating a variable can't hurt when tuning the car for track conditions.

9. If you can't science out a starting-line bog, try this. Run -10 lines to the carbs. Most racers use -8, but we've heard reports that after installing a high-pressure fuel system, a -10 line seems to help. Basically, you get a reserve in the lines to feed the carbs during the initial launch g-shock. The reason you need that is when the g-shock adds to the psi in the lines, the regulator, which is set at 9 psi, will shut fuel flow off and momentarily starve the carb. The preceding scenario assumes the lines are laid so the force of the launch pushes the fuel in the lines toward the carb and regulator. You also can drill out the opening in the carb by 0.050 inch and blend the angles. Don't use a larger-diameter drill bit; any bigger and you won't get a secure seal.

4.1.4
HOW TO WORK WITH DIRECT PORT PLUMBING

Plumbing the nitrous and fuel hard lines on a direct-port injection system isn't as easy as it looks. Here we show you how the professionals at NOS approach the craft of bending tubes.

4.1.4.1
INSTALLING THE NOZZLES

1.
Before you can select the mounting location for the distribution block, you've got to design around the throttle linkage. The throttle linkage has to go where it has to go. The installer places the throttle linkage fulcrum on

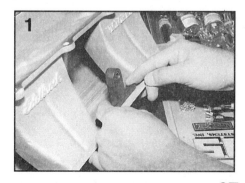

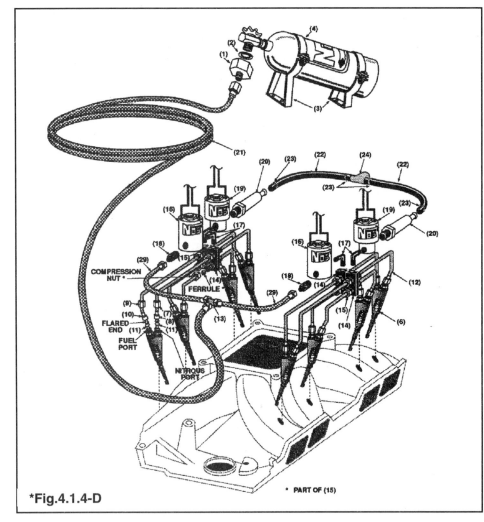

COMPRESSION NUT *

FERRULE

FLARED END

FUEL PORT

NITROUS PORT

*Fig.4.1.4-D

* PART OF (15)

runner. We'll put the first standard two inches from the flange for the height reference. Repeat for each runner. The second standard is the center line of the port. Again, repeat the process for each runner.

3.
Where the standard lines intersect, punch mark the position for each nozzle.

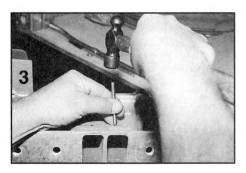

4.
With the nozzle positions marked, the next step is to drill them out. Our installer prefers to use a drill press. He says this keeps all the holes on the same plane. He also uses the drill press to tap the holes.

5.
When tapping the holes, do not run the tap all the way through the hole. These are pipe threads, and as such are tapered. If you run the tap all the way through, you won't have the taper to cause a bind and force an interference fit. When you install the nozzle, it will thread, but it will be far too loose.

the manifold to visualize the configuration of the plumbing system.

Imagine where your linkage is going to be; it's usually 1½ inch to either side. The pole to the throttle pedal is to the inside; the pole to the carburetor is to the outside. You have a pole coming from the throttle this width, and you have a pole going to the carburetors up this way, so the back-side of the distribution block will be outboard roughly one inch. The photographs will make this more clear.

Once you've compensated for the throttle linkage, the distribution block must be positioned so that there's

adequate clearance on either end to allow you to mount the solenoid. (Refer to Figure 4.1.4-D.)

If you're not experienced in tube bending, make a sample tube using either a piece of brakeline or a coat hanger before you bend each solenoid extension tube. This practice will help you minimize errors and produce an aesthetically pleasing plumbing job.

2a, 2b
This plumbing would normally have two reference lines that vary with the location of the nozzle in the intake

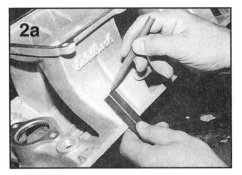

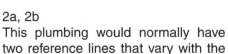

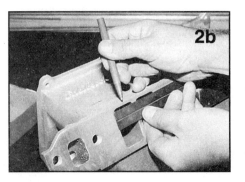

6.

You also can adjust how far you put the nozzle into the runner by how far you run the tap into the hole. This is where you need to exercise judgment. The idea is to spray the nitrous and fuel into the port. If the nozzle is too shallow it will hit the runner wall, causing the fuel to stick to the wall and the nitrous to cool the metal instead of the intake charge.

7.

Screw in the nozzles in four turns. This should have three threads showing, which puts the nozzle at 0.600-in. above the base.

8.

When you're mocking up your system, you can dry fit the plumbing, but fit it loosely. Don't tighten. Otherwise you can gall the fittings and they won't seal correctly. Also during final assembly don't over tighten. Run it in until the fitting is tight, then give it one more turn.

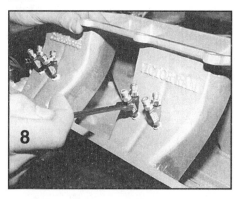

9a, 9b.

Be sure to use thread sealant with Teflon on final assembly.

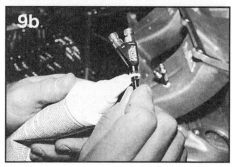

10a, 10b.

Once you've installed the nozzles, check alignment with a straight edge. If one or two nozzles are low, correct by screwing the higher nozzles farther into the manifold.

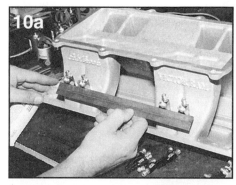

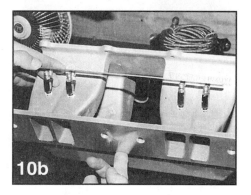

4.1.4.2
BENDING THE TUBES

Always start on the throttle linkage side. This allows you to set the height of the distribution block in relation to the throttle linkage. If you start on the other side, you may put the distribution block too low or too high.

The order of attachment to the distribution block is as follows: Working from the inside nozzle outward, connect hard line to the bottom inside port of the distribution block first; then outward.

Double-flare fittings have a thicker flange. Single-flare fittings have a thinner flange. This means you have to adjust the length, making the down length longer. Where you have the line, you have to draw it past that. In other words, move your reference point on the bender about 0.050 to 0.075.

11.

For professional-looking results, the following steps need to be performed with a quality tube-bending tool. NOS sells a tool for this purpose under Part # 15991. The Imperial Eastman No. 364FH tube-bending tool which retails for about $40, is highly recommended. You need a good tube bender, one with reference marks to do this job right.

Select two of the 12-in. solenoid extension tubes (13). Install blue sleeves (8) and B-Nuts (7) over flared-end solenoid extension tubes. Mark tubes at desired height above nozzle for first bend. Mark should be a minimum of 1-in. from end of tube. Make the desired bend in the solenoid extension tubes at mark. Bend should start at mark and proceed away from flared end of tube. (Figure 4.1.4-C)

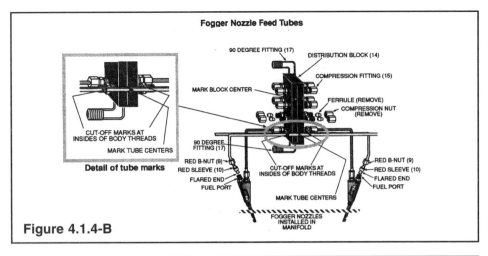

Figure 4.1.4-B

Fogger Nozzle Feed Tubes

90 DEGREE FITTING (17)
DISTRIBUTION BLOCK (14)
COMPRESSION FITTING (15)
MARK BLOCK CENTER
FERRULE (REMOVE)
COMPRESSION NUT (REMOVE)
90 DEGREE FITTING (17)
RED B-NUT (9)
RED SLEEVE (10)
FLARED END
FUEL PORT
CUT-OFF MARKS AT INSIDES OF BODY THREADS
MARK TUBE CENTERS
RED B-NUT (9)
RED SLEEVE (10)
FLARED END
FUEL PORT
FOGGER NOZZLES INSTALLED IN MANIFOLD

CUT-OFF MARKS AT INSIDES OF BODY THREADS
MARK TUBE CENTERS
Detail of tube marks

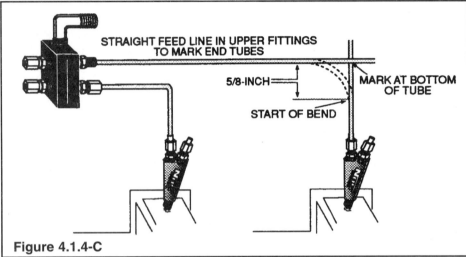

Figure 4.1.4-C

STRAIGHT FEED LINE IN UPPER FITTINGS TO MARK END TUBES
5/8-INCH
MARK AT BOTTOM OF TUBE
START OF BEND

12.
Install two bent solenoid extension tubes, blue B-Nuts, and sleeves on the Fogger nozzles closest to the distribution block (make sure tubes are attached to the nitrous ports on Fogger nozzles) with the two long legs of tubes crossing. (Figure 4.1.4-B). Measure between the insides of the tubes and place a center mark across the tubes.

13.
Next, take your block and center it between the two nozzles. Mark the tubes using the block as a guide.

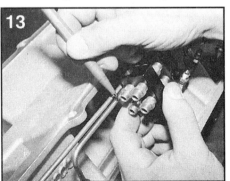

14.
Put the top of the B-nut right on the first scribe mark then bend it 90 degrees. Repeat, making two inside 90-degree tubes. These will be your standard.

15.
Take the tubes, put them side by side, then mark the spot in the middle of the scribe marks you just made referencing the distribution block. This gives you the length of the tube necessary to touch the face of the compression fitting. Then put it next to the compression fitting and mark it at the end of the threads on the inside (that's

where the end of the tube should butt against) then cut.

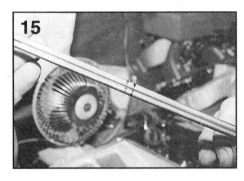

16.
At the NOS shop, the installer uses a band saw to cut the tubes. For those less fortunate, a hacksaw works fine.

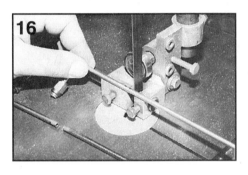

17.
Be sure to deburr the cut ends of all tubes.

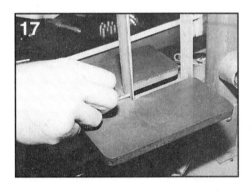

18.
Chamfering the inside edge removes burrs and loose metal from the saw cut. Loose material easily can become dislodged and clog a jet.

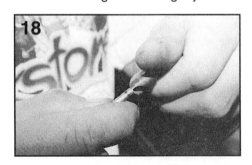

19.
A drill bit provides the final deburring touch to the tube's interior.

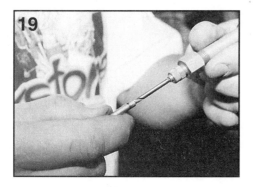

20.
The two tubes, completed, center the distribution block. Now it needs to be bent out to allow room for the linkage.

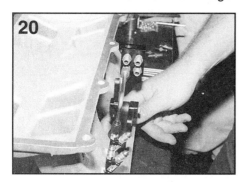

21.
This move requires some feel for the metal you're bending. How the installer accomplished this is by fitting the tube bender to the tubes in place, adjusting the tool to place the bend exactly where he wanted it, and then applied force smoothly to bend the tube.

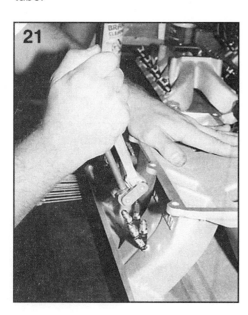

22.
Shown are the desired results. Notice that the throttle linkage will now have adequate room to operate without binding with the distribution block.

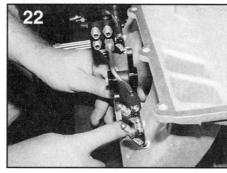

23a, 23b.
The next task is to finish the tubes for the remaining ports. Our installer uses a modified eight-port distribution block to help him set the plumbing. The block is drilled through, allowing the uncut tubes to stick through. This makes marking the correct cut lines easy since the block serves as a guide.

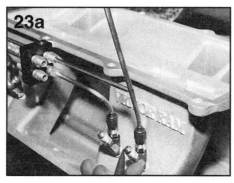

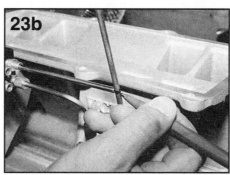

24a, 24b.
Learning to bend the tubes to fit correctly with a pleasing shape takes practice. it's hard to know which direction to bend the tube because the bending tool is designed to bend to the right. Sometimes you have to turn the tube over in order to get a left-hand bend.

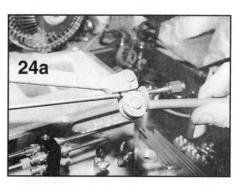

4.1.4.3
INSTALLING FLEXIBLE LINES

A nitrous system isn't all hard lines. You have to contend with the flexible braided steel lines that deliver both fuel and nitrous to your system. The following chart from Aeroquip says it better than we can, so we'll just leave it at that. See Fig. 4.1.4-A on next page.

4.1.5
HOW TO DESIGN A
NITROUS-PROOF WIRING SYSTEM

It wasn't that long ago when racers wouldn't put fuses in the electrical systems on their race cars, and early in the development of modern automotive nitrous systems, nobody bothered to use relays, either. But time, and a few electrical fires, have a way of changing things.

Wiring is simply one of those unpleasant facts of high-performance life. You have to have it, and there's just no easy way to lace a car chassis with all the cables and wires necessary for a modern, high-performance car. Of course, lacing and running the cable is only half of it. You also have to properly connect several separate components not only so they'll function, but will continue to function in the demanding automotive environment.

Granted, getting a nitrous system wired isn't a simple task. Fortunately, most systems come with about all the wiring components and accessories you'll need to let the juice flow. In addition, there are a host of companies from the autosound industry that cater to this occasionally frustrating but exceedingly important aspect of electrical and electronic component installation. Firms such as Scosche, Esoteric Audio, Metra, and even manufacturers of high-end mobile audio equipment have designed and supply a full range of specialty cables, fasteners, and connections for the auto sound enthusiast that gearheads can use to their advantage.

This chapter is designed to introduce you to some of the more common problems and obstacles associated with wiring a nitrous system and how to overcome them. To be sure, having a reliable system isn't magic, but comes from attention to detail and the fundamental laws of physics.

The first rule of wiring your nitrous system is to use the best quality cables, wires, and connectors you can afford. If you have to make budget adjustments, use the wiring kit that came with your system. But upgrade as soon as you can afford it. The second rule is to decide where you will mount each component before you lace a single strand of wire. This locates the component, allowing you to then establish wiring routes and distances. The third rule is to keep your wires and cables as short as possible. Longer cables use more energy than shorter ones, but shorter ones are preferred because they require less power. Naturally, you have to have a cable that is slightly longer than the pure physical distance between components but, exercise judgment when deciding how much excess you need. The fourth rule is to work with wiring in the following sequence: First disconnect the negative terminal of the battery. Second, route the main power cables and ready the fuses for each component. Be sure to leave excess at each end for adjustment and working slack. Third, make the final connections working your way toward the control unit (if your using electronic system controls) from the component that is farthest from it. The fourth rule is to learn all the rules, including the ones

that we've left out, misplaced, or forgotten, so that you can break the rules when the situation calls for it.

4.1.5.1
MATCHING POWER CABLE GAUGE TO POWER DEMAND

A direct current electrical system, such as that in your car, behaves almost exactly as a hydraulic system under pressure. In this metaphorical system, psi is to hydraulics what volts are to an electrical system—namely electrical pressure or force. The wires and cables are as tubes and pipes. A battery is a chemical reservoir of voltage just as a water tower is a reservoir of water pressure. In automotive electrical systems the pressure standard is 13.8 volts, although everyone refers to them as 12-volt systems. Now that we understand volts, the next concept is current flow.

Current flow in electrical or hydraulic systems are directly analogous. It's the amount of water or electricity that passes through a given point in a given amount of time. In electrical systems the current flow is measured in amperes, or amps, for short.

There are two ways to get more amperes (current) flowing through a circuit. You can increase voltage or reduce resistance. The limitation to current flow in a circuit is resistance. Resistance is friction within the circuit or wire that resists the flow of electricity. Electrical friction, called resistance, generates the heat that will melt your wires and blow your fuses. Resistance is measured in ohms. Ohms' Law states that the ratio of the potential (voltage) difference between the ends of a metallic conductor and the electron current flowing through it is a constant. Expressed mathemati-

cally: 1 ohm = 1 volt/1 ampere.

Ohms' Law rules electronics, and it's just as important to power delivery cabling. In a perfect world you'd have 0.00 ohms—no resistance in all your circuits. Unfortunately, we can't reach that theoretical ideal, but we can get close.

The fundamental import of ohms' Law as it affects power cables is this: Given a constant gauge of cable, the longer a cable is, the more resistance it will generate; hence, a longer cable will show lower voltage and amp values than a shorter one. The way around this resistance limitation is to use larger-gauge cables because larger gauge cables have less resistance for a given length. So large gauge wires are in order for 12V systems. That's why it's important to choose and use the right gauge power cable when you're designing your system.

To do this you need to know the current demands that will be placed on the cables. The nitrous solenoids are the most current-hungry devices in a basic nitrous system. For example, the Cheater and Pro Shot nitrous solenoids pull between 12 and 16 amps each; the Power Shot and Super Power Shot pull about four or five amps each. The fuel solenoids demand far less, somewhere on the order of one to 1.5 amps each, because they don't have to over come the high pressures of the nitrous line. That doesn't mean you can ignore their amperage draw; you have to design the system to provide power to all components. If you have a bottle warmer, remote valve controller, and/or other electronic components added to a staged nitrous system, the total current draw can be substantial.

Determining the power draw for your nitrous system can be an exact science, but we don't really need to go

---

NITROUS AND FUEL SOLENOID CURRENT DRAW

System	Amps	System	Amps
Power Shot/ Super Power Shot Fuel Solenoids	1.0 Ampere Ea.	Power Shot/ Super Power Shot N20 Solenoids	4-5 Amps
Cheater/Pro Shot Fuel Solenoids	1.5 Amperes Ea.	Cheater/Pro Shot N20 Solenoids	12.-16 Amps

to those lengths; an approximation should do fine. As we said, the nitrous solenoids are the most power-hungry components in the system, so we've provided a chart with the peak current draw of several popular solenoid sizes. You'll have to measure the other components' current demand with a multi-meter.

Fundamentally, you need to add up the amperage values of all the components on a circuit. For example, if you have a pair of Pro Shot solenoids on a circuit, you have to have a cable that will carry 32 amps before it splits off to each unit, where the cable only has to carry 16 amps. By breaking down your system in such a way and adding up the amperage draw, you can arrive at the total current your main power cable will have to carry.

By the way, if you have components in the circuit that are rated in watts, you can convert watts to amps by dividing the wattage by the volts of the system. In this case it's Watts/13=Volts. Once you have your amperage figured out, you can measure or estimate the length of power cable needed to reach from the battery to the distribution block and from the fuse block to each device needing power. Then refer to the "Power Cable Length Calculator" chart on page 65, and it will guide you to the proper cable gauge.

Those are the essentials on how to choose power cable gauge. The only other thing is to always use the same gauge ground cable as for the positive power cable. Remember, with an automotive electrical system, although a portion is lost in heat, what goes in has to be returned to the battery. So it's best to err on the high side and build in reserve current capacity. It's not only safer, but your system will be more reliable and perform as designed.

4.1.5.2
ROUTING POWER CABLES

Routing power cable correctly is one of the secrets that keeps your system trouble free.

Routing along the perimeter of the body or along the transmission tunnel also is acceptable. Occasionally, it's necessary to route the cable under-

neath the vehicle. Be sure to provide adequate protection for the cable. Adequate protection is at least using split loom covering and routing the cable above the frame or subframe members.

Use a grommet to protect the cable from being cut and grounding out when ever a cable is run through a wall or bulkhead. Also be aware of potential snags or other obstacles in the path of the cable that could cut through the insulation forcing a short circuit.

Good installers use grommets to protect cable from the sharp metal edges on the car body whenever they have to drill a hole to run cable through a wall.

The most misunderstood connection is the ground connection. Improperly grounded equipment is the cause of at least 90 percent of all problems in your system. The best way to ground your equipment is to have a single ground path to the negative side of your vehicle's electrical system for all your equipment. Then you have to route that common heavy gauge ground wire to a point on the vehicle body or frame that you're certain is part of the negative side of the car's electrical system. The best ground point of all is the battery.

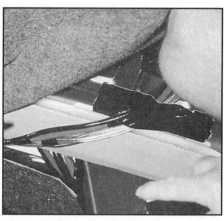

As you run cable along, around, and through the structures of the vehicle body, taping them into place keeps them from moving. By keeping them stationed, you reduce the chance of a breach in the insulation caused by abrasion. Besides, it just looks cleaner.

4.1.5.3
MAKING RELIABLE ELECTRICAL SYSTEM CONNECTIONS

Good wiring habits keep your system performing better longer. It's that simple. First you need to do is decide where you're going to mount all your new components. Second is make a sketch of the wiring system. This gives you a map to guide you and helps you determine cable gauge and lengths, as well as what type of connections you'll have to make.

That is what this section is concerned with: how to make reliable automotive electrical system connections.

The two primary methods of making connections in automotive electrics are soldered and solderless. In addition, there are the mechanical means manufacturers use for power, input, and output connections to their components.

There are many opinions about whether it's better to solder a connection or to use solderless connectors. But the consensus is that it depends on the connection. Both methods are used and each has its benefits.

There are a couple of common soldering techniques that are easy to learn and use. First is standard soldering. You heat the ends of the wires you wish to join until they are hot enough to melt the solder. When the joint reaches such temperature, the solder flows into it. Remove the solder iron from the joint as you hold the joint still until it cools slightly and the solder becomes rigid again. You then have your joint. The next operation is slipping the shrink tube around the joint and with a heat gun apply heat until the shrink tube shrinks, sealing and insulating the joint. That's it.

The second soldering method is a modification of the first and is known as tinning the joint. This just means that you heat and flow solder into each side of the joint separately. Then all that's needed to join the two ends is place them together, holding the soldering iron to them until the solder melts. Remove the soldering iron and hold until the solder freezes. As always, use a shrink tube to insulate the joint.

Note: Solder melts quickly. Use on tricky joints, or on devices that are heat sensitive such as solenoid terminals.

If you terminate your wires with solder, use a heat-shrink tubing to insulate the joint. A heat-shrink tube is the right way to insulate a joint, but friction tape will work…for a while. It's best just to use heat shrink, but if you run into a jam….

Solderless connectors are the quick alternative to soldering every connection. Solderless connectors come in all forms, from the common butt connector (which connects the ends of two wires) all the way to heavy duty high current battery ring-terminals.

Solderless connectors work by forcing a mechanical grip on the wire end. This is done by squeezing the connector, with the wire in place, with a special pair of pliers nicknamed "crimps." The crimps have a curved area that puts pressure on the seam in the shaft of the connector so that it bends in, clamping the wire in place. It only sounds complicated when you have to write it out. Doing it is simple. In fact, you've probably used solderless connectors before.

The other type of connection is the screw type. You strip the wire back a bit, insert it and tighten a screw. Simple, effective, and usually nice looking as well.

Tinning just means that you heat and flow solder into each side of the joint separately. Then place them together, holding the soldering iron to them until the solder melts. Remove the soldering iron and hold until the solder freezes.

WIRING HARNESS

The NOS wiring harness is designed for simplifying the chore of wiring Power Shot, Super Powershot, Cheater, or Big Shot nitrous systems. Quality features include easy-connect wiring, 15-amp fuse, abrasion proof wrapping, and pre-sized lengths to fit most installations.

Part # Description
15836 Wiring harness for Power Shot, Super Powershot, Cheater, and Big Shot systems.

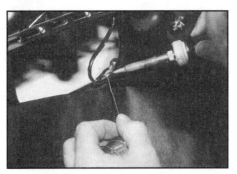

Heat the ends of the wires you wish to join until they are hot enough to melt the solder. When the joint reaches such temperature, the solder flows into it. Remove the solder iron from the joint as you hold the joint still until it cools slightly and the solder becomes rigid again. Notice the use of electrical tape to insulate the joint. That's not exactly the right way to do it, but it's not wrong, either.

This installer soldered and used heat-shrink tube on these set of Scosche goldplated spade connectors. Notice that the installer used equal gauge Scosche cable for the positive and negative leads.

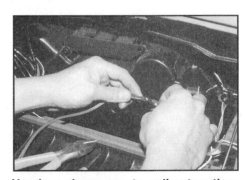

Here's a clever way to splice together heavy gauge cable. You simply blend the wire strands together before flowing solder onto the joint.

These goldplated Stinger spade connectors crimp on quickly. Slip the insulating collar over it and you have an instant connection.

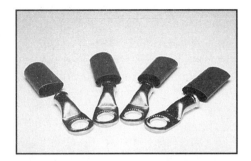

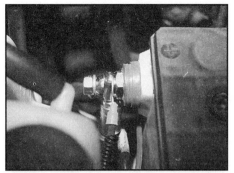

Power cable screw-type terminals. A quick way to a nice-looking connection. Use them with trick battery terminal adapters such as this one for GM cars and trucks.

Use ring terminals for ground connections. Notice how the paint is sanded from the area of the ground. This ensures optimum electricity flow.

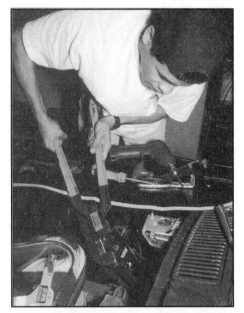

A set of StreetWires goldplated ring terminals for high current flow complete with heat-shrink tube. You have to use a special crimping tool to mash these babies on the end of an 1/0 power cable.

This installer is using heat-shrink tubing to bind split the loom to a waterproof fuse holder.

CABLE GAUGE GUIDE

	0-4 ft.	4-7 ft.	7-10 ft.	10-13 ft	13-16 ft.	16-19 ft.	19-22 ft.
300-225	1/0-gauge	1/0-gauge	1/0-gauge	1/0-gauge	1/0-gauge	1/0-gauge	1/0-gauge
225-150	2-gauge	1/0-gauge	1/0-gauge	1/0-gauge	1/0-gauge	1/0-gauge	1/0-gauge
150-125	2-gauge	2-gauge	2-gauge	2-gauge	1/0-gauge	1/0-gauge	1/0-gauge
125-105	4-gauge	4-gauge	4-gauge	2-gauge	2-gauge	2-gauge	1/0-gauge
105-85	4-gauge	4-gauge	4-gauge	2-gauge	2-gauge	2-gauge	2-gauge
85-65	4-gauge	4-gauge	4-gauge	4-gauge	2-gauge	2-gauge	2-gauge
65-50	8-gauge	8-gauge	4-gauge	4-gauge	4-gauge	4-gauge	4-gauge
50-35	8-gauge	8-gauge	8-gauge	4-gauge	4-gauge	4-gauge	4-gauge
35-20	8-gauge	8-gauge	8-gauge	8-gauge	8-gauge	4-gauge	4-gauge
20-0	10-gauge	10-gauge	8-gauge	8-gauge	8-gauge	8-gauge	8-gauge

HOW TO SOLDER CONNECTIONS
4.2.0
INSTALLATIONS

4.2.0.1
LT-1 VS. 5.0
THEY'RE BOTH ON THE BOTTLE, BUT WHICH ONE'S QUICKEST?

Dry manifold nitrous systems come in several varieties. Two of the more popular variations are found the Camaro and Mustang. Since these two cars have a natural rivalry, why not exploit it and put on a drag race?

Each car is sporting an NOS dry manifold system of equal power boost. The Mustang harnesses the engine's power with a manual trans; the Camaro with an automatic. Since the Mustang's stock clutch is no match for the nitrous system, the owner installed a McLeod clutch and Accufab clutch cable and pivot, as well as running a D.O.T drag-racing "slick." That's the extent of the modifications with the exception of the nitrous systems on each car.

So, how did they perform?

Both started as 14-second cars. The Mustang ran 14.55 at 100.19 mph; the Camaro ran 14.50 right at 95 mph. On the bottle, the Mustang's best run out of three was a 13.15-second pass at 102.43 mph. The Camaro ran quicker and faster with a best blast of 13.11-seconds at 109.48 mph.

The results, for the most part, are

To ensure precision clutch operation, the Mustang was also equipped with a high-performance clutch cable quadrant from Accufab.

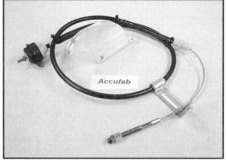

The manual transmission equipped Mustang was upgraded with a McLeod high-performance clutch, pressure plate, and throwout bearing assembly to take the abuse of the nitrous-equipped 302 engine.

obvious. The ETs are indicative of the disparities between the rear suspensions. The Mustang is at a disadvantage, but the liability is compensated by the use of drag-racing tires. The drag-racing tires prove their worth by allowing the Mustang to run similar ETs as the faster Camaro.

In terms of horsepower, the faster speed of the Camaro shows the wisdom of the axiom that there is no substitute for cubic inches. The 5.7-liter Chevrolet engine made more power than the 5.0-liter Ford, even though both cars were equipped with equal nitrous systems jetted to produce about the same amount of power increase.

4.2.1.
INSTALLING A DRY MANIFOLD SYSTEM ON A '66 LT-1 CAMARO

PLUS: HOW TO ACCESSORIZE THE LT-1 CAMARO

Dry manifold nitrous systems are perhaps the easiest systems to install. You don't have to worry about routing a fuel line, and installing the spray nozzle is a relatively easy procedure. That being the case, why not burn up some excess energy and money for that matter and install a few more goodies to make the system operation blend with the normal performance of your car so that you can devote all your concentration on driving (with the exception of a wee small corner of your mind to experience the rush of explosive acceleration that only nitrous can supply).

Editor's note: numerals in parentheses refer to Figure 1.

INSTALL THE BOTTLE FIRST

The first thing you must do to install your nitrous system is to decide where to put the bottle. (See section 4.1.1 Bottle Installation and Safety for details.) After you have determined the location and orientation of the nitrous bottle, use the following procedures to install the bottle.

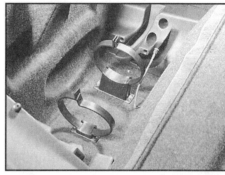

Install bottle nut adapter (2) and washer (3) on nitrous bottle (1), and tighten securely. Then loosely install bottle mounting brackets (4) and the blow-down tube (5) on the nitrous bottle. Now locate the bottle assembly in desired mounting area, ensuring that the location provides easy access to the bottle valve, hose connections, and bracket clamp bolts to make changing the bottle easier. Use assembled bottle/bracket/blow-down tube unit as a pattern to mark for hole drilling.

Drill four 5/16-in. holes for the bottle bracket bolts, a 1/2-in. hole for the blow-down tube and an 11/16-in. hole for the nitrous supply line. Mount brackets securely to surface (recommended minimum of 5/16-in. bolts). Tighten bracket clamps on bottle.

We went a little upscale on this installation. Instead of the rigid blow-down tube we installed a braided steel line using bulkhead fittings. A flexible blow-down tube makes changing bottles easier. We also installed the remote valve activation kit.

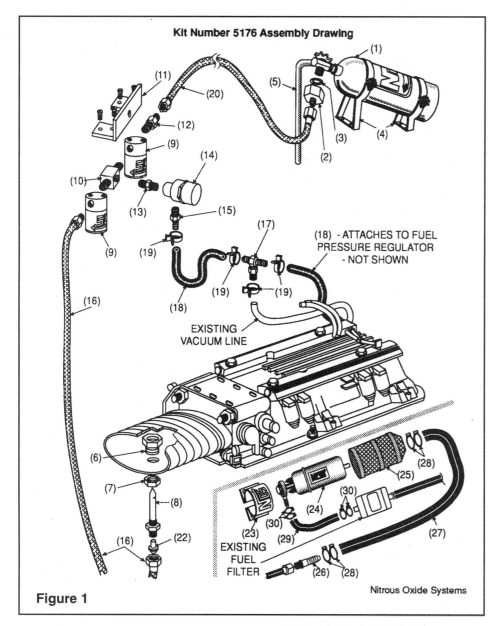

Kit Number 5176 Assembly Drawing

(18) - ATTACHES TO FUEL
PRESSURE REGULATOR
- NOT SHOWN

EXISTING
VACUUM LINE

EXISTING
FUEL
FILTER

Nitrous Oxide Systems

Figure 1

SPRAY NOZZLE INSTALLATION

You need to find a suitable location for the fan spray nozzle in the intake inlet duct. Check for interference between the spray nozzle and nearby components. On engines using mass airflow sensors, the nozzle needs to be mounted between the sensor and the throttle body (downstream of the sensor). After you've found the spot, mark it and remove the rubber air inlet duct from the engine. Drill a $\frac{7}{16}$-in. hole perpendicular to the inlet duct centerline through the inlet duct. Be sure to remove any drill shavings since they can severely damage your engine.

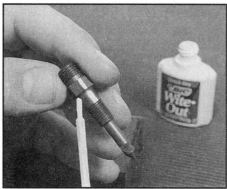

Mark the nozzle with a line of White Out or equivalent product. This lets you adjust the angle of the spray. Ideally, you want the spray to go with the flow of air, not against it, i.e., with the discharge pointed toward the engine. Insert the nitrous spray nozzle adapter (6) into a $\frac{7}{16}$-in. hole with the head on the inside of duct.

MOUNTING THE SOLENOID

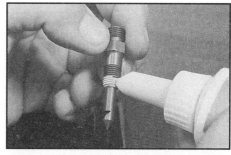

Severe engine damage can occur if the spray adapter/nozzle assembly works itself loose from the air inlet duct. Use Loc-Tite or a similar compound on the spray nozzle adapter threads and securely tighten spray nozzle adapter nut (7) to spray nozzle adapter.

Remove all the debris from the air inlet duct. Install the fan spray nozzle in the spray nozzle adapter with the discharge pointed toward the engine. The rubber air inlet duct will be secured in place later. For now, just put it in a safe place.

AND REGULATOR

Now we're on to the process of mounting the solenoid and regulator. But first a few caution signs. One: do not overtighten vise in the following procedure or the solenoid will be damaged. Two: apply a Teflon-based paste to all pipe fittings before assembling solenoids and regulators.

Clamp one nitrous solenoid (9) in a bench vise. Thread one side of the solenoid T-union (10) into the solenoid outlet port. The 1/4-in. NPT port should be facing outward, as shown in Figure ?. Thread the open side of the solenoid T-union into the inlet port of the second nitrous solenoid. Rotate the second solenoid so it's parallel to the first. Line up bolt holes on both solenoids with holes in solenoid bracket (11). Install nitrous filter fitting (12) into first nitrous solenoid inlet port. Install a 1/4-in. NPT nipple (13) into the nitrous pressure regulator (14) inlet port. Loosely thread the nitrous pressure regulator I nipple assembly into the solenoid T-union open port. If the regulator interferes with the solenoid coils, the coils may be temporarily removed. Thread 1/4-in. NPT-to-3/16-in. hose barbed fitting (15) into the regulator. Attach the solenoid mounting bracket to the nitrous solenoids. Thread a 3AN line male fitting (16) into the second nitrous solenoid outlet port. Remove the assembly from bench vise.

Ensure that the 2-ft. 3AN nitrous feed line (16) provided will reach the nitrous nozzle from the mounting location on the driver-side inner fender. Reinstall the inlet duct temporarily to check the fit. Attach the nitrous solenoid/bracket assembly to driver-side inner fender as close to the fuel pressure regulator as possible. Adjust the nitrous pressure regulator so the hose barb fitting points toward the engine fuel pressure regulator.

To make the fuel pressure regulator connection, remove the vacuum line from the fuel pressure regulator then install the pressure T-union's (17) center leg (denoted by blue nut), into the vacuum line. Measure and cut a length of vacuum hose (18) to run from one pressure T-union port to the fuel pressure regulator. Measure and cut a length of vacuum hose to run from the remaining pressure T-union open port to the hose barb fitting on the nitrous pressure regulator (11). Clamp the vacuum hose connections using the ratcheting hose clamps (19).

Nitrous Feed Line Mounting

Following the fuel lines along the left side of the vehicle and entering the engine bay near the master cylinder works well. Determine the route for your nitrous feed line to follow. Ensure that the path is clear of exhaust system, suspension, steering, wheels, electrical lines and components, and tires.

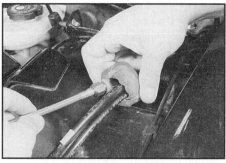

The safest route for the nitrous system fuel and nitrous lines is following the factory line. The factory has done crash studies and has determined the best route to keep the fuel line safe. Your first choice is always to follow the factory fuel line route. We started at the front and worked our way toward the rear of the car, first working the line through the fuel line grommet.

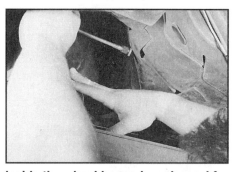

Inside the wheel house is a channel for the nitrous line, but you have to bend back the fender liner.

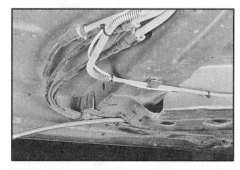

This is the nitrous line exiting the subframe structure. We ran the nitrous line inside the sub-frame rail.

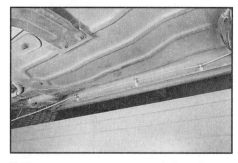

If it's necessary to support the nitrous supply line under the vehicle, use 1/2-in. Tinnerman clamps or nylon tie-wraps. Here we show a straight shot to the rear wheel house. Use a combination of clamps, tie-wraps, and body panels to lace the nitrous line away from the axle.

A body panel lip provided a good place to lace the line up to the point where we reentered the interior. The drain plug is an easy access point. Just punch a hole in it and run the line through it.

After reinstalling the drain plug and attaching it to the nitrous bottle, seal it with a liberal application of RTV. Sometimes attaching the nitrous supply line to the nitrous bottle valve adapter (3) requires using an optional 4AN to 4AN 90° fitting (21).

Before you attach the nitrous supply line to the nitrous solenoid inlet port (Using the optional 4AN to 4AN 90° Fitting (21), if necessary), purge the nitrous supply line by wrapping the end of the nitrous line with a rag and holding it securely. Point the opening away from people and briefly open the bottle valve.

SOLENOID/FAN NOZZLE NITROUS LINE CONNECTION

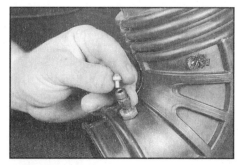

Place #67 flare jet (22) in fan spray nozzle (8) inlet.

Connect and tighten 3AN line (16) to solenoid outlet and from spray nozzle inlet.

FUEL PUMP INSTALLATION

The following procedure requires the disconnection of fuel lines underneath the vehicle. Empty the vehicle of fuel before attempting to disconnect the fuel lines.

Trial fit fuel pump (24)/fuel pump bracket (23) and sock (25)assembly to the driver-side floorpan of vehicle. Make sure that the assembly is higher than the lowest part of the rear frame rail and below the rear axle brake line.

Remove the driver-side rear seat bottom, pull the carpet out from under the side panel (armrest/speaker cover panel). Lift the carpet to gain access to the fuel pump mounting location. Using the fuel pump/fuel pump bracket and isolator assembly as a template, mark and drill four 3/8-in. isolator mounting holes in the floorpan. Install the fuel pump assembly and replace the carpet and seat cushions. Bleed off the residual fuel pressure at the fuel rail test port. Refer to Figure 2 for the location of the fuel rail test port. It has residual pressure of approximately 30 psi after the engine has been shut off. Be sure to bleed off the fuel pressure before loosening the fuel lines.

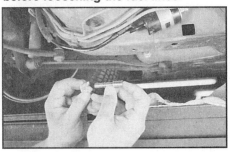

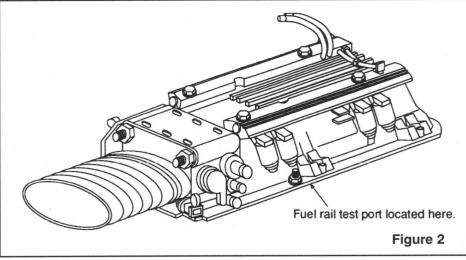

Fuel rail test port located here.

Figure 2

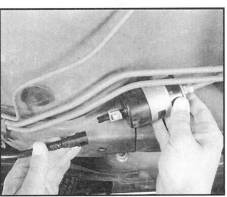

Disconnect the plastic fuel line from the inlet of the fuel filter. Remove the plastic retaining clip from the inlet of the fuel filter and install it on the fuel line hose barb (26). Install the fuel line hose barb in the end of the plastic fuel line. Connect the fuel line hose barb to the inlet side of fuel pump using a ½-in. rubber fuel hose (27). Double clamp both ends of the hose with large hose clamps (28).

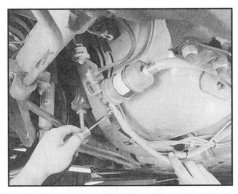

Connect the outlet side of the fuel pump to the inlet side of the fuel filter using 3/8-in. rubber fuel hose (29). Double clamp both ends with small hose clamps (30). Make sure that the fuel hose is pushed on far enough that the hose passes over the barb on the fuel filter inlet. Lubricating the inside of the hose greatly will ease this operation.

ELECTRICAL INSTALLATION: FUEL PUMP

Remove the cover from the spare tire well in the cargo area of vehicle. Select a mounting location for the 30-amp relay (33) and relay harness in the spare tire well and secure it in place. If you intend to secure the relay in place with a screw, be sure that the screw hole does not penetrate into any critical components. Do not drill any holes in the shock absorber mounts. Connect the fuel pump (+) pole to the blue wire from the 30-amp relay. Connect the green relay wire to the chassis ground. Connect the red relay wire to the factory fuel pump power wire (wire should be gray in color) usinga scotch lock connector (34). Connect the orange relay wire to the battery or vehicle accessory power supply (it should be located on the right side front fender well). If connecting to an accessory power supply, make sure that the circuit will support the additional 7-amp draw required by the fuel pump. A convenient route for the power supply wire is to have it follow the nitrous supply line to the front of the vehicle. Replace the spare tire well cover. Reinstall the rubber air inlet duct before operation.

ELECTRICAL SYSTEM INSTALLATION LT-1 NON-EMISSIONS LEGAL

Use the following procedure and refer to figs. LT-1-A, B, and C for electrical system installation on the non-emission-legal 5176 kit for the LT-1 Camaro/Firebird. Death or injury may occur from working on a charged elec-

Nitrous Oxide Injection Guide

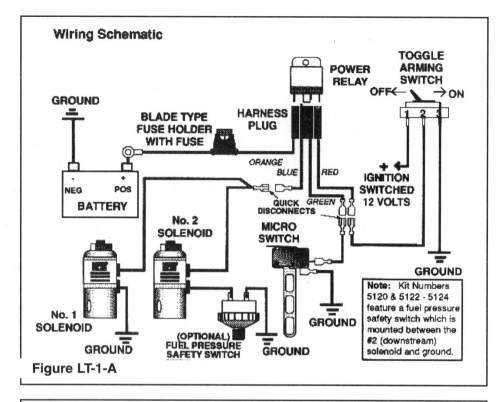

Wiring Schematic

GROUND

BLADE TYPE FUSE HOLDER WITH FUSE

HARNESS PLUG

POWER RELAY

TOGGLE ARMING SWITCH

OFF ← → ON

BATTERY NEG POS

ORANGE BLUE RED

No. 2 SOLENOID

MICRO SWITCH

QUICK DISCONNECTS

GREEN

IGNITION SWITCHED 12 VOLTS

+

No. 1 SOLENOID

GROUND

(OPTIONAL) FUEL PRESSURE SAFETY SWITCH

GROUND

GROUND

GROUND

Note: Kit Numbers 5120 & 5122 - 5124 feature a fuel pressure safety switch which is mounted between the #2 (downstream) solenoid and ground.

Figure LT-1-A

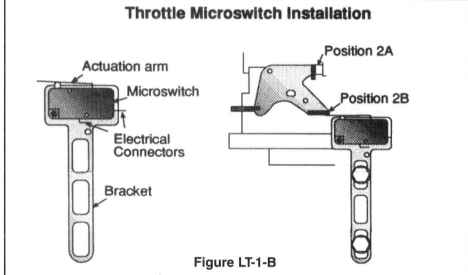

Throttle Microswitch Installation

Actuation arm

Microswitch

Electrical Connectors

Bracket

Position 2A

Position 2B

Figure LT-1-B

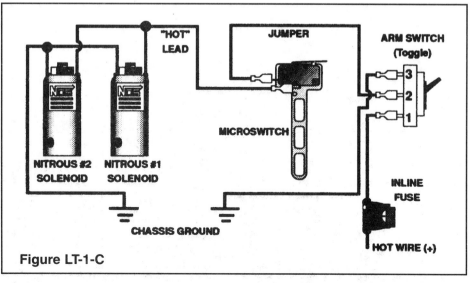

"HOT" LEAD

JUMPER

ARM SWITCH (Toggle)

3
2
1

MICROSWITCH

NITROUS #2 SOLENOID

NITROUS #1 SOLENOID

INLINE FUSE

CHASSIS GROUND

HOT WIRE (+)

Figure LT-1-C

trical system, so disconnect the battery before beginning.

Install the microswitch (31) on the throttle body so the microswitch is triggered by the throttle linkage at wide-open throttle (WOT). Figure 8 shows the suggested mounting configuration. Binding or dragging the throttle linkage will create a potentially dangerous stuck-throttle condition. Ensure that the microswitch doesn't interfere with normal throttle linkage operation. The microswitch may be mounted to the bracket in a variety of positions or on either side of the bracket. The bracket may be bent to suit your application. Mount the throttle microswitch on the intake manifold so the microswitch is triggered by the throttle linkage movement. Adjust the microswitch to trigger at WOT by adjusting the microswitch's position to ensure that the actuation arm of the microswitch "clicks" at the same point the throttle linkage reaches WOT against the throttle stop. Ensure that the throttle and switch can reach the activation position shown in Figure LT-1-B by using the accelerator pedal. Have an assistant slowly press the pedal to floor while you listen for the "click" of the microswitch.

ELECTRICAL INSTALLATION: LT-1 CAMARO EMISSIONS-LEGAL KIT

Emissions-legal kits use a WOT switch that works with the factory ECU. See Figure 4 for wiring details.

Install the NOS arming toggle switch (32) in the vehicle interior within easy reach of driver. Connect terminal #1 on the arming switch to an ignition switched +12V source using the fused red wire provided.

When selecting an ignition switched + 12V source, ensure that your source is capable of handing the amperage of the fuse provided by NOS. Connect terminal #2 of the arming switch to one post of the throttle microswitch (either post will do) with the blue wire provided. Connect terminal #3 of the arming switch to ground. (You must not skip this step; if you do, the light in the arming switch will not illuminate when the system is armed).

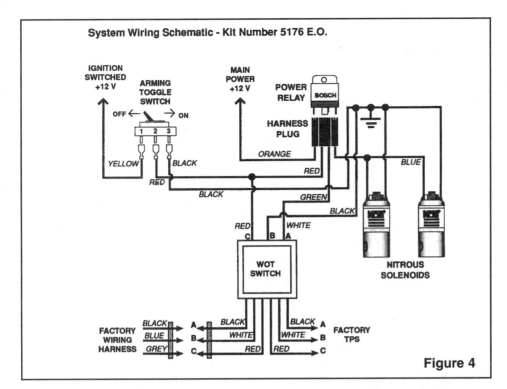

System Wiring Schematic - Kit Number 5176 E.O.

Figure 4

Tuning Information

Configuration: 5176 E.O.
NO Jetting: 0.067
Fuel Quality : 92+ Octane
Ignition Timing: Stock
Plugs: NGK

4.2.2
WET AND WILD

Installing an Edelbrock Quicksilver Carb and NOS Wet Manifold System on a Harley-Davidson Motorcycle

Harley-Davidson motorcycles aren't particularly known for searing acceleration and smooth throttle response—at least not right out of the box. On the bright side, though, the marque enjoys tremendous aftermarket support. The only limits to customizing your Harley is your bank balance.

However, the combination we present here is, dollar for dollar, the best performance buying decision you can make for your Harley. The first step we suggest, of course, is installing a nitrous system. The second is installing one of Edelbrock's "Quicksilver" line carburetors on your Harley. The Quicksilver carburetor delivers a smooth fuel curve for crisp throttle response, power, and satisfying driveability all the way through the power band. The Edelbrock carburetor also makes it far easier to install the micro-switch, a convenience you can appreciate only if you've ever had to fabricate a bracket.

Now let's get to the details of the installation.

Installing the Bottle

The first item to install is the bottle. Well, at least you have to decide where you're going to install it so you'll know how to route the nitrous line to the nozzles. Check out the section on bottle orientation earlier in this book.

The same physics apply to motorcycles as to cars but the layout of your 'cycle forces you to consider several additional factors. Basically, you have to find a mounting area for the bottle

Connect the open post of the microswitch to one wire from each solenoid (either wire will do; the solenoids are not polarized) using the blue wire provided. Connect the open wire from each solenoid to ground.

Ignition

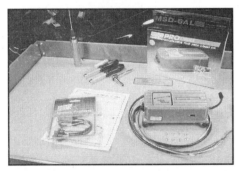

We also installed an MSD 6AL. The power-capacitive discharge, multiple-spark unit features MSD's Soft Touch Rev Control built right in to protect your engine from over-revving. It comes with several rpm modules that plug right in. Since this kit can only activate at WOT, the MSD unit is the perfect accessory to keep all that nitrous power under control and under the redline.

The plug with the skinny, long ground strap came from this '96 Camaro. The other plug is an NGK unit with a shorter, thicker ground strap. The stock Camaro plug will cause detonation with any amount of nitrous. Do not use your stock spark plugs with your nitrous kit.

This is the final check list before operating your new NOS nitrous system:

1. Start vehicle.

2. Examine auxiliary fuel pump to ensure operation. The fuel pump should run whenever the vehicle is running. If the pump is inoperable, refer to the Troubleshooting Guide.

3. Open the nitrous bottle valve. There should be no change in engine idle speed or exhaust tone. If either change is noted, refer to Appendix A, Troubleshooting Guide.

4. Inspect the nitrous lines and fittings for leaks.

5. Enjoy!

Here's where we mounted the auxiliary fuel pump—under the fuel tank. There isn't much space here, but it's about the only placed to put it.

Slip the bottle mount bracket onto the bottle, mount the bottle bracket to the frame, and tighten the bracket fasteners.

on the frame that's at least six inches from the exhaust system; and don't fasten it to any suspension components.

Installing the Solenoids

The next step is to install the solenoids. Due to the lack of space on a bike, your mounting locations are limited, but it can be done. You can mount the solenoids at any attitude, upside down, sideways, whichever way necessary. In addition to the limited space, you also face the following obstacles: keeping the solenoids and lines away from the exhaust, mounting the solenoids above the nozzles ,and positioning the solenoids near the nozzles to keep the lines short. Because space is limited and fitting the solenoids correctly is so critical, NOS supplies an additional bracket so you can mount the solenoids separately or together as required for your circumstances. In all cases, you

This is how we mounted the nitrous and fuel solenoids.

should trial fit the solenoids with all lines attached.

Installing the Fuel Pump

About the only place to install the fuel pump on this bike was under the fuel tank. Fortunately, this position satisfied all the criteria for proper performance. You should mount the fuel pump away from heat, and it should be as low as possible in relation to the fuel tank. This is a gravity-fed pump, so a longer column of fuel in the longer fuel line tends to work better.

Installing the Nozzles

The first thing to do, obviously, is to decide where to install the nozzles. On the Harley you have to install two nozzles, one for each cylinder. (See figure 2.) Because when the nozzles are mounted with the discharge end up fuel seeps down the nitrous line to contami-

nate the nitrous solenoid seal, we mounted them with the discharge end pointed down.

Since the Harley has metal intake runners, we drilled a ¼-in. hole and tapped it with a ⅟₁₆-in. NPT tap. Next we applied Teflon paste to the threads and screwed them into the manifold.

Then we measured and cut a length of poly line, enough to connect the Fogger nozzle fuel port to the fuel solenoid and did the same to the nitrous solenoid and nozzle port. Then we checked the baseline tuning chart and installed the recommended nitrous and fuel jets. Installing the poly line into the nozzles required slipping a blue B-nut and ferrule on the nitrous-side poly line and a red B-nut and ferrule on the fuel side before tightening them. Since this installation uses a pair of nozzles, we routed the supply lines to each solenoid to a T-fitting.

Mounting the Nitrous Feed Line

Determine the route for your main nitrous feed line, making sure the path is clear of the exhaust system, suspen-

You can clearly see the placement of the nozzles in the two runners. It uses two nozzles because the Harley has a short intake manifold that Ys off from the carburetor to each cylinder. The nozzles are close together and use black nylon rigid tubing to deliver the nitrous and fuel.

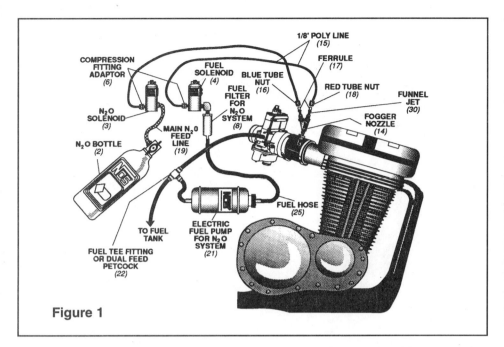

Figure 1

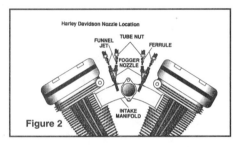

Figure 2

This shows the microswitch on the back side of the air filter mounting plate. It bolts to the carburetor and is fairly rigid. All we had to do was make a little aluminum spacer to raise it off the plate and the arm went right underneath the throttle linkage. When the throttle linkage arm came down, it centerpunched the microswitch just as it should. You also get a close look at Edelbrock's powerfully smooth "Quicksilver" carb.

line to the nitrous solenoid, you need to purge it. Wrap the end of the nitrous line with a rag and hold it securely. Point it away from yourself and others and briefly open the nitrous bottle valve. Now you may attach the feed line to the bottle.

Installing the Microswitch, Arming Switch, and Wiring

Most motorcycles activate their horn through a ground trigger. However, some motorcycles, including Harley-Davidsons', activate through a positive trigger. We have included two wiring diagrams that encompass both triggering schemes. The mounting position of the activation button is user defined, or wherever you feel comfortable.

Generically speaking, the microswitch goes anywhere on the throttle linkage where you have a solid mount that lets it activate reliably at WOT.

The rest of the wiring is straightforward. Just follow the appropriate wiring diagram for your particular horn configuration. Now all that's left is to button up your Harley and prepare to operate your new nitrous system.

sion, electrical, chain, and tires—in short anything that it can interfere with or which interferes with it. Once you've laced the line, secure it with nylon tie wraps. Be sure to shield painted components from the stainless braided line since it's extremely abrasive. Finally, attached the line to the bottle.

Before you attach the nitrous supply

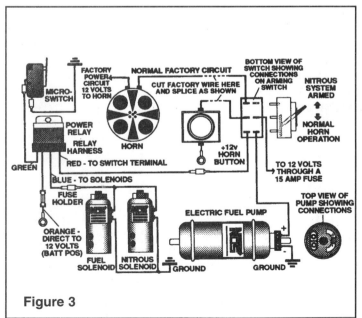

Figure 3

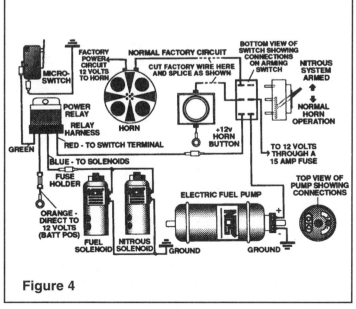

Figure 4

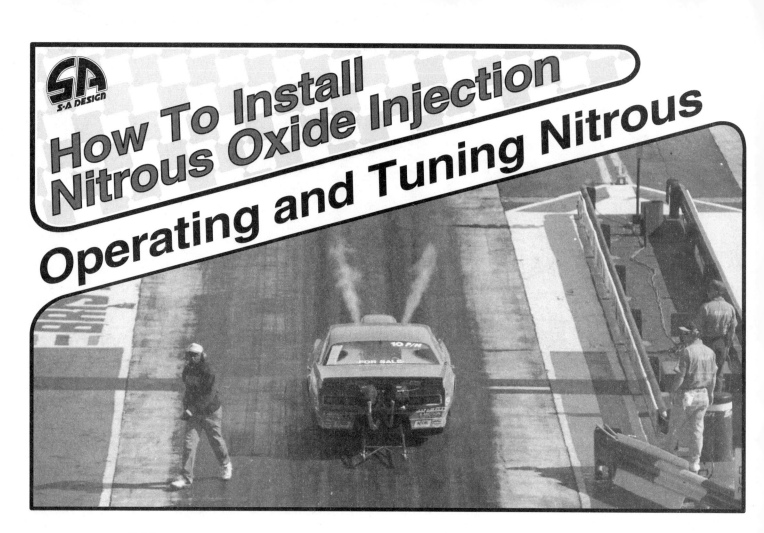

5.1.0
INITIAL SYSTEM CHECKS

Before you take your nitrous-enhanced machine down the track, always take a few moments and perform a system check. The purpose of these checks is to verify that the nitrous circuit and the fuel circuit are both operating correctly. Make this procedure a habit before racing and you'll spend more time running and less time on the trailer.

There are two scenarios regarding system checks, depending on whether you have a dry manifold system or a wet manifold system.

5.1.1
DRY MANIFOLD SYSTEM CHECK

To check a dry manifold system, first energized your car's ignition. Then check all fuel and vacuum lines for leaks. It's pretty easy to spot fuel leaks, but vacuum leaks are harder to see. Generally, a vacuum leak causes the engine to idle rough if it's bad enough.

Assuming the fuel and vacuum lines check out, start your engine. While the engine is running, open the nitrous bottle valve. Listen carefully to your engine as you open the valve. You should not hear a difference in idle speed or exhaust tone. If you notice either one of these changes—or both—your system has a defective nitrous solenoid. That means you have to remove and inspect the solenoid and repair or replace as needed. See the section on troubleshooting for more information.

Let's hope you won't notice any change in idle speed or exhaust note, leaving you free to inspect the nitrous lines and fittings for leaks. Leaks in the nitrous supply line will be obvious because they'll be covered with frost.

If there are no leaks in the nitrous supply line, you're cleared for take-off.

Dry Manifold Initial Checklist

1. Energized ignition
2. Check fuel and vacuum lines for leaks
3. Start engine
4. Open nitrous bottle valve—check for stable idle speed and exhaust tone
5. Inspect nitrous lines and fittings for leaks
6. Go faster

5.1.2
WET MANIFOLD SYSTEM CHECK

To check a wet manifold system, first turn on the fuel pump then check the lines and fittings for leaks. Next, arm the system by switching the arming toggle switch to "on." Rev the engine to 2000 rpm and hold it steady. Briefly activate the nitrous system by pushing, or squeezing, the button. You should notice a decrease of engine speed because, assuming the fuel system is working properly, the engine should be running pig rich right now. If not, you've probably wired the system incorrectly, have a restrictive fuel line, or a malfunctioning fuel solenoid. See the troubleshooting section for more information.

If the fuel circuit checks out, open the nitrous bottle valve. With this test you don't want any changes in engine speed or tone. If you notice such, you have a broken or defective nitrous solenoid that needs replacing or repairing. If the system passes this system check, inspect the nitrous lines and fittings for leaks. Once again if the system passes this check, you're ready to run.

Wet Manifold System Checklist

1. Turn on fuel pump
2. Check fuel lines and fittings for leaks
3. Turn arming toggle switch to "on"
4. Set engine speed at 2000 rpm
5. Briefly push N_2O activation button. Engine speed should decrease.
6. Open nitrous bottle valve. Engine speed should remain stable
7. Inspect nitrous lines and fittings for leaks
8. Go Fast

5.2.0
NITROUS TUNING TACTICS

5.2.1
TUNE YOUR ENGINE WITHOUT NITROUS FIRST

You should get your engine running right without the nitrous system first because 90 percent of the time you'll be running on the motor alone. You don't want to jet the carburetor to add fuel or anything like that. You want all the additional fuel to come through the nitrous system. Next, start tuning the nitrous system with the fuel jets to bring it back to a better state of tune.

Typically you should start with a conservative jetting combination and tune toward higher output. You don't want to start at the leanest jetting and break your engine right at the gate. If you don't have a reference point, then you're much better starting off conservatively. It's much more fun installing larger jets than sweeping up your engine.

Just keep putting in larger jet sizes, fuel, and nitrous, or alternate between the two until the plugs read as they would if naturally aspirated. If you have the jetting correct the plugs should read almost exactly like a naturally aspirated engine only you're running nitrous and they see a lot more fuel. You don't have to run a nitrous system so rich the plugs are black.

While it's true it's safer to run the mixture rich and that some engines will make more power on the rich side than on the lean side, these observations come about from distribution problems rather than from the characteristics of the chemical reaction of fuel and nitrous.

Regarding spark plugs: the ground strap on spark plugs is usually longer on stock engines because the combustion temperatures aren't as hot. The problem with running these types of plugs with nitrous is that the heat path is so long that the ground strap becomes red hot, the plug turns into a glow plug, and you get detonation. Even if you use a plug a few steps cooler like the nitrous kit manufacturers suggest, you can still run into this problem. Again, it's the style of plug with a long ground strap that causes the problem not necessarily the heat range.

What you really need is a plug with a short, wide, thick ground strap. Louie Hammel says he even cuts the ground strap so it isn't over the electrode so the spark can jump from the corner of the electrode. Hammel says he keeps the same gap, but because this shortens the strap, it gets the heat out of the strap quicker and is less likely to force detonation. You'll find this same approach on racing plugs that have a short ground strap mounted to the side of the electrode. On these plugs, the ground strap is short, thick, and wide so it transfers the heat to the cylinder head more effectively .

You choose the heat range of the plug for the type of duty the engine sees. If you go too cold, the plug won't clean itself and the cylinder won't fire. If you go too hot, you can get into detonation and even melt and crack the plug. With nitrous, you don't have to use a non-projected style plug such as a racing plug, but you do have to change the style of ground strap.

5.2.2
CARBURETED ENGINE-TUNING STRATEGY

At the risk of stating the obvious, with carbureted cars, the carburetor is the source of naturally aspirated engine performance in that it mixes fuel with air so that combustion can occur in the cylinders. Furthermore, it must do so in a specified proportion commonly referred to as the air-to-fuel ratio (a/f ratio). The a/f ratio that's accepted as safe and will produce the most acceleration from a high-performance gasoline-fueled internal combustion four-stroke engine is 12.8:1, or a brake specific fuel consumption (BSFC) of 0.50. Advanced engine tuners can run an a/f ratio of 13:1 or 0.45 BSFC to get the most steady-state power from an engine. Keep in mind you're getting closer to the lean side of the fuel curve, and if you're not completely dialed in, you can get into detonation. By the way, these ratios are for full- throttle, high-load situations. When you're cruising under low-load conditions, you can run right at 14.7:1 or stoichiometric and lower without problems. As long as it's not too lean.

From a performance standpoint, though, the job of a drag-racing carburetor is to deliver a constant a/f ratio of 12.8:1 throughout the rpm range of the engine. Simple enough. However, there are physical obstacles to achieving the desired result.

The carburetor is a mechanical device that regulates the amount of air and fuel the engine receives to control rpm and power output. The carburetor allows the engine to idle, hold a certain rpm level, and to rev up to the limits (and sometimes beyond) of engine combination. It does this by the physical dimension (or size) of the throttle bores and the angle (or opening) of the throttle plates that control the amount of airflow, as well as the various sizes of orifices and jets that comprise the idle, acceleration, mid-range and high-speed fuel-metering circuits.

Because of the subtle complexities of mixing fuel into air—that is at times traveling faster than sound—within the carburetor and changes temperature, density, and humidity levels, it so far has been impossible to design a carburetor that will deliver a constant a/f ratio throughout the entire engine rpm range. If you graphed the fuel curve as the carburetor throttle blades are opened, the engine rpm increases, and the various fuel metering circuits come into play, you'd see it zig-zag around. What the manufacturers do is arrange to have the variations of the fuel curve head toward the rich side. This is because less power is lost on the rich side of the curve and there's less potential for engine damage. Custom carburetor builders and blueprinters take this one step further in that they increase the CFM capability of the carburetor and modify the fuel metering circuits and structures so that the carburetor is able to deliver precisely controlled a/f ratio within specific rpm ranges where your particular engine combination performs best.

That said, it's easy to see why becoming a mix-master approaches the art of mastering a science. And while we can't turn you into a ninth-degree black-belt carburetor guru just by reading this book, we can at least help you get started on the three-fold path to peak horsepower.

First you need to understand how air density effects the fuel curve of your carburetor. Second, you must know how to choose the correct carburetor for your engine combination and purpose. And, third, you must become a diligent observer, note taker, and tester in order to establish a baseline carburetor tune.

5.1.3
HOW AIR DENSITY AFFECTS AIR/FUEL RATIO AND POWER OUTPUT

In general, the power output of a naturally aspirated engine is at the mercy of the prevailing atmospheric conditions. That is, the denser the air, the lower the altitude; the lower the humidity and temperature, the more power an engine can generate. Air density changes with altitude and temperature and is a major factor in tuning your carb to meet weather and track conditions.

To this end we enlisted the aid of mixmaster Bruce Huggard of B&G Racing Computers. B&G Racing Computers manufactures a racing weather station, which along with computers, has become essential tools for improving racing performance. To be consistently quick, a racer needs to understand how air density affects performance and be able to measure air density and make appropriate adjustments to the carburetor.

"The aeronautics industry has described a standard column of air as one that, at sea level, has a barometric pressure of 29.92 inches of mercury and is 59 degrees Fahrenheit and which loses one-inch of mercury, or barometric pressure, and 3.5-degrees per 1000-feet of altitude gain. What that means to the racer," Huggard continues, "is that elevation and temperature are the main factors determining air density. Therefore, if you are at a track elevation of 1000 feet, the relative air density could be similar to that found at 4500 feet in a standard column of air, if the temperature happens to be high."

"If you go to a different track with a big difference in elevation, you will notice a change in the performance of your equipment because of the large change in barometric pressure. But once there you'll find that the barometric pressure will remain nearly the same except when the temperature changes. Humidity will affect performance, but not as much as elevation and temperature. The exception is when you get an increase in humidity at a high temperature. This is because the relative air density is low to begin with, and with more water in the air to displace the oxygen content of a given volume of air and the amount of fuel that can be suspended, then the power potential of your engine is reduced under such conditions.

"Now let's learn a little about fuel mixture and it's effect on performance. Figure 1. illustrates a fuel mixture curve for horsepower. As you can see ,the slope on the left, or rich side, is closer to horizontal than the left or lean side of the curve. Which means horsepower drops off more rapidly when slightly lean than when slightly rich. In addition, engine damage is most likely to occur when running lean.

"Most stock or mild engines are set on the rich side so they can run all year round and travel from a higher altitude to a lower altitude without running too lean. This is why during a race performance will usually pick up as the air gets cooler at night. Cooler air means a lower density altitude and thicker air. If the fuel remains the same, the mixture will get leaner. As the mixture gets leaner, the engine develops more power because it's approaching the maximum horsepower point from the rich side of the curve. It's desirable to stay slightly on the rich side for two reasons. First, there's only a minimal loss of power; second, you can hurt your engine if the air-to-fuel ratio is just slightly on the lean side. If you're already operating on the lean side, and the air gets better, your vehicle will slow way down and the probability of hurting your engine goes way up. If this happens, immediately go up four jet sizes to improve performance and get a safety margin."

5.1.4
HOW TO BASELINE YOUR CARBURETOR JETTING

To be consistent, you need to do research. Fortunately this kind of research is fun because you get to do it at the racetrack. The purpose of baselining your jetting is to establish a standard that you can refer to under varying weather conditions. Your baseline is a reference point to help you regain your bearings and proper tune for your car.

Baselining carburetor jetting is a simple but time-intensive task. The goal is to find

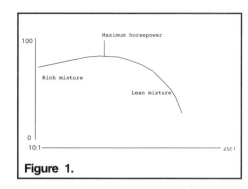

Figure 1.

the best jetting combination for your car at a specific air density. This is how you do it.

Start with a properly adjusted carburetor. For example, check that the throttle opens 100 percent, the linkage is satisfactory, float levels and fuel pressure are correct, etc., and jetting that you know is too rich for the altitude and temperature at the test site. The reason you start from the rich side is because it's safer and because the power levels are not affected as much coming from a rich condition as coming from a lean condition. When in doubt go rich.

If you're not sure of the current jetting and whether or not it's too rich, physically inspect the system and write down on the carb, firewall—or even a piece of paper—the number or orifice size; then ask some of the faster racers at the track for guidance.

Generally, the stock jetting is on the rich side, but if you're running a high -rpm combination, heads ported with a massaged manifold, big cam, and headers, you need to be at least two jet sizes up from what's considered stock.

Run your car down the track, changing jets until you get the fastest mph. It's best to stay in the same lane for your test runs in order to reduce variations in traction, even though the mph at the end of the quarter-mile is the significant figure. While you're establishing a baseline, remember to only make one change at a time. Do not change timing, adjust the lash, or any other tuning procedures. Simply change jets until you get the fastest speed in the quarter mile. The mph at the end of the quarter mile indicates horsepower generated.

Once you found the fastest mph in the quarter, note which jet sizes are installed. Take a temperature reading in the shade with open air and make a note of it. Also note the altitude of the test track. Keep a log of the best jets for the altitude and temperatures, and it'll help you tune for various conditions. Of course, buying a weather station and racing computer is the best scenario, but good record-keeping can create a firm database from which to make tuning decisions if you're on a tight budget.

5.2.1
TUNING THE NITROUS SYSTEM

The timing and control of peak pressure during the power stroke is the Holy Grail of engine tuners. Get the timing right and the pressure builds gradually to force the piston down the cylinder with greater intensity for a longer time. It's a good thing to have the pressure build gradually because burning fuel inhibits detonation and lengthens the amount of time the expanding charge exerts the most force against the piston without destroying it. The longer and more intense you can make cylinder pressure at the right time, the more power an engine will produce.

Having all the fuel ignite at once, or detonate, destroys engines, and while it's doing so does not create much power. A four-cycle gasoline-fueled engine cannot capture much energy from detonation-generated pressure spikes. All the energy of the intake charge is released too quickly, focusing the force on the top of the piston. It's sort of like the difference between driving a stake into the ground with a sledgehammer and shooting the end of the stake with a hunting rifle. There's so much force generated so quickly during detonation that it can crush the top of the piston, collapse the upper ring lands, punch holes through the pistons, destroy rod and main bearings…the list of bad things detonation can do to an engine just goes on and on. So it's important to control how quickly the fuel burns.

There are four techniques to control burn rate in order to avoid detonation and time peak cylinder pressure. One is the compression ratio of the engine. Second is the octane rating and chemistry of the fuel you choose. Third is the amount and ratio of oxygen to fuel present in the combustion chamber. And forth is ignition timing. Balancing these four factors is really the essence of tuning an engine.

Since you can't really tune the compression ratio of the engine, it's more of a combination choice having to do with the rpm range at which you want the engine to make power and a few other considerations. We don't need to talk about "tuning" the compression ratio. The compres-

sion influences the tune, but that's it. Fuel choice is another factor that influences the tune of your engine. You don't necessarily tune with fuel, but it does have a substantial impact on the tuning calibration of air, fuel, and nitrous ratios. That leaves air/fuel/nitrous ratios and ignition timing as your primary tuning channels.

Of course you have to know how to properly use these channels. Here's a quick overview of the tuning process.

1. Start with the calibration recommended by the manufacturer of your nitrous system. Usually that'll be conservative, i.e., less nitrous more fuel. You always adjust the power up as you tune. If you try dumping a ton of nitrous on your motor the first shot you'll be amazed at all the holes in your pistons.
2. Set your desired power level by providing the engine with the amount of fuel required for that much power. (See the section on Advance NOS tuning theory.) The power comes from the fuel, not the engine or the nitrous. If the fuel isn't there, the power won't be either. At the first sign of detonation, backfire, or misfire, *always reduce the nitrous jet first!* Don't think you can "cool things down" by adding more fuel. Since nitrous oxide is an oxidizer, the safest approach is to reduce the nitrous first, identify the problem, and go from there.

3. Gradually adjust the nitrous, beginning with too little, until the fuel is burned at a normal rate. Read every spark plug just as you would without nitrous. Not enough nitrous results in a rich, sooty, black plug coloration. This coloration means the fuel is burning too slowly. Too much nitrous will exhibit high heat in the form of a bluish or rainbow-like coloring on the plug's metal surfaces. This means you're engine is about to or is detonating, and you know what that means.

When you check the spark plugs, check *every* plug: Don't just spot check the easiest plug you can get to. Due to the wide possibility of air/fuel mixture variations, you need to check every plug for signs of detonation or other problems.

4. Nitrous oxide makes fuel burn more quickly. As you add nitrous, pull out ignition timing advance. The actual amount of ignition timing advance depends on your engine combination. Every engine is different. Adjust the timing down (less

advance before TDC) until there's a noticeable loss of power, then go up two degrees. If you don't already have an electronic retard box, buy one and install it. Buy one that only comes on when the nitrous is on. Set it to retard the timing by the amount you just determined was correct. If you use one of these boxes, don't forget to set your timing to a normal, non-nitrous number so it runs well with the nitrous system off.

5. Check the fuel and nitrous filter screens on a regular basis. This rates right up there with the most common problems that can lead you in circles for days. It doesn't take much to alter the calibration. Even a small scrap of pipe sealing tape can cause big problems.

6. If, when your system is activated something doesn't feel or sound right, *back off.* If you hear any detonation or feel anything unusual, get off the throttle. It's a lot easier to check everything over than it is to just try to drive through it and break a lot or expensive parts.

5.2.2
ON SPARK PLUG CHOICE

The spark plug has virtually no influence on how the engine burns fuel or runs in general.

Spark Plugs and Nitrous Oxide: What Works, What Doesn't, and Why

Over the years there seems to have been a great amount of technical material written about the simple operation of a spark plug and what it can do in relation to the way an engine runs. There are a few basic characteristics about spark plugs that you need to know to make an intelligent choice about the correct spark plug for your application.

First, and most important, a spark plug must be designed correctly to operate within the environment of your engine, not the other way around. This means that the spark plug has virtually no influence on how the engine burns fuel or runs in general. The correct spark plug will simply survive the conditions present in your engine. A spark plug must maintain a certain temperature to keep itself clean. The wrong heat range can cause an overheated or fouled plug. The heat range

The plug with the skinny, long ground strap comes a from a '96 Camaro. The other plug is an NGK unit with a shorter, thicker ground strap. The stock Camaro plug will cause detonation with any amount of nitrous. Do not use your stock spark plugs with your nitrous kit.

refers to the temperature of the ceramic material surrounding the center electrode.

Lean a/f ratios are more difficult to ignite because there are fewer fuel molecules in the area of the plug gap when the plug is scheduled to fire. Projected nose plugs were designed for late-model lean-burn engines as a solution to this condition, and modern high-energy ignition systems also allowed larger plug gaps. Igniting a lean mixture to reduce emissions and improve fuel mileage is one thing. Making power with nitrous oxide is an another.

Quite often, a factory type, wide-gap projected nose plug will produce a misfire condition after only a few seconds of nitrous use. The misfire is not due to the heat range. The misfire occurs because the ground strap of the spark plug turns into a glowing ember because it's too long to dissipate the extra heat produced by a nitrous-accelerated burn condition. The correct solution is to replace the plugs with units that have shorter ground straps. By doing this, you will shorten the heat path from the ground strap to the plug case.

Extra HP	Jetting N_2O/Fuel	Fuel Octane (R+M/2)Timing	Ignition	Spark Plug Heat Range
Super Power Shot				
100 HP	-0.047/0.053	92+ pump gas	Std	Std
125 HP	-0.055/0.061	92+ pump gas /B	Std to 2° retard	Std to1 step colder
150 HP	-0.073/0.082	92+ pump gas /B or 100+ racing gas	2° retard	1 to 2 steps colder
175 HP	-0.082/0.091	105 octane racing gas	4° retard	2 to 3 steps colder
Cheater System				
100 HP	-0.047/0.053	92+ pump gas	Std	Std
125 HP	-0.055/0.061	92+ pump gas /B	Std to 2° retard	Std to 1 step colder
150 HP	-0.073/0.082	100+ pump gas /B or 100+ racing gas	2° retard	1 to 2 steps colder
175 HP	-0.082/0.091	105 octane racing gas	4° retard	2 to 3 steps colder
200 HP	-0.093/0.102	110+ octane racing gas	6° retard	3 to 4 steps colder
250 HP	-0.102/0.110	110+ octane racing gas	6° retard	3 to 4 steps colder
Dual Shot Cheater System, Stage 1				
100 HP	-0.047/0.053	92+ pump gas	Std	Std
125 HP	-0.055/0.061	92+ pump gas /B	Std to 2° retard	Std to 1 step colder
150 HP	-0.073/0.082	92+ pump gas /B or 100+ racing gas	2° retard	1 to 2 steps colder
Dual Shot Cheater System, Stage 2				
150 HP	-0.063/0.071	100+ pump gas /B or 100+ racing gas	2° retard	1 to 2 steps colder
180 HP	-0.073/0.082	105 octane racing gas	4° retard	2 to 3 steps colder
210 HP	-0.082/0.091	110+ octane racing gas	6° retard	3 to 4 steps colder
250 HP	-0.093/0.102	110+ octane	6° retard	3 to 4 steps colder
Multiple Carburetor Cheater System				
100 HP	-0.033/0.037	92+ pump gas	Std	Std
125 HP	-0.038/0.043	92+ pump gas /B	Std to 2° retard	Std to 1 step colder
150 HP	-0.052/0.059	92+ pump gas /B or 100+ racing gas	2° retard	1 to 2 steps colder
175 HP	-0.059/0.065	105 octane racing gas	4° retard	2 to 3 steps colder
200 HP	-0.065/0.073	110+ octane	6° retard	3 to 4 steps colder
250 HP	-0.073/0.078	110+ octane	6° retard	3 to 4 steps colder
Big Shot System				
175 HP	-0.073/0.082	92+ pump gas /B or 100+ racing gas	2° retard	1 to 2 steps colder
225 HP	-0.082/0.091	92+ pump gas /B or 100+ racing gas	2° retard	1 to 2 steps colder
275 HP	-0.093/.102	105 octane racing gas	4° retard	2 to 3 steps colder
325 HP	-0.102/..110	110+ octane	6° retard	3 to 4 steps colder
350+ HP	-0.120/0.116	110+ octane	8° retard	3 to 4 steps colder
Two-Stage Big Shot System, Stage 1				
100 HP	-0.047/0.053	92+ pump gas /B or 100+ racing gas	Std	1 to 2 steps colder
125 HP	-0.0550/.061	92+ pump gas /B or 100+ racing gas	2° retard	1 to 2 steps colder
150 HP	-0.063/0.071	100+ pump gas /B or 100+ racing gas	2° retard	1 to 2 steps colder
180 HP	-0.073/0.082	105+ racing gas	4° retard	2 to 3 steps colder
210+ HP	-0.082/0.091	110+ octane	6° retard	3 to 4 steps colder
250+ HP	-0.093/0.102	110+ octane	6° retard	3 to 4 steps colder
Two-Stage Big Shot System, Stage 2				
175 HP	-0.073/0.082	92+ pump gas /B or 100+ racing gas	2° retard	1 to 2 steps colder
225 HP	-0.082/0.091	92+ pump gas /B or 100+ racing gas	2° retard	1 to 2 steps colder
275 HP	-0.093/0.102	105 octane racing gas	4° retard	2 to 3 steps colder
325 HP	-0.102/0.110	110+ octane	6° retard	3 to 4 steps colder
350+ HP	-0.1200/0.116	110+ octane	8° retard	3 to 4 steps colder
Multiple Carburetor Big Shot System				
150 HP	-0.052/0.058	92+ pump gas /B or 100+ racing gas	2° retard	1 to 2 steps colder
225 HP	-0.059/0.065	92+ pump gas /B or 100+ racing gas	2° retard	1 to 2 steps colder
275 HP	-0.065/0.073	105 octane racing gas	4° retard	2 to 3 steps colder
325 HP	-0.073/0.078	110+ octane	6° retard	3 to 4 steps colder
350+ HP	-0.085/0.082	110+ octane	8° retard	3 to 4 steps colder
Pro Racing Plate System, Each Stage				
100 HP	-0.047/0.053	92+ pump gas	Std	Std
125 HP	-0.055/0.061	92+ pump gas /B	Std to 2° retard	Std to 1 step colder
150 HP	-0.063/0.071	100+ pump gas /B or 100+ racing gas	2° retard	1 to 2 steps colder
180 HP	-0.073/0.082	105 octane racing gas	4° retard	2 to 3 steps colder
210 HP	-0.082/0.091	110+ octane	6° retard	3 to 4 steps colder
250 HP	-0.093/.102	110+ octane	6° retard	3 to 4 steps colder
Multiple Carburetor Pro Racing Plate System, Each Stage				
Note: Special tuning combinations will be required if both stages are to be applied simultaneously.				
100 HP Std	-0.033/0.037	92+ pump gas		Std
125 HP	-0.038/0.043	92+ pump gas /B	Std to 2° retard	Std to 1 step colder
150 HP	-0.052/0.059	92+ pump gas /B or 100+ racing gas	2° retard	1 to 2 steps colder
175 HP	-0.059/0.065	105 octane racing gas	4° retard	2 to 3 steps colder
200 HP	-0.065/0.073	110+ octane	6° retard	3 to 4 steps colder
250 HP	-0.073/0.078	110+ octane	6° retard	3 to 4 steps colder

Extra HP	Jetting N_2O/Fuel	Fuel Octane (R+M/2)Timing	Ignition	Spark Plug Heat Range
Pro Fogger System				
100 HP	-0.018/0.022	92+ pump gas	Std	Std
125 HP	-0.020/0.024	92+ pump gas /B	Std to 2° retard	Std to 1 step colder
150 HP	-0.022/0.026	92+ pump gas /B or 100+ racing gas	2° retard	1 to 2 steps colder
175 HP	-0.024/0.028	105 octane racing gas	4° retard	2 to 3 steps colder
250 HP	-0.028/0.032	110+ octane	6° retard	3 to 4 steps colder
300 HP	-0.032/0.036	110+ octane	6° retard	3 to 4 steps colder
350 HP	-0.036/0.040	110+ octane	6° retard	3 to 4 steps colder
400 HP	-0.040/0.046	110+ octane	6° retard	3 to 4 steps colder
500 HP	-0.043/0.052	110+ octane	6° retard	3 to 4 steps colder
4-Cylinder Sportsman Fogger System				
50 HP	-0.018/0.022	92+ pump gas	Std to 2° retard	Std to 1 step colder
75 HP	-0.022/0.026	92+ pump gas /B or 100+ racing gas	2° to 4° retard	1 step colder
100 HP	-0.024/0.028	105 octane racing gas	4° to 6° retard	1 to 2 steps colder
125 HP	-0.026/0.030	110+ octane	4° to 8° retard	2 steps colder
150 HP	-0.028/0.032	110+ octane	6° to 10° retard	2 to 3 steps colder
6-Cylinder Sportsman Fogger System				
75 HP	-0.018/0.022	92+ pump gas	Std to 2° retard	Std to 1 step colder
100 HP	-0.022/0.026	92+ pump gas /B or 100+ racing gas	2° to 4° retard	1 step colder
125 HP	-0.024/0.028	105 octane racing gas	4° to 6° retard	1 to 2 steps colder
150 HP	-0.026/0.030	110+ octane	4° to 8° retard	2 steps colder
175 HP	-0.028/0.032	11O+ octane	6° to 10° retard	2 to 3 steps colder
8-Cylinder Sportsman Fogger System				
100 HP	-0.018/0.022	92+ pump gas	2° retard	Std
125 HP	-0.020/0.024	92+ pump gas /B	Std to 2° retard	Std to 1 step colder
150 HP	-0.022/0.026	92+ pump gas /B or 100+ racing gas	2° retard	1 to 2 steps colder
175 HP	-0.024/0.028	105 octane racing gas	4° retard	2 to 3 steps colder
250 HP	-0.028/0.032	110+ octane	6° retard	3 to 4 steps colder
300 HP	-0.032/0.036	110+ octane	6° retard	3 to 4 steps colder

You can use the same heat range, you just have to use a non-projected nose plug.

5.3.1 CLEANING THE NITROUS SOLENOID FILTER

When nitrous bottles are refilled they can become contaminated with debris if the retailer does not have an adequate filter in his transfer pump mechanism. Contaminants in the bottle will eventually become lodged in the nitrous solenoid filter fitting. Periodically, after every 20 to 30 pounds of nitrous usage, examine the mesh in the nitrous filter for debris.

Clean the filter using the following procedure:

1. Close valve on nitrous bottle.
2. Empty main nitrous feed line.
3. Disconnect main nitrous feed line from nitrous solenoid.
4. Remove nitrous filter fitting from nitrous solenoids.
5. Remove all Teflon paste debris from solenoid inlet port threads and from nitrous solenoid filter pipe threads.
6. Examine the mesh in the nitrous filter fitting for contaminants. Blow out debris with compressed air if necessary.
7. Apply fresh Teflon paste to nitrous filter pipe threads. Reinstall filter in nitrous solenoid.
8. Reconnect main nitrous supply line to nitrous solenoid.

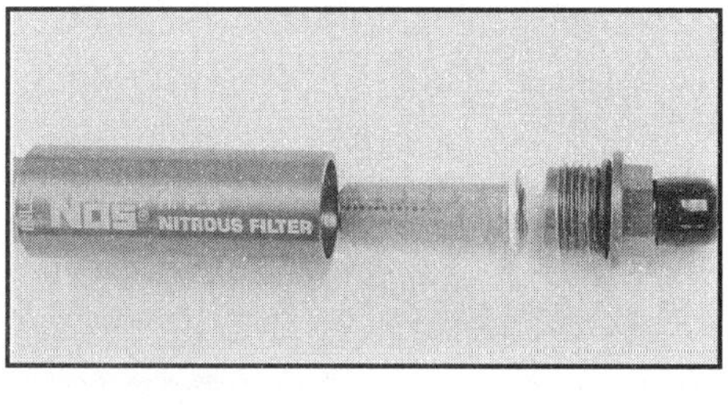

5.3..2 NITROUS SOLENOID PLUNGER MAINTENANCE

The seals use in Nitrous Oxide Systems' solenoid plungers are constructed from materials designed for use with nitrous oxide. When kept free from fuel contaminants or from being over-pressurized, they should provide trouble-free performance. However, you should examine the seal in the nitrous solenoid plunger after using about 20 to 30 pounds of nitrous.

The seals are designed to work at pressures up to 1100 psi. Exposing the plunger to excessive pressure (whether the vehicle is sitting or in-use) can result in the seal in the plunger swelling or, in extreme cases, disintegrating. The seals have a fail-safe feature. If they fail, they will not leak, nor will they flow nitrous. If the nitrous solenoid plunger seals swell, that will reduce nitrous flow and cause the nitrous/fuel ratio to become overly rich and reduce engine power.

If an NOS solenoid fails to operate correctly, the problem usually stems from chemical incompatibility, contamination from debris, or coil failure due to overheating. Chemical or debris contamination can result in flow reduction or flow stoppage. Coil failure will cause flow stoppage. Occasionally, plunger seals chip or crack from contamination, resulting in solenoid leakage.

An engine that suddenly is running lean may indicate a problem in the NOS fuel solenoid. Suddenly running rich is characteristic of a trouble in the NOS nitrous solenoid.

Disassembly and inspection of NOS solenoids is easy.

1. Close valve on nitrous bottle.
2. Empty main nitrous supply line.
3. Remove retaining nut from nitrous solenoid.
4. Remove coil and housing from nitrous solenoid base.
5. Unscrew stem from nitrous solenoid base. Do this by double-nutting the stem or by using a solenoid stem removal tool. Do not use pliers on the solenoid stem or you will damage it.
6. Remove stem, spring, and plunger from the solenoid base.
7. Examine the plunger seal for swelling. The seal service should be flat except for a small, circular indentation in the center of the seal. A chemically contaminated seal will protrude from the plunger and be dome-shaped.

A chemically contaminated seal will return to its original shape if left out in fresh air for several days. It may then be returned to service. Seals that are damaged should be replaced. A persistent seal swelling problem will require corrective action.

Some fuel additives are not compatible with NOS gasoline solenoids. Changing brands of fuel may cure this condition. NOS nitrous plunger seals will swell when exposed to fuel. A swollen nitrous seal is indicative of fuel collecting in the NOS nitrous solenoid. This problem can be cured by moving the NOS nitrous solenoid higher and/or farther from the injection orifice.

PROBLEM

No change in engine speed when fuel solenoid is activated

Probable Cause	Diagnostic Procedure	Corrective Action
System wired incorrectly	Compare wiring to schematic	Wire per instructions
Restricted fuel line	Inspect fuel line for restrictions	Remove restrictions
Malfunctioning fuel solenoid	Turn arming switch on; activate microswitch. Solenoid should make "clicking" noise	Repair/replace solenoid problem

Change in engine speed when nitrous bottle valve is opened

Probable Cause	Diagnostic Procedure	Corrective Action
Malfunctioning nitrous solenoid	Remove and inspect solenoid	Repair/replace solenoid.

Engine runs rich when system is activated

Probable Cause	Diagnostic Procedure	Corrective Action
Bottle valve not fully opened	Check bottle valve	Open valve fully
Bottle mounted improperly	Check bottle orientation	Mount bottle properly
Plugged nitrous filter	Inspect filter	Clean/replace filter
Low bottle pressure	Check bottle temperature	Set bottle temperature to 75° to 85° F
Poor nitrous supply	Weigh bottle	Fill bottle
Mismatched N_2O/fuel jetting	Compare to recommended values	Install correct jets
Excessive fuel pressure	Install fuel pressure gauge, such as NOS part #15931 in the fuel line. Measure the pressure during acceleration with the system activated	Regulate pressure down or install smaller fuel jetting
Loose nitrous solenoid wiring	Inspect solenoid wiring	Repair wiring
Malfunctioning nitrous solenoid	Close bottle valve. Disconnect nitrous solenoid outlet port. Disconnect solenoid (+) lead. Open nitrous bottle valve. Connect +12V to solenoid. Solenoid should make clicking noise	Rebuild solenoid

No change in performance when system is activated

Probable Cause	Diagnostic Procedure	Corrective Action
System wired incorrectly	Compare nitrous wiring to schematic	Wire system per instructions
Loose ground wire(s)	Connect 12V test light to battery (+) terminal. Check for continuity at grounds noted in schematic	Tighten/repair loose ground(s)
No power to arming switch	With vehicle ignition on, connect 12V test light to battery (-) terminal. Check for power at pole #1 on arming switch.	Repair wiring
Malfunctioning arming switch	With vehicle ignition on, turn arming switch on. Connect 12V test light to battery (-) terminal. Check for power at red wire on arming switch	Replace arming switch
Malfunctioning throttle microswitch	Close N_2O bottle. Empty N^2O supply line. Remove fuel solenoid shell. Turn ignition on. Turn arming switch on; Short across terminals on microswitch, +/-, solenoid should click	Replace throttle microswitch
Malfunctioning Power Relay	Temporarily disconnect /injector plug. Connect 12V test light to (-) battery terminal. Turn arming switch on. Manually set microswitch on. Use test light probe to check for continuity at blue wire on power relay	Replace Power relay
Malfunctioning pushbutton	Turn bottle valve off. Turn arming switch on. Connect 12V test light to battery (-). Turn pushbutton switch on. Check for continuity at pushbutton output pole	Replace pushbutton. Overly rich fuel condition
	Check for black smoke or backfiring through exhaust with system activated	Install smaller fuel jet or decrease fuel pressure.

PROBLEM
Engine detonates mildly when system is activated

Probable Cause	Diagnostic Procedure	Corrective Action
Excessive ignition timing	Check ignition timing	Reduce timing in 2° increments, up to 8° from non-nitrous conditions.
Inadequate octane fuel		Use higher-octane fuel; up to 116 VPC-16.
Spark plug heat range too high		Reduce spark plug heat range (Max: two-steps colder)
Too much nitrous flow		Reduce nitrous jetting

PROBLEM
Engine detonates heavily when system is activated

Probable Cause	Diagnostic Procedure	Corrective Action
Way too much N_2O		Reduce nitrous jetting
Poor fuel delivery due to:		
• Plugged fuel filter	Inspect fuel filter	Clean or replace filter
• Crimped fuel line	Inspect fuel line	Replace crimped line
• Weak fuel pump	Install fuel pressure gauge such as NOS Part # 15931. Run engine under load at wide-open throttle with system activated. Fuel pressure should be at least 5 psi on carbureted kits. Fuel-injected dry manifold kits should read higher. Check owner's manual for specific fuel pressures	Repair/replace fuel pump

PROBLEM
High-rpm misfire when system is activated

Probable Cause	Diagnostic Procedure	Corrective Action
Excessive spark plug gap	Inspect spark plugs	Set spark plug gap at 0.030 to 0.035 in.
Weak ignition; ignition component failure	Inspect components (plug wires, distributor cap, etc.)	Replace worn components.

PROBLEM
Surges under acceleration when system is activated

Probable Cause	Diagnostic Procedure	Corrective Action
Poor nitrous supply	Check bottle weight	Replace with full bottle
Bottle mounted incorrectly	Compare bottle position and orientation to instructions	Mount or orient bottle correctly

PROBLEM
Two-Stage system does not switch between stages correctly

Probable Cause	Diagnostic Procedure	Corrective Action
Improperly wired	Compare nitrous wiring to schematic	Wire system as instructed

5.3.3
COIL MAINTENANCE

Coil failure can occur if an NOS solenoid is held open too long or if it's forced to operate at pressures above which it's rated. Coils easily may be checked using a voltage-ohm meter. Proper resistance values are listed in the solenoid characteristics chart in Section 3.

5.3.4
SOLENOID STEM

The solenoid stem will not fail if it is not inadvertantly abused during disassembly/assembly. The solenoid stem is frequently crushed by mechanics who grip the stem with pliers or clamp it in a vise. If there are scratches visible on the stem, check the inside bore of the stem for damage. Slide the plunger inside the stem and check for binding. Components that bind should be discarded.

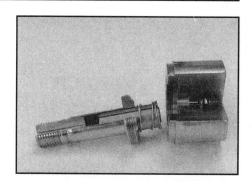

How To Install Nitrous Oxide Injection
Basic Engine Dynamics

FOUR STROKE FUNDAMENTALS

Your engine's a self-driven air pump; all internal combustion (IC) engines are. However, there are several designs of IC engines: two-stroke, four-stroke, Wankel or rotary engines, even turbine engines. For the sake of brevity, we're restricting our discussion here to four-stroke engines.

A four-stroke engine has valves and a cam that opens these valve in relation to a piston traveling up and down a cylinder bore. By manipulating the timing of the valve openings we get the four-strokes by which this engine design is sometimes known.

Briefly, they are: 1) intake; 2) compression; 3) power; 4) exhaust.

Your engine's camshaft determines its power curve. By opening and closing the valves with precise timing in relation to the position of the piston and crankshaft, the cam determines where in the rpm range an engine makes the most power and torque.

Of course the cam is dependent on the intake and exhaust tract design efficiency, i.e., how well these channels flow throughout the rpm range of

the engine as well as the pressure curve in the cylinder dictated by the motion of the piston. The cam can't flow any more than these tracts allow. What it can do is optimize the physics of the air moving through these tracts within an rpm window in order to best fill the cylinder with air and fuel.

The physics of the intake and exhaust tracts come down to accelerating columns of air and using the inertia of that column to increase the volumetric efficiency of the cylinder. As the piston recedes to bottom dead center (BDC) it creates a low-pressure area that's filled by atmospheric pressure (in an normally aspirated engine) forcing air through the intake manifold into the cylinder. What the manifold does is make the air into columns. When you get a column of air moving it doesn't want to stop, so more of it packs in the cylinder. By the way, air columns in the intake runners behave more like a Slinky than a column of liquid. By timing the intake and exhaust valve opening and closings—let's call these events from now on—you can catch a little more air and fuel and have a cleaner mix for each power

stroke.

The amount of air you can stuff into a cylinder per intake stroke is a measure of the engine's volumetric efficiency. If it can capture its full cubic capacity, it's said to have 100 percent volumetric efficiency. By tuning the intake dimensions, head port configuration, and cam profile and timing, you can, within a certain rpm window, get more than 100 percent volumetric efficiency. (Depending on the efficiency of the intake and exhaust systems.) Generally the torque peak occurs at peak volumetric efficiency. It should be obvious that volumetric efficiency of the cylinder is a primary factor in determining power output of an engine. Turbos, superchargers, and nitrous all work because they increase, by mechanical—or in the case of nitrous—by mechanical as well as chemical means, the volumetric efficiency of your engine. These techniques literally squeeze more air into the cylinder per cycle, allowing the engine to burn more fuel and make more pressure.

Volumetric efficiency falls off as engine rpm increases because there's less time to fill the cylinders. That's why a cam is designed to work with specific intake and exhaust system flow characteristics within an rpm window. Cams designed to work best at high rpm have a long duration, meaning they hold the valve open longer. Holding the valves open longer gives the cylinder more time to fill, so the power band is moved up the rpm range. In addition, high-rpm cams have a lot of what is called overlap. Much of the work of designing and tuning a cam has to do with how the intake charge and exhaust charge interact in the "overlap zone."

Overlap is when both the intake and the exhaust valves are open. This occurs when the piston is near TDC on the exhaust stroke. Figures 2.1-A through E walk you through the valve events of the four-stroke engine cycle.

We mentioned that it's important to get an uncontaminated charge into the cylinder. That means we have to expel the charge that was burned in the power stroke. That's what the exhaust stroke does. It forces the hot and expanding gases out the exhaust tract. But the real exhaust cycle begins a few degrees back on the power stroke before the piston reached BDC. Because the gas is a gas, it's compressible, so it behaves sort of like a spring. During the power stroke, the gas is expanding and forcing the piston down the bore, generating power, so it's under really high pressure. One of the things engine tuners have discovered is that, if you open the exhaust valve near the bottom of the power stroke, you can use some of that energy to get the exhaust gases out of the cylinder. (Opening the exhaust valve while the gases are still burning gives an internal combustion engine its characteristic exhaust sound.) Then the piston comes up the bore and forces most of the rest of the spent gas from the cylinder.

The exhaust stroke by itself can't get all the spent gas out of the cylinder because the piston doesn't completely fill the combustion chamber at the top. Ashes don't burn, and that's basically what's left after the power stroke; removing them so the next charge is as uncontaminated as possible helps make power. Engine

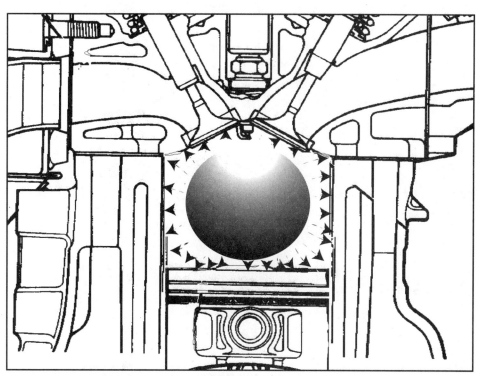

On the power stroke, most of the work is done in the first 90 degrees of crank rotation. As the piston gets near BDC, it's not putting as much pressure on the crank to spin it. The gases are still hot and expanding, but for the most part their job is done.

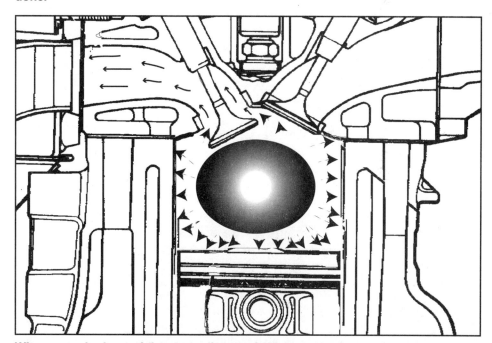

Why waste the heat of the expanding gas? Why not use its energy to help evacuate the cylinder? That's what engine tuners are up to when they get the cam to open the exhaust valve while the piston is still on the power stroke. Near BDC the exhaust valve pops open and the expanding gases punch into the low pressure of the exhaust system.

tuners use the same strategy at this end of the four-stroke cycle as they do on the exhaust cycle. That is, they open the intake valve before the piston reaches TDC and before the exhaust valve closes.

Engine tuners also discovered that, by using the inertia of the escaping exhaust gases, they could pull in a little extra fresh charge air and use it to push out the residual exhaust gas, or what's called "scavenging" the combustion chamber of spent gases. It's a pretty cool trick that's totally dependent on proper timing of the opening of the intake valve and the closing of

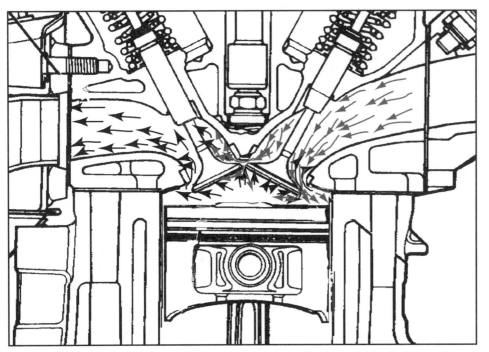

Just as the exhaust valve opens on the power stroke, so does the intake open on the exhaust stroke. At high rpm, a certain amount of overlap helps improve the quality of the intake charge by using the exiting exhaust pulse's low pressure to draw intake air through the combustion chamber. At low rpm, too much overlap results in low intake pressure and intake charge contamination because the high-pressure exhaust gases bleed into the low-pressure intake. This results in a lopey idle and loss of low-end power.

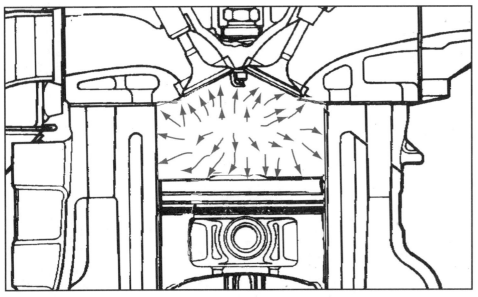

The point-of-intake valve closing influences how much intake charge the cylinder captures as well as the dynamic compression ratio. Closing the intake valve too late causes a loss of some intake charge because it's forced back into the intake manifold. For high-rpm power, you need a cam that closes the intake later in the cycle because you need the duration.

the exhaust valve.

Overlap is a critical area of four-stroke engine tuning. Lots of things happen here. The intake valve is opening and the exhaust valve is closing as the piston is rushing toward it, so valve-to-piston conflict can occur here. But most important is how the phasing of the valve events at overlap influence the performance of your engine—mainly in shifting peak power at different rpm levels.

If the intake is opened too soon, you get too much exhaust gas pulsing into the intake tract. Let's face it: the intake manifold has much lower pressure than the cylinder at this point. You always get some if you have overlap, but too much hurts engine performance. If too much exhaust gas gets into the intake, you have a contaminated intake charge. Because of the scavenging effect we talked about earlier, most of the contaminated intake air is drawn through the cylinder and out the exhaust as it should be. Keep in mind that if you have too much scavenging, a lot of the intake charge air will rush through the cylinder and out the exhaust leaving you with a lean cylinder. Again, tuning is always a balancing act.

The efficiency of the scavenging effect rises with engine rpm, which is reasonable since the gases have a higher velocity (and therefore less pressure) and more inertial energy to do the work of pulling the intake air through the cylinder. It's also influenced by the efficiency of the exhaust port and related manifolding such as headers, exhaust tube diameter, and muffler. If the exhaust system is highly efficient, you don't need to open the exhaust valve as soon as you would if the exhaust was slightly restricted.

It's interesting to note that intake contamination isn't usually a problem at high rpm because the tendency for exhaust gas to pulse back into the intake is most pronounced at low rpm. This is why long-duration cams with lots of overlap idle so poorly. The exhaust stroke is, in addition to recycling spent mixture, pumping pressure into the manifold, so it messes up the vacuum signal to the carburetor on carbureted cars and sends a confusing manifold absolute pressure (MAP) reading to the computer. It's not until you speed up the charge air velocity at higher rpm that the engine starts to make good, smooth power.

6.1.1
VALVETRAIN DYNAMICS

For the cam to make power, the valve train has to follow the lobe "signal" of the cam. The more precisely the valves do so, the more power you can make and the more reliable your engine will be.

To set a standard by which to judge the performance of current valvetrain technology, let's imagine what characteristics the ideal valvetrain should have. If it were possible, the ideal

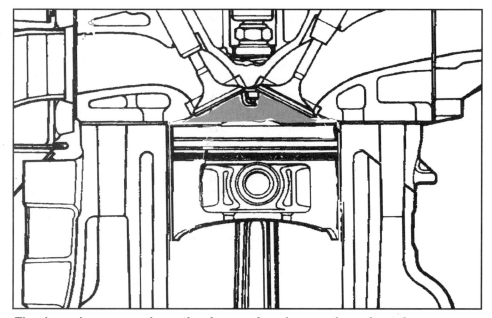

The dynamic compression ratio of an engine changes throughout the rpm range. A cam that closes the intake early and has little overlap makes good bottom-end power and idles smoothly. It also has a dynamic compression ratio closer to that of the static compression ratio. Closing the intake late means you lower dynamic compression, but you can gain high-rpm power.

valvetrain would instantly open and close the valve at precisely the right moment. Further, these valve timing events could be varied during engine operation to optimize power throughout the entire rpm range. In addition, there would be no valve head to inhibit charge flow through the port into the cylinder. And, of course, all this would occur without any friction whatsoever.

Unfortunately, the current state of valvetrain technology cannot achieve such performance. What we're stuck with is a mechanical compromise built from materials that have mass that's accelerated, and therefore inertia that must be managed. (For a valve system to instantly open and close and not self destruct, it would have to be composed of material without mass. It just ain't going to happen in this dimension.)

The valvetrain is a mechanical leverage system that converts the rotating eccentric of the cam lobe to a straight line reciprocating motion at the valve. Between these components there is space, called lash, which is needed to compensate for the expansion of the metals of the valvetrain components and the engine as it heats up.

The job of the camshaft, in addition to its lift and duration duties, is to open the valve as quickly as possible (accelerate) but not so fast as to

cause the valvetrain components to lose contact with the cam (valve float) after full lift is reached. And then to close the valve as quickly as possible, again with out valve float, or slamming the valves down on the seat so hard they break. This is a delicate balancing act and these requirements are what, literally, shapes the lobes of the cam.

In Figure F-6.1 on page 47 we have a map of the cam lobe sections. Compare the cam profiles of these theoretical cams and notice the difference in ramp angles in relation to crankshaft degrees of rotation. The steeper angles accelerate/decelerate the valves quicker. A square wave would represent the ideal instant response.

These angles, or rates of lift, are determined by several interdependent limiting factors.

First is the desired valve lift and duration. Lift is important because, to achieve maximum head-port flow rates, the cam has to get the valve head away from the seat.

Duration is related to lift in that more and quicker lift means more duration, since it takes time to lift the valve higher. Doing so means the port is flowing at max volume and velocity for a longer period of time and therefore fills the cylinder in less time. Time limits become critical as engine rpm

increases, and is a limiting factor in power output.

To move the valve off the seat to max lift and then to set it back on the seat means that the valvetrain must be accelerated and decelerated. And that means the cam designer has to deal with inertia. The quicker the valve is accelerated, the more inertia it has. Inertia is that quality of mass that, according to Newton's second law of motion, tends to stay in motion or at rest unless acted on by an outside force.

The cam profile, then, has to overcome the valvetrain's resistance to being accelerated, manage its resistance to slowing down and changing directions at the top of the lobe and accelerating back down toward the seat, then finally coming to rest upon the seat. In addition, taking up the lash, or the space between the valve train components, has to be accomplished without destroying components.

Referring to Figure F-6.1 again, we can see how this is accomplished. If you study the curve you'll notice that the entrance to the acceleration ramp of the cam has a shallow slope and therefore a slow acceleration rate. This is to take up the lash slowly and cushion the valvetrain before being accelerated to the top of the lobe. If this area of the cam wasn't shaped as it is, the cam would slam the valvetrain as if it were a sledgehammer. The shock of such an acceleration profile would soon destroy some component of the valvetrain.

Once the lash is taken up, the flank of the cam is designed to achieve maximum acceleration for a given rpm limit. The limits to the rate of acceleration, or ramp angle, is defined by the resilience of the valvetrain components to withstand the forces of acceleration and the tension, or pressure, of the spring. In other words, as engine rpm increases, the quicker the valve is opened, and consequently more force is generated.

The next limit is the inertia of the valvetrain as it reaches maximum acceleration rates. Notice on Figure F-6.1 that the curves near the top of the cam once again become shallow. This accomplishes two things. First, it extends the amount of time at max lift and therefore extends the time the open valve allows the cylinder to be filled. Second, it slows down the valve to reduce the magnitude of inertia to a point that the spring tension won't allow it to "ski-jump" off the top of the cam lobe, which is commonly referred to as valve float. Valve float is what destroys your valvetrain. (See figure G-6.1 for a description of the function of the shape of the cam lobe.)

Actually, the valvetrain doesn't jump off the top of the cam. What happens is the valve is accelerated to such an extent that the valve spring can't resist its motion. The valve goes slightly farther than the rocker arm on single overhead cam (SOHC) or overhead valve (OHV) engines, or the cams on double overhead cam (DOHC) engines, push it. When this happens, once again there's space between the components, (remember lash), but instead of the slack being taken up slowly, the components can slam back together with explosive force and that's when parts break.

A related observation to the cause of valve float is that the weight of the valve and keepers tends to be the most influential factor in determining the acceleration rate at which a valve floats. In other words, the lighter the valves and spring retainers, the higher the rpm capability of the valvetrain before reaching the point of valve float. On SOHC and OHV engines, this effect is amplified because the valve is moving farther, by virtue of the rocker arm ratio, and therefore faster than the rest of the valvetrain. This is also one of the reasons four-valve-per-cylinder engines rev much higher than than two-valve-per-cylinder engines. By having two intake and two exhaust valves you've divided the mass that each cam lobe and valve spring has to control.

At this point the spring pressure comes into play. The pressures rated in lb./in. that are seen with either the valve open or closed are important factors on how quickly the top of the cam lobe can decelerate the valvetrain. Valve springs have been a weak link in the valvetrain chain because they're subject to fatigue. And the higher the valve lift, the more fatigue becomes a problem. As the spring compresses, friction causes the springs to heat up, thereby changing the metal and losing some of it's resilience, or spring rate. When the spring rate is reduced, the cam lobe becomes too aggressive compared to the spring rate, and the valves will float at a lower rpm. That's why all racers using exotic cam lifts are constantly changing valve springs. Cam manufacturers have been diligently researching this problem and several now are offering springs made from new alloys that have a longer service life.

Spring pressures, in addition to cam lobe profile, impact the design of the rocker arms. When a higher spring pressure is used, more force is required to open the valve, so these components have to be built strong enough to physically overcome the spring pressure and not break. But at the same time they have to be as light as possible to reduce the inertia of a heavy mass. What this means in reality is that the components between the cam and the valve tend to flex. The more spring pressure and quicker the acceleration curves are, the more pronounce the flexing tends to be. In fact, if the spring pressures are high enough, the cam will actually bend slightly, enough to cause a loss of lift and duration at the valve. And when the rocker arm, or even the rocker mount, bends slightly, the valve doesn't follow the cam lobe profile.

It's really amazing how much the valvetrain flexes at high rpm. And because of the flex, some of the lift and duration of the cam is lost, and valve opening and closing event timing becomes skewed. Obviously, the better engineered and matched the valvetrain components, the closer it will follow the lobe profile and, hence, the engine will tend to produce more power. This subtle but critically important point is why you should always use the combinations that the cam manufacturers recommend. Unless you really know what you're doing and have experience to prove it, mixing components can rob you of power and reliability.

Valves tend to bounce when set back on the valve seat. The amount of bounce is directly associated with the lobe profile, how it ramps back on the base circle. This deceleration curve is designed differently for intake and exhaust valves. The intake can hit the seat harder than the exhaust valve because it's cooler. The exhaust valve is hot and therefore softer, and must be decelerated more before hitting the valve seat.

While we have barely exposed the subtle complexity of valvetrain dynamics, the main point of this discussion is that the valvetrain is a system. All the parts must work in relation to the others to balance the forces required to

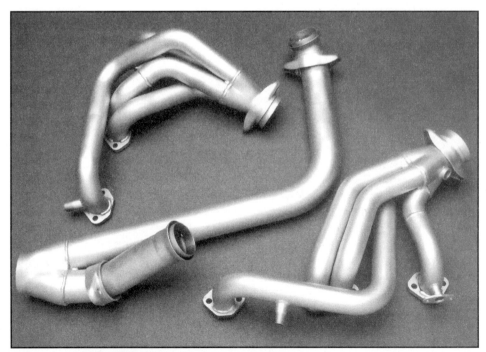

Exhaust system design is critical to extracting maximum performance from a nitrous oxide injected engine.

operate the valves accurately and reliably.

EXHAUST HEADERS

Exhaust Header Theory

It's time for more engine theory. Nothing too intense, just a quick theoretical model of what goes on in the exhaust system after the exhaust pulse leaves the combustion chamber. (Yeah, right.)

The exhaust system is the tail end of the flow path that we discussed in some detail in the previous section. The airflow concepts presented there are generally valid for the exhaust side; however, now we're talking about super-heated gasses that are cooling and slowing as they're pumped from the high pressures of the combustion chamber to ambient atmospheric pressure, i.e., 14.7 psi. As in the intake side, we're still concerned with the velocity of the gas through the flow channel, only this time, we're trying to use its energy to help evacuate the cylinder and begin the process of filling it during overlap—the old scavenging effect.

The way to do that is with pressure. Only instead of positive pressure to fill the cylinder, you need negative pressure to help suck the spent gasses from the cylinder. The trick is to develop negative pressure and to control the timing of when it hits the port of the next exhaust event. The power curve of your engine is, to a large degree, determined by how the exhaust header controls these two factors.

Header designers have only two main tools to work with: diameter and length. Historically, engines are most sensitive to changes in primary diameter. The primary diameter seems to establish the horsepower peak, while the length of the primary tube tends to shift the rpm range where the peak occurs. In general, a longer primary shifts the power peak to a lower rpm and vise versa. Of course, this relationship doesn't always hold true for every engine and application. When we talked to AEM's John Concialdi about header design, he was candid about header design being a bend, weld, and test item. AEM was testing

header designs for a BMW and found the most horsepower with the broadest torque curve with a small-diameter primary that was miles longer than anything he thought would work. So you never really know until you test it.

Dialing in exhaust headers is a tricky business because you're trying to synchronize a sound wave and the incredible shrinking/slowing exhaust gas pulse traveling down the tube with another cylinder and it's valve timing events. Remember in the section on valve-timing events, how the exhaust valve opens near the end of the power stroke? As soon as that valve cracks open, a sound wave punches out at the speed of sound, around 18,500 inches per second, followed by (well it's actually sort of part of) the exhaust gasses slamming down the pipe at about 3600 inches per second. When the high-pressure part of the sound wave pass through the collector, the low-pressure side of the wave (you can't have up without down) reaches back through the other tubes and, with the low pressure behind the exhaust gas pulse, pulls the next exhaust pulse out of the cylinder. Assuming of course, you've got all your dimensions right. Check out figures 4.6-3.1 through 3.4; these drawings show the timing relationship between all the events. Admittedly it's simple, but, hey, it's only a model; use it as such.

You may have noticed that what we've been describing sounds suspiciously like a 4-into-1 header, while the figures show a 4-2-1 configuration. What gives? Basically, ground clearance, or rather a lack of it. A 4-into-1 header with a fine-tuned collector is the best for peak power. The trouble is to make it work you have to introduce the primary tubes into the collector stacked two on top, two on bottom. It doesn't work if you collect the tubes side by side. The next best solution is a 4-2-1. When matched with properly sized tube diameters and length for your combination ,you're within about three to five horsepower of what a similarly matched 4 into 1 system would do.

Whether it's a 4-2-1 or a 4-into-1 header, the basic tuning theory of small-diameter, long tubes for torque and larger-diameter, short tubes for

high-rpm horsepower usually holds true, but there are always exceptions. Especially with 4-2-1 headers because you have the secondary tubes to play with as well as the primaries. Ultimately, an exhaust header only can be tuned to be really effective within a fairly narrow rpm range, say around 1000 rpm. So you've got to make you combination choices to work best around that range. You don't want to have a wicked mega-duration high-lift high-rpm cam with head porting and manifold with headers tuned to make power at 3000 rpm.

That wraps up our quick review on engine basics. Next we'll get into the subtleties of how nitrous affects the engine.

6.2.0
AIR FLOW FUNDAMENTALS

6.2.1
YOUR ENGINE IS A SELF-DRIVEN AIR PUMP

How to Get 125 Horsepower at Peak Torque and 140 Horsepower at Peak Power

It is possible to achieve the above numbers with 1.25 SCFM in a four-cycle engine if properly tuned. Our source for this generality is from some of SuperFlow's technical literature, which states: "As a rule, an engine consumes approximately 1.25 SCFM of air per horsepower at peak torque and 1.4 SCFM at peak power." This, according to engineers at the firm, is a pretty good rule of thumb. Not gospel. Just a good yardstick by which to measure and compare the state of tune of your engine with other parameters, such as Brake Specific Fuel Consumption (BSFC), Brake Specific Air Consumption (BSAC), and Volumetric Efficiency (VE).

We begin this section with that observation to express the importance of air flow through an engine. Since an internal combustion engine is an air pump, it has to move air through it in order to make power. No air, no power. Of course, an engine also requires fuel, but airflow is of such basic importance to the power output of an engine that we thought it logical to begin our discussion of basic engine theory with, well, the basic ingredient.

By the way, the goal of this section is to provide you with a basic theoretical model of how an engine works. Once you've grasped the fundamentals, we'll address some of the more vital essentials of tuning an engine using nitrous oxide in the section on Advanced Engine Theory.

To get a better understanding of this we need to get down to the molecular level. The air we breathe is two thirds nitrogen and less than one third oxygen. Oxygen molecules are the ones that combine rapidly with the molecules of the fuel to create heat and raise the pressure in the combustion chamber to make power. Nitrogen doesn't burn, but it sure takes up a lot of space in the intake manifold and combustion chambers. So does water vapor, i.e., humidity, suspended in the intake air. Adding fuel to this mix changes the temperature and therefore the pressure and density of the intake charge as well as taking up its own space. All these factors affect flow. The idea we're trying to highlight is "air" is not just "air." It's not a static value, so there are many factors that affect the amount of air/fuel you can flow through your engine. But neither is its behavior completely random. In fact, it's quite predictable, allowing us to shape intake and exhaust passages that improve flow.

An engine ingests air and fuel to make power and torque. Air alone doesn't catch fire when the spark plug strikes. You need some fuel mixed with the air to start such a reaction. So when we talk about airflow, we need to include the fuel as part of the equation. Admittedly, modern port-injection systems have intake manifolding optimized for dry airflow (no fuel); however, the port design has to take into consideration the need to transport and keep the air and fuel vapor thoroughly mixed.

Now since we're discussing what happens inside a tube, such as an intake runner or port, we have to consider the walls, or sides, of the tube. To simplify our discussion, let's first look at flow in two-dimensions. The long-side and short-side radius have the greatest impact on fluid flow because gases and fluids have mass

and therefore inertia. The gas and fluid flow on the long-side radius will pick up speed, forcing a pressure drops in that area. Meanwhile, the fluid flow on a short-side radius slows down because the flow separates and tumbles, and then you get a pressure increases in this area. Daniel Bernoulli, a mathematician who lived from 1700 to 1782, first described this effect with his equations. And so this principle of physics has come to be known as the Bernoulli effect. In essence, Bernoulli's equations state that if air speed varies as it flows around an object, the pressure of the air will vary inversely to the square of the air speed. That means as air speed increases, its pressure will drop; as air speed decreases its pressure will rise. In an unevenly shaped tube such as an intake runner, the consequence is you get less average mass flow through it compared to a plain straight tube. The runner itself becomes a restriction.

Let's add the third dimension and consider the shape through which gas or fluid flows best. Obviously, a straight tube offers the least resistance to flow. But the realities of packaging an engine to fit under the hood of a passenger car almost always take that option away from us. So if we have to turn the fluid, what shape generates the least turbulence while allowing maximum flow?

Air behaves like water except that it expands when its temperature rises. At certain speeds it really acts as a fluid. That's why aerodynamicists use fluid dynamic equations and oil filled "wind tunnels." What engine builders have found is that a fluid, and therefore a gas, flow smoothly over the walls and shape of a tube until it has to make a turn greater than about 9 or 10 degrees. Smooth airflow that's attached to the surface of a structure is called laminar flow. In other words, laminar flow is when the gas or fluid "seems well organized," as Joseph Kats put it in *Race Car Aerodynamics*. Laminar flow tends to, but not always, produce the most volume flow with the least amount of drag. Turbulent flow is when the air starts to tumble. It becomes disorganized and tends to generate friction, slowing the gas or fluid flow. When you force a

fluid to turn more than 10 degrees, it wants to separate from the shape over which it's flowing.

In general, we only have a few shapes that are practical: square and rectangular; round and oblong; and hybrids of these, such as a D-shaped port. But the question remains, which one is best? Of course, the answer is all of the above. Let's get more specific.

Each shape has its own particular effect on flow depending on how it's positioned relative to the changing direction of the airflow. For example it's easy to see that a circle has less square area than a square, so a square shape has more area to flow air mass. Now bend the air and use a round shape on the long-side radius. What happens? The gases respond as Bernoulli's equations state. The air on the long-side radius, since it has to travel farther, wants to speed up and drop pressure. But the round shape has less area than a square port, so comparatively, the airflow will slow down and keep its pressure more consistent with the short side. This minimizes tumbling, keeping the air more organized, and lets the port flow more mass. For a performance engine that's a good thing.

Sometimes the engine architecture, headbolts, water passages, etc., won't allow you to use the optimum shape. Then you have to figure out the next best choice and apply it. The bottom line is that, by precisely controlling runner shape and volume, you can get the airflow to all the intake valves just about even with sufficient mass to make power within a predetermined power band.

Once you get the air to the valve, you have to make a sacrifice, because the air has to turn. It can't flow through the metal of the valve. That means you're going to generate turbulence and lose mass flow. The only thing you can do is try to minimize the flow loss.

The general strategy for minimizing flow loss through the valve is to make as direct an approach as possible to the valve seat. The idea is to direct the column of air in such a way as to set up a cone-shaped flow of air around the full circumference of the valve. We're talking intake side here, but essentially you try to get the cone-shaped flow

Two images of a highly efficient combustion chamber. Notice that the area around the valves (arrows A and B) are tapered away from the valve head to help form the flow cone. In the areas next to the cylinder walls (arrows C) there isn't much you can do. But notice how this head porter chose to give the exhaust valve a little more breathing room in this area.

pattern around the exhaust valve as well; you just have to use different shapes to get it.

Speaking of shapes, airflow in the cone around the valve seat is critically dependent on the angles you use on the seat and the shape within the combustion chamber, particularly on the shrouded side. In general, you get better flow with a series of sharp edges on the cuts than blending the cuts together.

Of course, flow is only part of the power equation. How dense you keep the charge, i.e., how cool you keep it until it get into the combustion chamber, has a great impact on performance. In general the power output of a naturally aspirated engine is at the mercy of the prevailing atmospheric conditions outside the engine as well as inside. That is, the denser the air, (i.e. the lower the altitude), the lower the humidity and temperature, the more power an engine can generate. Air density changes with altitude and temperature. And while you

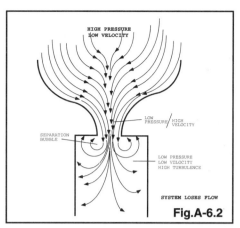

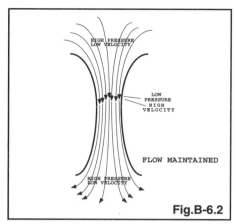

Managing airflow is critical in a high-performance engine. In Fig.A-6.2, the runner wall terminates, suddenly releasing pressure and throwing the flow into turbulence. This causes the system to lose flow and is the main reason you should match the ports of your intake and exhaust manifolds to the head ports. In Fig.B-6.2, the runner wall gradually slopes away, keeping the flow organized to maintain a high rate of flow. This, more than anything, should clue you in to seeing that the shape and the entire flow channel, up- and downstream, i.e., intake manifold, head ports, and exhaust system, impacts airflow.

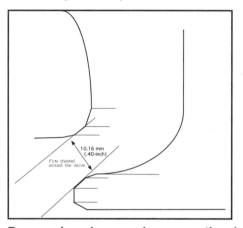

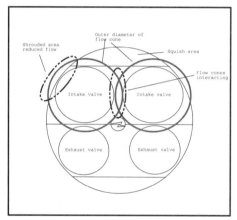

Runner size, shape, and cross-sectional area are important. But the bottom line is that the air and fuel have to go around the valve to get into the cylinder. The passage isn't wide but it does go around the entire circumference of the valve. Unless, of course, the valve is positioned extremely close to the cylinder or combustion chamber wall. Then it's said to be shrouded, a condition that inhibits flow.

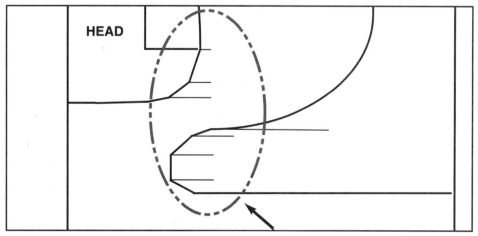

Valve face and seat angles have the most influence on low lift flow. Getting good low lift flow numbers makes an engine come alive. Sharp angles seem to work the best. Blended angles appear to increase the boundary layer and reduce the effective channel size. The flow cone forms at a certain lift depending on shape of the port surfaces and those in the combustion chamber around the valve. After the flow cone forms, raising the valve further does not increase airflow. The only reason to lift the valve further is to increase the duration that the valve is open.

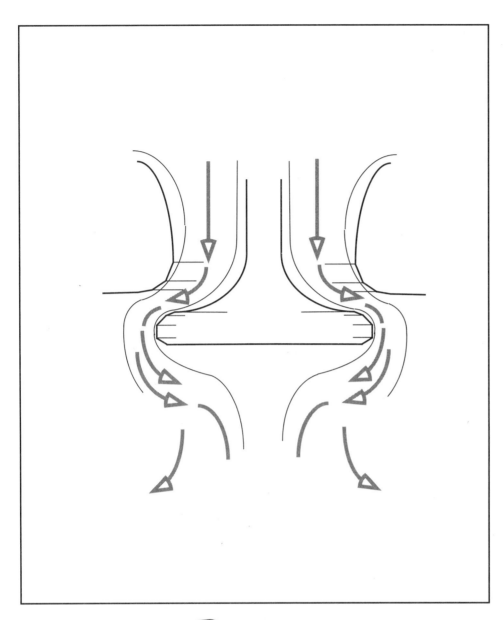

can't really control the altitude change, you can, within limits, control the heat injected into the intake system. Removing heated water lines from the intake or using ice on the intake before a run can help. Perhaps even using heat barrier coatings on the intake. Remember, air expands when it gets hot. That doesn't create any more oxygen to combine with the fuel, it only takes up space and reduces the amount of oxygen available to burn with the fuel. When injecting N_2O the super-cooled gas minimizes these concerns but doesn't erase them. If you want maximum performance you should address these issues.

Ultimately, however, it comes down to the combination. Everything in an engine affects everything else. You can have perfectly sized and matched intake runners and port and not realize the power potential of your higher airflow capacity because the stock fuel-injection system doesn't recognize the changes; or you have too much or too little carburetion for a carbureted car. To make an engine really sing, you have to have it all together. That's why if you just have the head massaged to flow more air without making equal improvements in the intake manifold, the exhaust manifold, and the fuel management system, you don't see improvements in power. The most important concept to get in high-performance tuning, with and without nitrous oxide, is that the engine is a combination of systems that work together to make power.

COOL AIR IS WORTH HORSEPOWER

Check this out. For every 11 degrees F you can lower the intake air temperature, you're rewarded with approximately a one-percent horsepower increase. If you're underhood temps are in the 165-degree F range and it's 80 degrees F outside, you'll get a 7.7-percent increase by ducting outside cool air to the intake. If you're running at 100 horsepower, that turns into a cool 107.7 horsepower. Free.

EXTRUDE HONE

Extrude Honing uses a heavy semi-liquid that carries a cutting media. Because air flows like liquid, the theory behind extrude honing is that, as this heavy liquid is forced through the channel, it removes more material from where the channel causes the air to change directions. It shapes the channel as it removes the material in such a way to enhance the laminar flow and therefore the flow capacity of the channel.

One of the main benefits of extrude honing your intake and heads is increasing the flow capacity of the channel, but keeping the volume of the runner close to original so you don't lose low-rpm velocity of the charge air. This broadens the power curve instead of tuning the engine to produce more power within a narrow high-rpm range. Of course you can use the process to "hog out" an intake or port if you have specific requirements.

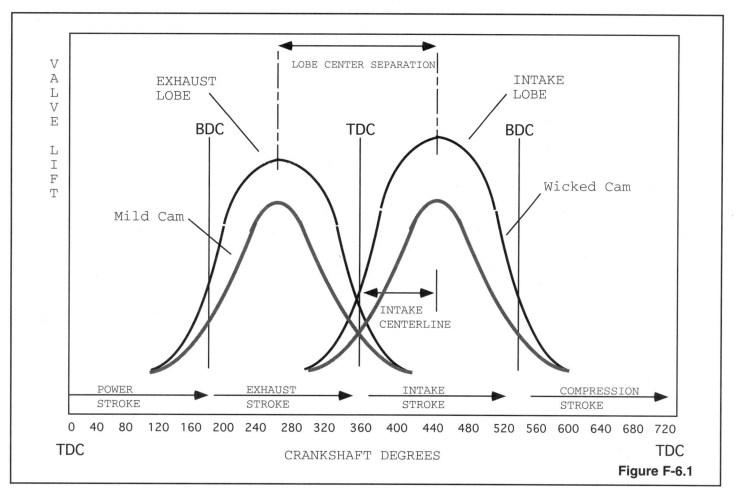

Figure F-6.1

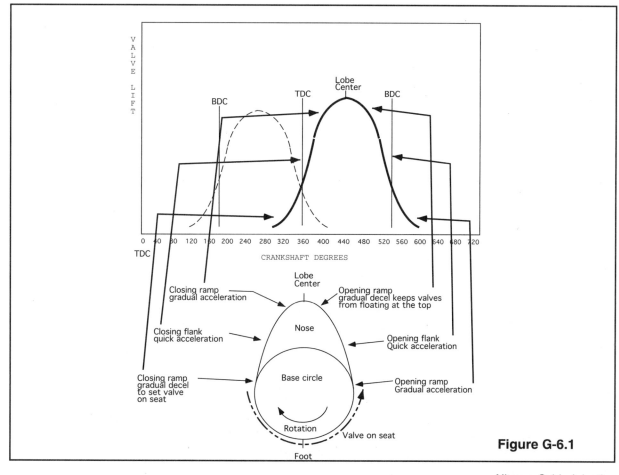

Figure G-6.1

How To Install Nitrous Oxide Injection
Advanced Nitrous Tuning

7.1.0
HOW TO BECOME AN EXPERT NITROUS TUNER

This section is devoted to advanced tuning theory. That's really just a fancy way of saying we're in the gray area where the "science" of engine tuning becomes art, or at the least a high craft. Which is to say, not even the experts can predict exactly what's going to happen. They, like you, have to try it, observe it as objectively as possible, quantify it, and, decide on the best course of action.

What these experts have that you don't is an ingrained, virtually instinctual model of the complex mechanical and chemical processes happening in an internal combustion engine. It's as if their central nervous systems are branded by experience, bitter and victorious, so much so that they see things other's don't—noticing the imperceptible hidden in the obvious. While we can't give you an expert's experience, we at can least give you a rudimentary model to guide you on your way to becoming an expert nitrous engine tuner.

7.1.1
THE MOST OVERLOOKED TUNING "SECRET"

Let's start things off with a concept that always gets lost in the search for peak power, more torque, and achieving optimum nitrous-to-fuel ratios. This most overlooked concept is that, even with healthy doses of nitrous, you're only increasing the oxygen content of the charge by just a few percent. That's wild when you think about it. Just a scant few percent increase in the oxidizer content of the intake charge and you get incredible power output.

This should show you just how sensitive gasoline and other fuels are to oxygen, which, by the way, precludes using pure oxygen as an induction agent. If you did it would probably use your pistons for fuel along with the fuel and the cylinder walls. And we don't want to have to measure the Brake Specific Aluminum Consumption of that combination.

Think about this for a second. You're doing a lot of work to set up a system to deliver super-cooled nitrous oxide into your engine. The upshot of this is that you gain a few percent increase in the oxydizer content, which allows you to react to more fuel more quickly to create more heat and pressure to push down harder on the top of your pistons, which drives the wheels that win the races. Really, that's all we're doing here. But it's so easy to get lost in the forest looking at the trees that you need to step back and just get the basics. And this is the most basic and most overlooked concept regarding tuning a nitrous system.

Measured by volume, air is about 20.95 percent oxygen and 78.06 percent nitrogen, with the remaining 0.99 percent taken up with trace elements like helium, hydrogen, carbon dioxide, etc. By weight, nitrogen makes up 75.5 percent of the atmosphere's mass, with oxygen contributing 23 percent of the mass; the remaining 1.5 percent is contributed by the aforementioned trace elements.

Of course, it's the oxygen content that reacts with fuel to make power, so we're interested in that portion of the atmosphere. In a conversation with Ken Duttweiler at the '97 NHRA Winston World Finals, he noted those figures may be accurate for a global average, but in the environment from which engines draw air, oxygen usually accounts for around 19 percent of the mass of the intake charge. It does fluctuate, but he said 19 percent is a good working number, so that's the one we'll use in this exercise.

Nitrous oxide, measured by volume is 33 percent oxygen; 66 percent nitrogen. Measured by weight, 36 percent of its mass is oxygen with 64 percent nitrogen. When you first hear the numbers you think you're going to get a big jump in the oxygen content of the intake charge with nitrous oxide. But you don't get the whole 17 percent increase (36 percent minus 19 percent = 17 percent) because you're not running the engine solely on the nitrous system. You're augmenting the atmospheric charge with nitrous oxide, blending two oxygen sources, each with a different amount of oxygen. How much of a blend is what tuning is all about.

Complicating the tuning process is the usual motor mayhem of pulsing flow, changing rates of volumetric efficiency through rpm range, combined with the flat flow rate of nitrous systems. Put roughly, a nitrous system makes prodigious force at the torque peak because at that point in the rpm range you get the highest percentage of nitrous oxide to air. At higher rpm, the engine still makes more horsepower, but as the airflow demands outpace the flat flow rate of the nitrous system, you get a lower percentage of nitrous oxide to air and power falls off. Unless, of course, you have a staged system that increases nitrous flow as the engine demands. More on these systems later.

Because of the rate and volumetric efficiency variations of piston engines, it is advantageous to build on your understanding of nitrous systems, if we confine our discussion to the nitrous vs. airflow rates at the torque and horsepower peaks. By looking at the differing nitrous to air ratios at these points, you'll understand that these ratios change dynamically as the engine runs through its rpm range. Let's present a simple model in order to make the math and the concept as plain as possible. Let's have a look at the torque peak first.

7.2.0
MODELING A NITROUS SYSTEM

The gearheads at SuperFlow, Inc., makers of some of the better dynos, flow benches, and other power and flow measuring equipment on the market, say that, in general, an engine flows approximately 1.25 SCFM per horsepower at peak torque and 1.4 SCFM per horsepower at peak power. We'll use these values throughout our discussions.

Assume you're making 200 horsepower at the torque peak without nitrous. Using the SuperFlow constant, that cyphers out to about 250 SCFM When you hit the button, suddenly the engine thunders to 340 horsepower at the torque peak and the SuperFlow constant no longer is valid. The reason the constant (this goes for the peak power constant, as well) no longer is valid is because nitrous has a greater oxygen content than that of air, so it takes less nitrous oxide to react to a given amount of fuel. And if you've grabbed hold of the concept we've been repeating like a mantra throughout this book: "fuel makes power, not the nitrous," then this should make sense to you. If not, call the tech gurus at NOS and meditate on the concept while on hold.

In a perfect world, or at least in a world where reality conformed to wishes, we should be able to calculate a nitrous flow constant in the image of the SuperFlow constants used above and just nail the question of nitrous flow to the wall, shoot it through the heart, and end all these vague tuning decision once and for all. We can't exactly do that, but we can get close enough to be useful. And in the immortal words of Mary Poppins, "enough's as good as a feast."

If we just take the additional power gain, ordain its genesis as nitrous, and calculate what it would take to make 140 extra horsepower at the torque peak, we can estimate how much nitrous we need to run. This isn't a completely accurate model of the reality within our engine. Reality is always so much messier. The difficulty here is that not only do we have the ever-changing conditions of a pulse device running through its rpm range, but now we have an oxidizing agent that's active in two other ways. First, it cools the incoming atmosphere, increasing its density and thereby its oxygen content. Second, it also pressurizes the intake slightly, reducing the flow through the carburetor. What's a tuner to do?

The pros measure everything. They already measure the air and the fuel going into the naturally aspirated engine—with savvy nitrous tuners doing the same with the nitrous and the enrichment fuel. That's the way to do it if you have a dyno and generate BSFC data. For the rest of us, we've got to tune on the run, literally; but if you understand the relationships of the data from the dyno, you'll be able to make better tuning decisions at the track.

7.2.1
FUEL/NITROUS/AIRFLOW AT PEAK TORQUE

Since airflow constants aren't practical when using nitrous, the only other constant we can use is Brake Specific Fuel Consumption (BSFC). I've written about BSFC elsewhere in this book so I won't explain it here other than to say that BSFC is the ratio of fuel consumed to the power output. Suffice it to say that a BSFC value of 0.50 is about average for a well-tuned engine with roughly a 12:1 air/fuel ratio. The reason why it's a good value to use when working with nitrous is because, "fuel makes power, not the nitrous." If you know the total rate of fuel flow, you know, based on a 0.50 BSFC, approximately how much power that fuel flow rate will support.

To use our BSFC standard we need to convert the other values into like units of measure. Going back to our model, 200 horsepower at peak torque is about 250 SCFM, which if you reference ratio and flow charts in section 7.8, we find 250 SCFM is about 19.05 lb./min. That corresponds to a fuel flow at 0.50 BSFC of 100 lb./hr. (To convert the lb./hr. to lb./min. simply divide it by 60.), which converts to 1.67 lb./min. 19.05/1.67=11.4 a/f ratio. At the torque peak, an 11.4:1 a/f ratio isn't too far off for an engine tuned to accelerate.

Most engines accelerate quicker if they're slightly rich. Peak steady-state power comes with a much leaner mixture, somewhere around 13.5:1 depending on the combination.

Now lets do the math when we have nitrous to factor in. The extra 140 horsepower equates, at peak torque, to a naturally aspirated flow rate of 175 SCFM, or 13.34 lb./min. for air; for nitrous, it's only 50 CFM or 5.83 lb./min .at a N_2O/fuel ratio of 5:1 referenced to a BSFC of 0.50 for 1.17 lb./min. mass fuel flow. We come by the 5:1 N_2O/fuel ratio via the NOS crew. It found that 5:1 is a good, conservative, slightly fuel-rich beginning ratio. About the leanest mix it suggests is a 6:1 ratio, but you can go leaner if you've got the nerve. According to David Vizard, the chemistry suggests that stoichiometric, or complete reaction, would take place with a 9:1; however, that ratio won't make the best power. At the 6:1 ratio the figures break down like this: 61CFM or 7.00 lb./min.

Before we go on, let's explain where we got the CFM values of the nitrous at lb./min. flow rates. It's basically an estimate. If you check the reference chapter for the physical constants of nitrous, you see its specific volume at 1 atm. We've chosen the specific volume factor at 70°F of 8.726 ft^3/lb. Exactly what temperature and therefore volume it reaches in the engine before the intake valve closes, we're not sure, but this figure at least is a good estimate. We should also point out that as the engine heats during a power run or dyno pull, the intake temperature increases, and as it does the volume of the nitrous charge increases as its temperature increases as well. To recap, this is what we've done so far (see Chart 1).

7.2.2
NITROUS TO NATURALLY ASPIRATED MASS FLOW COMPARISON

If you compare the mass flow rate of a nitrous system-enhanced engine with that of a naturally aspirated engine of the same output, you'll see that the nitrous system generates much less mass flow—at least on the intake side of the equation; we'll get to the exhaust side later. That's one of the great advantages of nitrous. It packs in more oxygen in a smaller package than a naturally aspirated engine. How much? take a look at Chart 2.

The point of this exercise is to show you that, in spite of the big flow and horsepower numbers, a nitrous system doesn't have to supply huge rates of oxygen and you don't need unreasonably large quantities of enrichment fuel to add horsepower. Basically, we get back to the concept that fuel makes the power, and it takes X amount of fuel to make Y amount of power, no matter how you introduce the oxidizer. It doesn't matter to the engine if the oxygen is supplied by a compressor or a bottle of compressed nitrous oxide.

We've just taken an in-depth look at the air, oxygen, nitrous oxide, and fuel flow demands of an engine at peak torque. Peak torque usually occurs at an rpm level well before the horsepower peak. At those airflow rates, a nitrous system typically doesn't have a problem keeping up with the demand, so every intake cycle is rich with a relatively cool and dense oxygen and fuel charge. As the engine's rpm increases, so does the airflow rate. However, power falls off because friction increases with engine speed and the volumetric efficiency of the engine falls off because there just isn't enough time to fill the cylinders. How this affects the nitrous system is that less of the incoming charge is filled with the cold charge of oxygen that

Chart 2						
HP	Air CFM	Air Lbs/Min	Oxygen Lbs/Min	Nitrous CFM	Nitrous Lbs/Min	Fuel Lbs/Min
All Naturally Aspirated Suggested Beginning Ratio Nitrous Injection:						2.83
Natural Aspirated Portion:						
200	250	19.05	3.61			1.67
Nitrous Rates at 5/1:						
140			2.09	50	5.83	1.17
Totals:						
340	250	19.05	5.70	50	5.83	2.84
Nitrous Rates at 6/1:						
140			2.52	61	7.00	1.17
Totals:						
340	250	19.05	6.13	61	7.00	2.84
5/1 Percentages:				**6/1 Percentages:**		
Natural:		Nitrous:		Natural:		Nitrous:
HP:				**HP:**		
200/340=59%		140/340=41%		200/340=59%		140/340=41%
Lbs/Min Oxygen:				**Lbs/Min Oxygen:**		
3.6/5.70=63%		2.09/5.70=37%		3.61/6.13=59%		2.52/6.13=41%

nitrous oxide delivers which, again, conspires to reduce power output.

7.2.3
FUEL/NITROUS/AIRFLOW AT PEAK POWER

Here's a model of what happens at peak power. The engine is now consuming 1.4 SCFM of air per horsepower because it needs rpm and therefore airflow to make peak horsepower. On a typical small-block 350-cubic-inch V-8 street combination, peak power usually hits in the mid 5000-rpm range, so let's just use 5300 rpm. To calculate airflow at this rpm we need to know the displacement (350) the rpm (5300), and the volumetric efficiency, which typically is around 85 percent at this rpm.

To find CFM at the rpm and 85 percent, plug the values into this equation: (see Chart 3).

Compared with the rates of flow at peak torque, an engine definitely consumes more air and fuel at peak power. I don't mean to be redundant, just redundant enough to allow these concepts to sink in.

7.2.4
COMPARATIVE FLOW RATES AT PEAK TORQUE AND POWER AT 6:1 N2O FUEL RATIO

Chart 4 shows how our theoretical numbers add up during peak power. Notice that I didn't change the nitrous flow nor its enrichment fuel flow for the peak power model. Again, that's because a single-stage nitrous system is a constant-flow system. Still, you can see that a moderate dose of nitrous raises power impressively.

7.2.4.1
OBSERVATIONS AND INTERPRETATIONS OF THE PERCENT INCREASE FROM PEAK TORQUE TO PEAK POWER

These stats suggest a nitrous system

increases mass flow from the torque peak to the power peak 12 percent more than an all-natural combination. The 60 percent increase in mass flow with nitrous compared to the 48 percent increase of a naturally aspirated engine is consistent with the fixed flow of a single-stage nitrous system. This is explained as the natural consequence of the nitrous system supplying a greater percentage of the intake charge at peak torque, where air flow also is lower than at the power peak.

Analyzing the percentages for the volume flow in CFM, the values are different because the volume and weight of nitrous oxide and the atmosphere have different values. However, the explanation for the percent increase is the same as the increase of mass just given. Remember that we aren't accounting for volume increases due to intake manifold temperature increase and therefore charge temperature increase during a power pull.

The increasing proportion of oxygen is where it gets interesting. We get a 48-percent increase, true; that has to occur to support the power level, i.e., the amount of fuel available to react with the oxygen. The question we need answered in our quest for nitrous expertise is how much of the additional oxygen comes

from the nitrous system and how much from the atmosphere. According to the calculations, at peak power with a 6:1 nitrous-to-fuel ratio, 28 percent of the oxygen comes from the nitrous system; at peak torque, that value jumps to 41 percent. And check this out— at peak power, 17 percent of the mass contributes to 28 percent of the oxygen.

Included are the fuel and horsepower increases purely for reference, though these exhibit an interesting trend. They show a larger increase in fuel consumption compared to power output. This expresses the tendency of internal combustion engines to be more efficient at the torque peak. That being so, some of the power generated by the additional fuel at the power peak is being consumed by a higher rate of friction caused by the engine spinning at a faster rpm. But let's put that aside for now.

At this point we hope you've kept up with the mathematic modeling. Now we need to address the exhaust cycle quickly and by no means as thoroughly as we did the intake.

7.2.5
EXHAUST TACTICS

As we've just seen, even a mild nitrous system delivers much more fuel and oxygen to the combustion chambers than a naturally aspirated engine. Of course, if more goes in, then more has to come out. Traditionally, this is accomplished by choosing a cam with an exaggerated

	Air	Nitr	Air+Nitr	Fuel	Percent increase from peak torq
Chart 4					
			(All In Lbs/Min)		to peak horsepower
Peak Torque:					In Air Mass
340hp @ peak torque	19.05	7.00	26.05	2.83	With N2O (41.74/26.05=1.60) 60%
Percent Nitrous: 7.00/26.05=27%					Mass% NO2: PTorq=27%; PPwr=17%
Peak Power:					All Natural (48.00/32.39=1.48) 48%
450hp @ peak power:	34.74	7.00	41.74	3.87	**In Volume (CFM) with Nitrous:**
Percent Nitrous: 7.00/41.74=17%					**(517/311=1.66) 66%**
					All Natural (600/425=1.41) 41%
					In O2 (9.12/6.15=1.48) 48%
					% O2 From Nitrous @ PPwr:
					(2.52/9.12-0.276) 28%
					% O2 From Nitrous @ PTorq:
					(2.52/6.15=0.409) 41%
					In hp: (450/340=1.32) 32%
					In Fuel: (3.87/2.83=1.37) 37%

exhaust lobe. Usually this meant compromising engine performance when not on the bottle. Most "nitrous" cams traded throttle response and low-end torque for high-end performance because, in order to provide a good exhaust duration, the cam had to open the exhaust valve in such a way that the design had lots of overlap. For street cars, most enthusiasts opted for a cam that gave good performance without nitrous, knowing that the nitrous system would make serious power anyway.

With Competition Cams' new series of nitrous cams, compromising just may be a thing of the past. Because of innovations in valvetrain design, the firm's new Nitrous HP cams open the intake valve faster (resulting in more vacuum and more response) and close it sooner (resulting in more cylinder pressure and more torque).

The exhaust profiles are chosen to have enough area to scavenge the extra gases released from the combustion of oxygen-enhanced mixtures. The intake and exhaust centerlines are chosen to optimize responsiveness and power, while overlap area is maintained close to the optimum value. With this design strategy, most combustion pressure lost due to opening the exhaust valve early is somewhat compensated for by the improved intake profile.

That's a quick overview of cam strategy.

7.3.0
ANALYSIS OF COMPETITION CAM NITROUS HP CAMSHAFT DYNO DATA

To further illustrate our model of nitrous behavior, let us look at a couple of real-world examples. Competition Cams has developed several camshafts specifically for nitrous application. By comparing the dyno data from the naturally aspirated test with the nitrous-enhanced test we should be able to build a solid case for our theoretical model, as well as explore the effects of a fixed flow system on engine power.

7.3.1
THE TEST ENGINE COMBINATION

The test engine combination is as follows:

Camshaft part number: 12- 555-4
Designation: NX256H-13
Duration @ 0.006: 256/268
Duration @0.050: 212/222
Max lift w/1.5RR: 0.447/0.468
Lobe Separation: 113
Lobe ID numbers: 5441/5212
Intake Centerline: 108
Engine Type: Chevrolet 350
Bore: 4.040
Stroke: 3.480
Displacement: 356
Compression: 9.25: 1
Heads: Dart Sportsman II
Intake: Edelbrock Performer
Carburetor: Holley 750 DP
Exhaust: 1.75 headers
Nitrous system: Single-stage adjustable street plate system

Results:
Torque @ 3200 rpm: 371 ft./lb.
Power @ 5100 rpm: 326 hp
With N_2O: 600 ft./lb.
With N_2O: 439 hp
Manifold Vacuum: 16.5-in. Hg @ 800 rpm and 18.5-in. Hg @ 1000 rpm, no load

Comparing the chart of the dyno data for this cam, several trends become apparent. First, we notice the broad and smooth torque curve the engine produces without nitrous. The combination peaks with torque at 3200 rpm with 371 ft./lb., but it's making just over 314 ft./lb. at 2000 rpm and doesn't fall below that figure until 5500 rpm, where it still makes 306 ft./lb. Peak horsepower occurs at 5200 rpm with 329 ponies. The broad, even, torque curve gives the engine a broad horsepower curve as well. It has a window of 1500 rpm where it's making over 300 horsepower and a window of over 2000 rpm over 270 horsepower .

It's also tuned well. The air/fuel ratios are in the 11:1 to 12:1 range with a BSFC of a little over 0.50, about where you'd expect it. And to compare with our theoretical model of 1.4 SCFM air per horsepower at peak power, we get 1.32 by dividing 434.9 (measured airflow at that level) by 329 (peak power). This result indicates that the model's not that far off and we've got a well-tuned engine to start making power with nitrous.

When you apply nitrous to an engine on a dyno, the data can look misleading if you don't measure the nitrous and enrichment fuel going into the engine. Of course, that's the case with the set with which we're working. Still, the data shows how the nitrous system influences the carburetor and the resulting fuel curve from it. This is because the air turbine doesn't recognize the nitrous going into the engine; it only measures the air that flows through it. What happens when you activate the nitrous system is it supplies the intake manifold with an alternate pressure source so the flow through the carburetor drops while the nitrous system is on.

Granted, you have a drop in flow through the carburetor, but you have to know how much nitrous is going into the engine and what it expands to to get an idea volume-wise, i.e., cubic feet per minute, what's going on in the engine as you would with a normally aspirated combination. Of course, using the weight of the nitrous gives you an accurate account of the mass, and from that your can calculate the volume if you know the manifold temperature and time the nitrous charge resides in the intake. However, this information is difficult to gather, and to be absolutely sure you have to test and verify the flow of the jets, even the entire circuit, because line lengths, varying bends, and distribution blocks all change the flow rate of the circuit.

At this point we can't accurately measure the flow of the system in question, but we can deduce it from the power figures and the observed flow rates from the dyno. Because these aren't strictly objective, i.e., measured, quantified, and observed rates, regard this exercise as illustrative of the concept only.

Before we become involved in analyzing the dyno data from a few of these tests we need to back up a bit and get familiar with the airflow peculiarities of a four-stroke internal combustion engine and the flow characteristics of a nitrous system.

7.3.2
FIXED FLOW VS. DYNAMIC FLOW

That nitrous systems, when properly calibrated and maintained, deliver a steady quantity of nitrous and fuel, may or may not be news to you, but it's one of the key concepts concerning the tuning of your nitrous system. Speaking roughly, it means that optimum tuning is only achieved in a narrow rpm range.

The reason for this is the way your engine pumps air.

Looking at the airflow versus rpm chart (fig 7.3.2-1), you can see that at low rpm an engine pumps little air; as engine speed increases, so goes airflow. This chart displays airflow in CFM per rpm at 100 percent volumetric efficiency (VE). Naturally aspirated engines as a rule do not operate at 100 percent VE. A few combinations get close and some even surpass 100 percent VE within a narrow rpm band. But the average is closer to 80 percent VE. (See tuning your carburetor for more info.) A good rule of thumb is the VE curve of an engine closely follows the torque curve.

Horsepower is pretty much directly associated with airflow according to techies at SuperFlow Corp., the firm the makes SuperFlow Dynos and flow benches. Using Standard Cubic Feet Per Minute (SCFM) as our unit of measure—SCFM is what the airflow would be if the atmospheric conditions were measured at a barometric pressure of 29.92 inches of mercury, 60 degrees F, and no water in the air (dry vapor pressure)—a naturally aspirated engine will consume approximately 1.25 SCFM of air per horsepower at peak torque while using approximately 1.4 SCFM at peak power. This relationship is displayed in Figure 7.3.2-2 In this instance we used SCFM as the unit of measure; however, it's just as valid to use pounds per hour, or pounds per minute of airflow. The important idea, though, is power is directly proportional to mass flow through the engine, no matter what unit you use to measure it.

In a way, that's how a nitrous system helps an engine leap to super-power status in a single squeeze—by injecting additional oxygen and fuel mass into the cylinders where it can react to make heat and power. Of course, a nitrous jet and a fuel jet are fixed orifices and as such they only flow a specific amount at a specific pressure. Which means when you activate the system, it's flowing, almost instantly, a specific rate of mass determined by the jets and pressure behind them. Putting it as blunt as a boxer's nose, nitrous

systems are flat-line systems. They are completely dumb to the increasing air/fuel demands of your engine as it spins faster.

If you compare the airflow curve with the flat line of a nitrous system in figure 7.2.3-2 you should be able to see the situation quite clearly. Basically, all a nitrous system can do is deliver a constant amount of fuel and nitrous. This property is the primary reason for activating nitrous systems within a specific rpm band and multi-stage systems. In the first instance, activating the system at too low an rpm creates more cylinder pressure than the fuel can take so it detonates, because the piston isn't moving down the bore quickly enough to relieve the pressure. Additionally, since you're putting more nitrous and fuel into the manifold than is being consumed by the engine, you run the risk of igniting what amounts to a bomb in the intake, turning your trick manifold into shrapnel. In the second instance, when your engine surpasses the flow capabilities of the system, you switch to the larger system to deliver more fuel and nitrous. Exactly when you make the shift depends on your combination and includes decisions on gearing, tire diameter, and engine combination.

So far we've presented you with a basic model of engine airflow based on 100 percent VE. As you know, real naturally aspirated engines don't behave this way. Typically their VE is lower as the engine comes off idle, gets better as engine speed increases, and falls away as rpm increases to a point where the time allowed to fill the cylinder isn't sufficient to produce more power. In addition to the VE of the engine falling off, friction within the engine increases significantly. Both combine to reduce the engine's output.

Now let's get back to our analysis of Comp Cams' test engine dyno data.

7.3.3
ANALYZING BRAKE SPECIFIC AIR CONSUMPTION

Brake Specific Air Consumption (BSAC) shows us how much air the engine uses to make X amount of power. BSAC is defined as air in lb./hr. divided by horsepower. If you look at the trend line of chart (7.3.3-1) you

can see that the naturally aspirated dyno pull saw a BSAC that hovered around the 6.00 lb./hp./hr. mark through most of the test. In contrast, the nitrous-enhanced test shows a curve that is at first substantially lower, but then trends back toward a level that echoes, at a much lower rate, the naturally aspirated level.

The relationship between these two traces demonstrates the fundamental property of a nitrous-oxide injection system. The fixed flow rate of a nitrous system delivers more fuel and oxygen to the combustion chamber at lower rpm than at high rpm. As a result, nitrous-enhanced engines always exhibit huge increases in torque. The torque measurement is proportionally much higher than the power output; but horsepower being a function of torque, horsepower also jumps substantially. In this example, naturally aspirated at 3200 rpm the engine makes 370 ft./lb. and 226 horsepower while flowing 281 SCFM. With nitrous, at the same rpm, it makes 600 ft./lb. and 365 horsepower with a measured flow of 255 SCFM. That translates to 26 SCFM less flow making an additional 230 ft./lb. and 139 horsepower at 3200 rpm. That's a 62 percent increase in torque and a 61 percent increase in horsepower. With such a large power increase with less air consumed at this rpm point, you can see why the BSAC value changes so dramatically. Instead of dividing 1290 lb./hr. air/226 hp=5.71 BASC; you're dividing roughly 1170 lb./hr. air/365 hp = 3.20 BSAC. Of course, that last BSAC value doesn't contain the additional mass flow of the nitrous system, since the nitrous is injected after the carburetor. Again, this is consistent with a fixed flow device delivering a set rate of additional gaseous mass flow.

What the BSAC shows us indirectly the SCFM chart 7.3.3-2 tells us straight out. It tells us that even though a nitrous system flows mass at a fixed rate, i.e., X lb./hr., the volume of that mass changes, like that of any gas, with temperature. We contend that the variance between each SCFM curve reflects this affect. It seems logical that the marginal difference at the start of each dyno pull between the A/B test curves is explained by a rela-

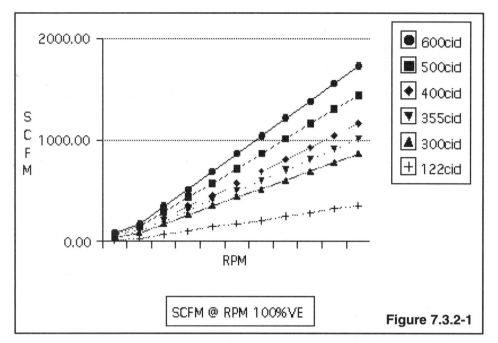

SCFM @ RPM 100%VE

Figure 7.3.2-1

tively cool intake tract. A cool intake doesn't cause the nitrous oxide charge to heat as quickly and therefore it has a smaller volume. As the intake gradually heats up, thereby causing the volume of the intake charge to become larger but less dense, it displaces progressively more of the normally inducted atmosphere.

If we look closely at the data, it should become clear that this is so. Recalling from our discussion of BSAC, this test engine made over 60 percent more torque and power at 3200 rpm with only 26 CFM drop in airflow. However, at the power peak at 5100 rpm, the engine made 113 more horsepower with a loss of just 49 CFM. This is displayed prominently in the CFM comparison trace of chart 7.3.3-2. The variance line, keyed with the triangles and beginning near zero, shows a trend away from the zero baseline, indicating larger variance as rpm rises.

The reason this observation is important is because it explains why nitrous oxide generates so much torque at first and why the torque curve falls off so quickly. To explain: one of the assumptions we made while modeling mass and fuel flow rates for a nitrous engine was to use the specific volume factor for nitrous at 70°F, which is 8.726 ft³/lb. The nitrous flow rate that supports the power increase is 5.5 lb./min. Assuming the charge reached 70°F, that flow rate would have a volume of

48 CFM, just one CFM shy of what the dyno recorded at the power peak. Just to be sure, we checked the CFM differences of several other tests made with the same engine combination but with different camshafts. All fell within a 43 to 49 CFM window at peak power. When we checked the difference at high engine speed of the test, we noticed a similar pattern with the upper limit being about 55 CFM. In addition, we noted a correlation between higher intake air, water, and oil temperatures and larger CFM differences. In fact, the dyno pulls made with the nitrous system active always produced a greater rise in oil and water temperatures than the naturally aspirated pulls. This is as expected since a naturally aspirated engine produces less power and heat. These observations seem to correspond and explain a warmer less dense, yet more voluminous intake charge.

7.3.4
ANALYZING BRAKE SPECIFIC FUEL CONSUMPTION

The Brake Specific Fuel Consumption chart 7.3.3-1 (BSFC) displays, once again, a predictable and consistent relationship to airflow through the engine from the naturally aspirated test and from the nitrous system active. The traces echo each other and show that the carburetor is doing its job metering fuel in proportion to air flow. It doesn't reflect the

enrichment fuel supplied by the nitrous system, but it does reflect the nominal and gradual increasing displacement of incoming atmosphere. The evidence for this is the variance trace's trend toward a lower flow rate signified by a greater variance.

That's our snapshot of this combination and of what the dyno figures can tell us about the nitrous system's behavior. The information's there; it's just in a negative form, much like looking at a photographic image. To a get a positive, (normal) look to the image, reverse it. We'll use our theoretical model to make this reversed dyno composite into a meaningful picture as far as nitrous use is concerned.

7.3.5
APPLYING THEORETICAL MODEL TO COMP CAMS' DYNO DATA

Let's analyze the engine's performance with the horsepower values. We'll model the engine keying off a BSFC of 0.50 first. Since the dyno operators at Competition Cams didn't measure nitrous flow and enrichment fuel flow, we'll have to make a guess about how efficient the engine is; a 0.50 BSFC tends to be a good standard. After that we'll see how well we can make the dyno data fit.

The engine produced 326 naturally aspirated horsepower and 439 horsepower enhanced with N_2O, resulting in a 113 horsepower difference. We assume that all 113 ponies were generated by injecting nitrous oxide, since, obviously, they weren't there before. Next we determine what fuel flow we need to support 439 horsepower at a BSFC of 0.5. Doing the math we find we need 3.65 lb./min. of gasoline. To support 326 horsepower at the same BSFC requires 2.71 lb./min. gasoline. The difference between the brake specific fuel consumption levels is: 3.65 - 2.71= 0.96

Working off the fuel requirement value we determine how much horsepower this fuel flow supports. Do this by referencing table 3.4.1, which lists air flow and fuel flow at various power levels. According to the chart, 0.96 lb./min. gasoline supports 115 horsepower. So we're real close to the difference of 113 horsepower at the power peak with the nitrous system active.

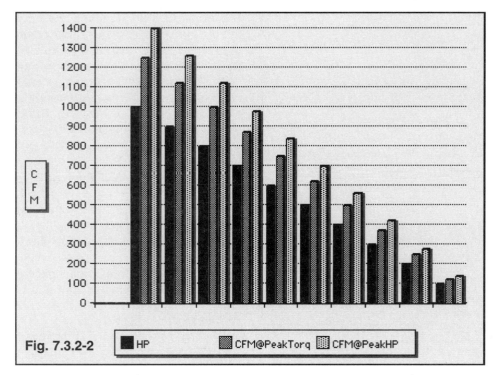

Fig. 7.3.2-2

Legend: ■ HP   ▨ CFM@PeakTorq   ▦ CFM@PeakHP

To make an educated estimate of how much nitrous needs to be poured on the fuel to make that much power, reference the "Equivalent Flow" tables at the end of this chapter. We're using the 6/1 nitrous to fuel chart since that's the ratio for which you should strive. The chart says that .96 lb./min. fuel calls for 5.75 lb./min. of nitrous flow at a 6/1 ratio.

The next value we need to determine. is CFM rate. Let's look at the dyno figures first. At power peak without the nitrous oxide system active, the engine consumed 431 CFM of air to generate 326 horsepower. At the power peak with the system active, according to the dyno, it used only 382 CFM to make 439 horsepower. Obviously, the dyno didn't measure the mass flow of the nitrous system.

Subtracting 382 from 431 we get 49 cubic feet per minute (431-382=49).

Using the conversion factor 8.726 and multiplying the nitrous flow rate of 5.75 lb./min. we get 50 CFM of nitrous flow. This 50 CFM of nitrous flow conveniently fills the CFM flow gap of the dyno figures to within one CFM. That's tells us we have a pretty good model from which to design a system and to predict power level response to tuning changes.

As we've seen, an engine is a self-driven air pump. But it's also an "air gate." It will only move a limited amount of air. Further, we can predict with a good degree of accuracy what that flow rate will be, and we can certainly measure it. Even if the engine is turbocharged or supercharged, at some point the engine and the super-

chargers reach a limit.

As this applies to nitrous, we have a naturally aspirated engine that will flow only so much air at a given rpm. We measure this on a dyno with a turbine on the intake or calculate it using the formulas above. When the nitrous is activated it displaces a certain amount of atmosphere. The volume it displaces is equal to the volume the nitrous charge reaches within the intake. As we've discussed above, the exact volume depends on the temperature of the charge. Therefore, given the flow properties of a naturally aspirated engine, we can use the measured flow difference to gauge the accuracy of our model.

7.4.0-
IGNITION TIMING TACTICS

7.4.1

IGNITION COMPONENTS AND HOW TO USE THEM

When you're using nitrous, your engine not only makes tremendous power, but that power can sometimes let it rev quicker than you can think. In addition, as we've discussed thoroughly throughout this book, you have to control timing advance accurately and appropriately to keep your engine together. There are several manufacturers of ignition components that not only deliver a solid, reliable ignition spark, but let you control when it's delivered as well as limiting and controlling engine rpm. Rpm activated switches can control your nitrous system's function. That said, the following quick buyer's guide should inform and enlighten you to your ignition and engine electronic control options.

MSD Ignition Controls
Street Performance

MSD 6 Series Ignition Controls Performance Benefits: Improves power, quickens throttle response, smoothes out idle and starting, reduces spark plug fouling, improves mileage and reduces emissions.

All sparks, including each multiple spark, is 110 millijoules of spark energy. It steps up the primary voltage to

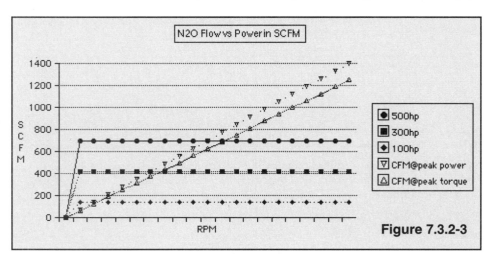

Figure 7.3.2-3

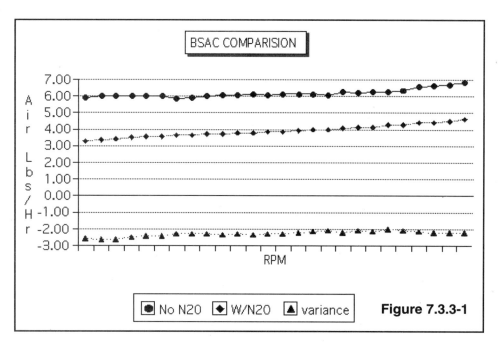

Figure 7.3.3-1

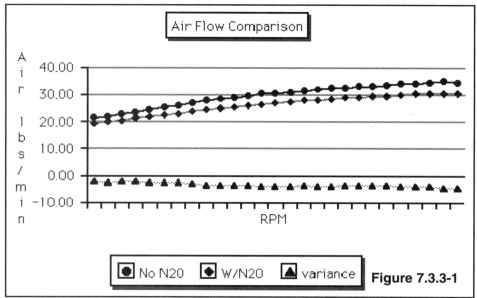

Figure 7.3.3-1

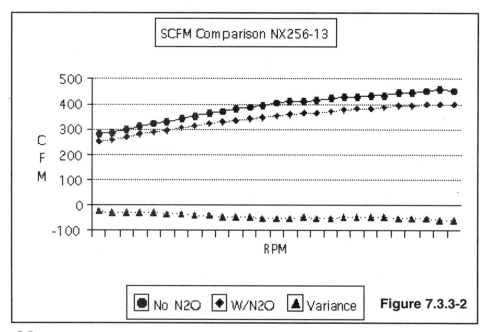

Figure 7.3.3-2

470 volts. The spark series lasts for 20° of crankshaft rotation and operates at full power with a supply of 10 to 18 volts and will run down to five volts. A cast aluminum housing and Humi-Seal-coated circuits protect the electronics. It can be triggered using points, electronic ignitions, or magnetic pickups.

MSD 6A, Part #6200

The 6A is MSD's base capacitive discharge, multiple sparking ignition. It will increase the overall performance of everything from the loaded work truck to bracket street cars cruising the boulevard. The hot multiple sparks ensure complete combustion of the air/fuel mixture even under the worst conditions possible. CARB-approved under E.O. D-40-14 for installation in all states.

MSD 6AL, Part #6420

The 6AL delivers everything the 6A does with the addition of a built-in Soft Touch Rev Control. This feature allows you to set an rpm limit to protect the engine from over-rev damage caused by driveline failure or missed shifts. Other MSD rpm controls can be connected to the 6AL such as a Three Step Module Selector (Part # 8737) or Rpm-Activated Switch (Part #8950). The 6AL also comes supplied with rubber shock mounts and 3000-, 6000-, 7000-, and 8000-rpm modules.

CARB approved under E.O. D-40-17 for installation in all states.

MSD 6BTM, Part # 6462

Supercharged or turbo engines will benefit from the 6BTM in more ways than one. Not only do the full energy

sparks help burn the fuel mixture, the 6BTM allows the driver to retard the ignition timing based on the amount of boost being produced by the supercharger. The timing is adjusted from a dash-mounted knob and can be retarded 1 to 3° per pound of boost with a maximum of 15°. There's also a built-in adjustable rev control to protect the engine from over-rev damage. CARB approved under E.O. D-40-17 for installation in all states.

HEI Module, Part # 8364
HEI Coil, Part # 8225

The GM HEI Distributor is a favorite among hot rodders due to its simple and clean installation. Unfortunately they lack real spark power. The MSD HEI Module and Coil increase the spark energy output throughout the entire rpm range of your engine. The MSD Module holds a more precise timing and dwell control circuit and produces a 50 percent higher coil drive current which saturates the coil faster giving you more spark energy at high rpm. CARB approved under E.O. D-40-15 and D-40-21.
Note: Can only be used on non-computer HEI Distributors (4-Pin modules).

MSD 7AL-2, Part # 7220

Powerful multiple sparks ignite exotic fuel in high-compression engines. The quick-charge/recharge CD ignition design produces full power sparks at high rpm. Built-in Soft Touch Rev Control protects the engine from over-rev damage. Twenty-degree spark duration helps burn the fuel mixture completely. The 7AL-2 is the choice of professional racers from six-second Pro Stocks to Monster trucks. The CD circuits deliver full energy sparks to the plug throughout 14,000 rpm, ensuring that even the most exotic fuel combinations are thoroughly ignited. A special coil coupler increases spark duration and protects the ignition in the event of coil failure. MSD's accurate Soft Touch Rev Control is built into the 7AL-2 so the Module Selectors and other rpm controls can easily be connected. To survive the demands of heavy-duty racing applications, the circuit boards receive a heavy-duty coat-

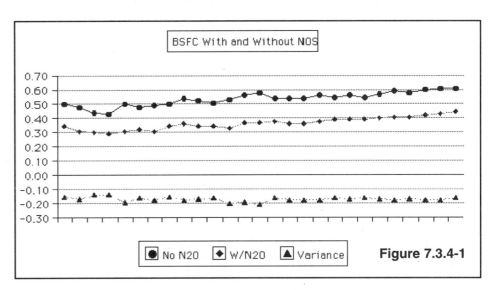

Figure 7.3.4-1

ing of Humi-Seal compound. This substance seals the circuits for resistance to vibration and moisture. Heavy-duty vibration mounts also are supplied. The 7AL-2 is a proven winner on tracks around the world.

Timing Computers

One of the foremost developments by MSD are its Timing Computers. These computers are designed to take the place of the mechanical advance mechanism inside the distributor. The weights and springs inside your existing distributor are removed and the mechanical advance is locked out. The timing is controlled entirely by the MSD Timing Computer.

By controlling the ignition electronically, the timing curves can be set faster, more accurately, and with more adjustability than mechanical advances. Also, mechanical advances can falter at high rpm, while the Timing Computer provides reliable operation throughout the rpm range. There's also a High Speed Retard function made available by

the Timing Computer that would be impossible to do with a standard mechanical advance.

MSD Timing Computers are available in two different models and must be used with the MSD 6, 7, 8, or 10 Series Ignitions. Part # 8980 is a pre-programmed Timing Computer that has a fixed curve, and part # 8981 is a Programmable Timing Computer that has an adjustable curve so you can tailor your ignition timing curves to the individual needs of your engine. Both Timing Computers are particularly useful when using a crank trigger, locked advance, or flywheel trigger ignition system as the initial timing can be set for easy starting and the advance curve can be tailored for various race conditions.

The 8980 Timing Computer has a pre-programmed timing curve that eliminates the need for a mechanical advance. As you start the car, the Timing Computer will retard the timing 20 degrees from the total timing. This allows easy starting and smooth idle. The timing curve begins when the engine speed reaches 1000 rpm, and then gradually increases until the total

timing is reached at 3000 rpm. The graph shows the relationship between ignition timing and engine rpm.

The Computer also has a High Speed Retard function that can be used in conjunction with the electronic advance or by itself. Drag racers and oval track racers can use this feature to increase mph and to prevent detonation at high rpm.

The Timing Computer will retard the timing the specified number of degrees when a driver, a shifter operated switch, or 'an MSD Rpm-Activated Switch triggers the Computer. The amount of retard is changed with plug-in modules. This unit is supplied with two-, three-, and four-degree modules. For other ranges, see the MSD Retard Module Kits. In applications where nitrous oxide is used, the Timing Computer can be used to retard the timing when the nitrous system is activated. This prevents detonation and possible engine damage.

The Timing Computer works on four-, six-, and eight-cylinder engines and must be used with an MSD Ignition.

Programmable Timing Computer

The MSD Programmable Timing Computer, part # 8981, has several features in common with the pre-programmed 8980 Timing Computer. Both are adjustable for four-, six-, and eight-cylinder operation and both models have the High Speed Retard function and are supplied with two-, three-, and four-degree modules. The wiring hookups for both Timing Computers are similar, and both models retard the timing 20 degrees for easier starting.

The difference between the two models is that the 8981 Programmable Timing Computer has an adjustable timing curve that can be tailored to fit the needs of any engine in any application.

Three adjustments have to be made to achieve the desired timing curve. First, the idle or initial timing must be set with the Initial Timing knob. This can be adjusted up to 20 degrees from full advance (total timing). Second, the rpm level where the timing will begin advancing needs to be

set. This can be set from 1000 to 3000 rpm using the rpm knob. The third adjustment is the slope. This is the rate (how fast) you want the timing to advance. The range of adjustment for this feature is from 0.5 degree per 1000 rpm to 20 degrees per 1000 rpm using the Slope knob. The timing will advance at the rate you select until it reaches the full (total) timing.

Rpm Accessories

Retard Modules and Module Selector

The MSD Retard Module Kits and Retard Module Selectors give you a full selection of retard values to choose from. The individual modules and Module Selectors plug into the MSD Multi-Step Retard. The MSD Module Selector is equipped with a positive stop knob that can be used to select any one of 12 different retard modules.

MULTI-STAGE TUNING TIPS

7.5.1
Timing is Everything

Each stage should have it's own optimum ignition settings. Remember, as you increase power with nitrous you always retard ignition timing. See the system-tuning basics section for a chart on suggested baseline tuning combinations.

Direct-port injection and plate systems can have different timing requirements. Take good notes on the ambient temp when you're tuning. A good racing weather station is ideal.

Plates give the charge more time to absorb heat from the engine. Sometimes you can get the mixture so cold, i.e., a port injection flowing huge amounts of nitrous, that it slows the burn rate to a point where you lose power. This can happen with subtle changes in ambient temperatures, such as the difference between day and nighttime. For example, a staged plate and direct port system that run fast during the day will lose power at night.

The reason, at least in Louie Hammel's opinion, seems to be that

the nitrous charge picks up heat from the intake manifold before being captured in the combustion chamber. The easy fix for this is to add timing depending on the temperature drop. If you track ambient temperatures with your tuning you'll have an advantage. Depending on your combination, a rule of thumb is to bump up the timing 0.5 to one degree for every 10 degrees drop in temperature from your baseline tune.

7.5.2
HEAT SOAK CHANGES
TIMING REQUIREMENTS

Another factor influencing timing and one that further complicates tuning a system, is heat soak. As you approach the end of the track, the temperature in the cylinder increases, which reduces timing advance requirements. This phenomenon happens so fast that it doesn't show in EGT or coolant temps—these will remain virtually constant, but the timing requirements can vary a lot. Be aware.

7.5.3
ONE BOTTLE PER STAGE

With multiple-stage systems, using a separate bottle for each stage is ideal because it allows you to evaluate the tune of each stage by accurately gauging nitrous consumption. It also gives you a better idea of how much power each stage is contributing. Using a separate bottle for each stage ensures that each starts with the correct bottle pressure. Consistent pressure equates to consistent flow. If you run two systems on the same bottle, the jetting will be corrupted because you can't know exactly how much pressure you'll have when you activate the second system.

Nitrous bottle temperature and pressure also must be constant. And don't forget, line length, diameter, distribution blocks, hard-line length, and amount of bends in a circuit influence flow rate and hence nitrous fuel mixtures.

7.5.4
SEPARATE FUEL SYSTEMS PER STAGE

Fuel delivery must be as constant as possible. As we've already stated in a previous section, you should use a separate system for nitrous and carb or fuel injection. Concerning multi-stage systems, if you have a pump that will deliver the volume and pressure, you can use a bypass-type regulator for each stage of multi-stage systems.

7.5.5
TRADE BALLAST BARS FOR BATTERIES

This is a tip for the truly hardcore racer racing without an alternator. Think about this: A hot ignition is going to pull 10 to 25 amps, a big fuel pump up to 10 amps, and if you're running one pump per each stage, that adds up quick. The bigger nitrous solenoids can pull 15 amps each. That's 30 amps for one stage of port nozzles. Dual-plate systems with two more nitrous solenoids adds another 30 amps. As you add stages, the current draw keeps going up. If you tax the battery on a run and voltage or amperage sag, the low-resistance solenoids, usually the fuel, will close first. Racers without alternators and elaborate systems run a risk of leaning out quick and unexpectedly. The moral: If you have the room, trade the ballast bar for batteries.

7.6.0
MORE NITROUS TUNING TIPS

The Mistaken Association of Bottle Pressure Surge Affecting the Power Curve

Transient flow effects—or bottle pressure surge, or initial plate flow surge and supposed power fluctuations—are greatly exaggerated. This was demonstrated by a series of tests performed by NOS. The test, originally conducted to map the effects of a nitrous solenoid orifice size change, also shows measurable transient flow effects in the flow trace of the nitrous solenoid and the fact that power output was not affected.

This series of tests was performed with a 454-cubic-inch engine installed on the NOS SuperFlow dyno using an off-the-shelf Super Power Shot kit. Steady-state dynamometer testing was conducted at 5000 rpm for each of the jetting combinations supplied with the standard nitrous kit. The test series was then repeated with a 0.072-in. solenoid installed in place of the 0.080-in. unit.

At each jetting level, nitrous flow rate was reduced slightly with the 0.072-in. solenoid but, horsepower was not significantly affected. In fact, with 73/82 jetting, horsepower actually increased slightly.

It's interesting to note the oscillating flow rates with a various nitrous jetting. Both solenoid orifice sizes exhibit the oscillating flow associated with transient flow effects. They also shadow each other's tracings in response to jet changes. For example, the larger orifice size ramps up to flow more quickly that the slightly smaller orifice. Then its flow rate tapers off as the smaller orifice begins to outflow the larger. In spite of an apparent higher flow rate, the smaller orifice makes slightly less horsepower on the dyno with the same jetting combination.

The greatest variation occurs with the smaller orifice flowing much less mass with more erratic behavior. However, in this case, the smaller orifice made more power than the larger. In no example does the power output follow the oscillating mass flow rates. So even though you can measure transit flow effects, they only seem to affect the test instrument, not the power output of the engine.

7.6.3
AIMING NOZZLES AND SPRAY BAR ORIFICES

Aiming nozzles or spray bar orifices aren't nearly as crucial as they have been marketed. As the plenum size increases it becomes even less of a concern. The reason is the severe pulsing of the intake tract. With all the flow changes, the moving air carries the nitrous fog with it no matter which direction it's introduced. Don't forget an engine isn't a linear device but rather a pulse flow device; the air is constantly changing direction in the intake.

7.6.4
UNEVEN AIR/FUEL DISTRIBUTION AND DETONATION

Making sure each cylinder receives the same amount of fuel is important when you're trying to get the last bit of power from your engine. If an engine has uneven distribution of the air/fuel mixture between cylinders, the leaner cylinders are more prone to detonate. That means you have to, or the computer has to, retard the timing for the mixture of the leanest cylinder. This most often occurs on carbureted cars, but it also happens to throttle body or port fuel-injected cars as the injectors get clogged or just weren't built right at the factory. Basically, if one cylinder is down on power, the rest of the cylinder are brought to that level by the computer as it retards timing.

A combination with poor distribution easily can turn into a broken engine once you hit it with nitrous. Be careful about this. Dial up the power and always read the plugs—all of them. Don't just spot check. If one of the cylinders is going lean, you better know about it before putting more nitrous into the engine.

7.6.5
TUNING HOW THE NITROUS HITS

This means the distance from release point, i.e. the solenoid, to the next restriction, or orifice. That distance is a chamber the nitrous has to fill and pressurize. The greater the volume, the longer it takes to pressurize. You can use this physical fact as a tuning aid. The longer it takes the nitrous to pressurize such a chamber, the softer the power comes on, the less you shock the tires. It's more of a roll-in feel. Adjust the nitrous side and leave the fuel side alone. This works best for traction-limited cars if you can't adjust the clutch.

7.7.0
ALL ABOUT THE FUEL

Fuel Fundamentals

A proper engine fuel provides quick starts, fast warmup, rapid acceleration, smooth performance, good mileage in various driving conditions and climates, and minimal engine maintenance. That's a hefty shopping list, but for the most part, pump gas provides all these benefits. Yet for high-performance applications, you need to use a racing gasoline. These are specially blended to resist detonation so you can run higher compression ratios than possible with pump gas. Racing gasolines also have more British Thermal Units (BTU) per unit of measure, about 1200 BTU more on average than pump gas. The BTU content of a fuel is a measure of the potential heat a given unit of fuel can produce. Heat is what makes the pressure in the cylinder, and that's where you get more power from racing gasoline.

We won't be able to tell you everything about pump and racing gasolines here. The purpose is really to get you acquainted with some of the basic concepts that will let you educate yourself more quickly and accurately as you start tuning your nitrous system to take advantage of racing gasolines.

Let's start with the engine factors that shape the properties needed in a good gasoline. The first is compression ratio. All the compression ratio does is heat things up. In effect, compressing the air/fuel mix heats it, getting it ready to be ignited by the spark plug.

So what's the advantage of a higher compression ratio? That's your control over the heat in the combustion chamber before you ignite it, which influences burn rate. With lower compression you can run more timing advance. This is because at lower compression ,when you start the mixture burning, it takes longer to heat and raise the pressure in the chamber. Basically its a tuning tool. Instead of lighting it off way early, as with a low-compression combination, you can fire the cylinder closer to dead center with a higher compression combination. Ultimately you have to get peak cylinder pressure at the same crankshaft degree for peak performance. So whether you use the pistons to heat the mix or burn it early to make heat is of little consequence. The real limitation is the fuel's resistance to detonation, called its octane rating.

The rule of thumb that raising compression makes horsepower is only partly true. The average engine is compromised in a lot of ways. It has to do a lot of different things in a variety of situations, particularly street engines. If you ran the engine at the highest compression that the fuel would support, the number of situations in which the engine would function properly would be few. About the only time you could drive such an engine would be on the coldest winter days. On hot summer days, forget it. You'd rattle the heads off the block.

You can optimize an engine for track conditions or for the type of racing, or sometimes you may have cubic-inch limitations, such as in NASCAR. If you have a cubic-inch limitation, you know you can't get power by making the engine bigger. The only way you can make more power is by doing more work in the same period of time. That means the engine will have to rev higher and make peak power at higher rpm: for example, a 355-inch small block revving to 10,000 rpm. The problem with running at 10000 rpm is that pump gas won't burn that fast nor remain stable because it's not that good of a fuel. If you use a good racing fuel that has the appropriate energy content and octane rating, you still have the problem of burning it at a rate that makes power at 10,000 rpm. To get racing fuel to burn fast, you have to get it close to its auto-ignition point, then light it off with a spark plug. With an engine combination design to make power at high rpm, there just isn't any other sound way to put a predictable amount of heat in the chamber before igniting the mix. The heat goes up in direct proportion to how much the gas is compressed. So compression ratio is simply part of the overall combination.

If you're burning alcohol, which takes a different temperature curve and has a slower burn rate compared to gasoline, then the compression ratio of that engine will be higher for most combinations. Most enthusiasts get excited by the thought that they can make all sorts of power with alcohol, but it's not all that simple. On one hand alcohol stays stable; it doesn't self ignite in conditions that gasoline does. The advantage of alcohol is that for the same amount of airflow, more energy is released.

There is a limit, both mechanically and chemically, as to how much you can raise compression ratios to get more efficiency from an engine. First, you have to have some clearance between the piston and the head, which is the mechanical limit. But more relevant to our topic is the limitation of the fuel. At some level of compression, an air and gasoline mixture will self-ignite; that's the chemical limit. When that happens, you've got detonation, and we've talked about that subject in depth in an earlier chapter.

In the broadest terms, you can get into detonation in two ways. One we've just discussed: a compression ratio that raises the pressure in the combustion chamber beyond the fuel's ability to resist self-ignition. The other occurs when the pressure in the combustion chamber rises to that point after the spark plug fires the charge. In this case, what happens as the main flame front travels across the combustion chamber and pressure begins to rise in the cylinder, a second flame front is generated by an area in the combustion chamber with raised temperature and pressures high enough where it self ignites in little pockets within the combustion chamber. The rattle you hear in severe detonation is the flame fronts colliding.

The most common causes of, let's call it dynamic detonation, is too much ignition advance and/or a hot spot in the combustion chamber. Obviously, if you light off the fuel too early, the piston isn't going to be heading down the bore soon enough to keep the pressure in the chamber from reaching self-ignition levels. A hot spot can cause this condition to occur in the chamber even if the timing is set properly for the fuel.

A gasoline's resistance to detonation is known as it's anti-knock rating or its octane value. The Octane rating on most pump and racing gas is an average of two laboratory tests using a single-cylinder engine with sensors to detect detonation. Research Octane Number (RON) is decided at 600 rpm and determines the fuel's resistance to detonation from compression. Motor Octane Number (MON) is determined at 900 rpm with the intake air heated and ignition advanced to get the fuel to detonate. A mixture of reference fuels, iso octane, and heptane are used and get a relative value from which to rate the test fuel. Add the Motor Octane value to the Research Octane value and divide the sum by two (R+M/2) gives you the average value. This is the octane rating you see on pump and on racing gas, although racing fuel usually has both listed in the literature.

A high octane number does not indicate a more powerful fuel. It indicates that, for example, your 10:1 compression ratio aluminum headed engine won't detonate on (R+M/2=) 92 octane premium fuel. That's assuming you haven't advanced the timing to get the two or three horsepower you can find at the expense of significantly higher cylinder pressures and a high risk of detonation.

Most modern fuel-injected stock engines, have sensors that allow you to use middle-grade fuel, such as 89 octane or lower. The sensors detect detonation and the computer retards the timing or adds fuel or a combination of both. Since the timing is retarded, the power stroke is shortened and therefore the engine loses some power.

What a high octane fuel does is lets the engine operate the way it was designed in so far as compression ratio and efficiency is concerned. For example, Unocal 100 octane unleaded racing gas is advertised for use in engines with up to 11:1 compression ratios. That means an engine in good operating condition and tuned, i.e., timed correctly with proper fuel curves, shouldn't start detonating with this fuel. Therefore, you won't have to back off the timing or fatten up the mixture to compensate for a problem.

The engine takes advantage of the high compression, has a powerful air/fuel mixture, and is timed for a long power stroke. That's really what an appropriate octane number is all about.

7.7.2
DETONATION CHECKLIST

Lean Fuel Mixture, or Too Much Nitrous. A lean mix may burn slower than a fat mixture, but the heat of combustion is higher. When you raise temperature, you also raise the pressure, and you're just asking to generate a second flame front and detonate your main bearings away.

Too Much Ignition Timing. Firing the cylinder too much before TDC means the piston is going to be dwelling at TDC when the cylinder reaches peak pressure. Because the piston isn't traveling down the bore yet to relieve the pressure, it builds to a point where the fuel self-ignites. Boom! You have detonation. Retard the timing to a point where peak cylinder pressure occurs just after the piston starts down the bore and you not only stay out of detonation, you make lots of reliable horsepower.

Compression Ratio. Compression ratio affects detonation, as we discussed above because it increases cylinder pressure.

Cam Choice. The timing of closing the intake and exhaust valves control the dynamic compression ratio of the cylinder and thus the cylinder pressure and potentially the tendency of a fuel to detonate. A cam with valve timing that fills the cylinder with more air and fuel promotes higher cylinder pressures and higher horsepower. It also increases the chances for detonation.

Coolant/Engine Temperature. You can get hot spots in the cylinder or combustion chamber from an inefficient or insufficient cooling system. Hot spots raise the temperature in the combustion chamber and, well, you know.

Cylinder-to-Cylinder Distribution. If an engine has uneven distribution of the air/fuel mixture between cylinders, the leaner cylinders are more prone to detonate. That means you've got to retard the timing for the mixture of the leanest cylinder. This most often occurs on carbureted cars, but it also happens to fuel-injected cars as the injectors get clogged or if they just weren't built right at the factory.

Carbon Build Up. If carbon builds up on the piston, valves, and combustion chamber surfaces, it can cause a hot spot. Need we say more? If you really get a lot of carbon built up, it can raise the compression ratio.

Oil in the Combustion chamber. If you get oil in the mix from worn or broken rings, a bad guide, or ring flutter, your engine will detonate.

Air Inlet Temperature. High air inlet temperatures can push an engine on the edge of detonation right over the cliff. The higher the inlet air temperature the more chance you have of detonating. Just one more reason not to put your air cleaner right by the exhaust pipes.

Combustion Chamber Shape. A pent-roof or clover-shaped combustion chamber with a centrally located spark plug and lots of quench area has the least tendency to detonate. A hemi-head/pent-roof head allows for faster combustion, allowing less time for detonation to occur ahead of the flame front.

Octane Number. If you haven't got it by now, let's go over it one more time. A high octane number is an indication of a particular blend of gasoline's resistance to detonation. If your engine has high compression, chances are it'll need a high octane number.

Spark Plug Choice. The proper heat range and spark plug type is a critical factor in keeping your engine from detonating, particularly on nitrous. See sidebar on choosing the right spark plug.

7.7.3
THE TRUTH ABOUT MAKING POWER WITH GASOLINE

The truth about making big horsepower numbers with gasoline is that, for it to burn, for it to react with oxygen, it has to be a vapor. We'll repeat that to make sure you get this point: Gasoline has to be suspended in the charge air to burn. Technically, this is known as atomization or vaporization. Vaporization occurs when liquid fuel turns to a vapor or gaseous state. If the fuel is still in a liquid form in the combustion chamber, all it does is take up space and raise the dynamic compression ratio. If you get enough fuel remaining in liquid form in your engine, you can raise the dynamic compression ratio enough to force detonation. This is an extreme case and is given purely to drive home the point that liquid fuel does not burn.

Fuel tends to do some weird things

if you put too much in the engine. It recombines, or goes from little droplets at the carburetors, and as it travels down the runner it starts forming bigger droplets. When it gets to the actual cylinder, it's a river, and is so heavy it just falls to one side. It doesn't burn in this form, only the surface of it burns. You may have a ton of fuel going through the engine, but little of it is burning when it needs to burn to make power. It gets spit out the pipe, where it absorbs heat from the exhaust tract, vaporizes, and then burns with a big flame out the tail pipe like a top-fuel engine.

The trick to making big horsepower with an internal combustion engine, particularly with nitrous, is getting the fuel vaporized. That's the job of the carburetor or the fuel injectors. These devices take liquid fuel and disperse it into the intake air in small droplets. Droplet size is critical to the rate at which fuel will then vaporize. Fuel can only vaporize from the surface area of the droplet.

The rate fuel vaporizes is key to how much power you can create. The intake charge is moving quickly and is in the engine only a short time before it's ignited. For a carbureted engine, all you have is the distance from the venturi to the chamber and the time it takes for the charge to travel that distance. On a port-injected engine there's even less time for vaporization.

Looking for more efficient ways to vaporize fuel and keeping it suspended in the charge air keeps engine tuners and the petroleum company's chemists employed. Manifold, carburetor, and fuel-injector designs are all the product of this pursuit. As simple a process as evaporation can become a serious challenge when you have only a scant few fractions of a seconds to work with.

Most of this work is done by the chemists that refine pump gasoline and racing gasoline. Their job is to blend several petrochemicals to produce gasoline that performs as stated at the beginning of this section. The way they do this is to blend certain elements that vaporize easily at low temperatures. These are usually called the front ends or light ends or volatiles. The petroleum companies

actually blend various ratios of these volatile compounds into pump gas to compensate for seasonal changes in average temperature. For example ,they put more volatiles in gasoline in the winter when it's cold to help cars start in the morning.

Most pump gas runs around 10 to 15 psi on the Reid Vapor Pressure test. This indicates how much of the gas is made of these light compounds. Racing gas, on the other hand, has a much lower RVP, around six psi, and isn't seasonally adjusted so you don't have to go chasing jet sizes or pulse widths to compensate for the fuel. That's why it's hard to start engines using racing gas in cool weather. But the pay-off to hard starting is that since the gas has less light ends or volatiles, it has more of the dense, high BTU content compounds.

Of course these dense high BTU content compounds have to vaporize to burn, too, so they can't be too dense. A compound can have all the BTUs in England, but if it doesn't vaporize in the cylinder it won't turn them into heat. It also has to vaporize enough to give you good throttle response. And that's perhaps the hardest trick the chemists perform: blending compounds to have a certain rate of vaporization for a given temperature rise.

This is known as the distillation curve. Most racing gasolines have an advertised distillation curve in its product literature. When it comes to choosing a racing gas for your combination, this is one your most valuable guides. (You might think the BTU content should be, but most racing gasolines are so close in BTU content it doesn't really matter.) What matters is how quickly and at what temperatures the gasoline turns to vapor.

Here's how it works. Trick 108 (R+M/2) octane racing fuel has an advertised distillation curve beginning with an initial boiling point (IBP) of 97° F. At 137° F, 10 percent of the gas has turned to vapor; at 202° F, 50 percent has turned to vapor; at 243° F, 90 percent has vaporized, and when it hits 295° F all of the fuel is vaporized. This indicates how quickly the heat in the engine will help turn

the fuel to vapor so it can burn to make power. While you want it as cool and as dense an intake charge as possible, as the distillation curve indicates, a little heat doesn't hurt. As the intake air travels through the manifold it picks up heat. Then the fuel uses the heat to vaporize, cooling back down the air. Then the charge gets compressed and heat from friction of the compression as well as from the engine surfaces raise the temperature of the charge and the fuel vaporizes completely to make some heat of its own.

Most people think that octane is an indication of how quickly or slowly the fuel burns. That's not correct. According to the chemists at Phillips Petroleum, the hydrocarbons used to make gasoline oxidize, or burn at virtually the same rate, given the same conditions. The rate of burn, or the speed of the flame front, is basically the same for all gasolines as long as it's not detonating. The controlling mechanism of burn rate or flame front travel is the amount of oxygen in the combustion chamber available to react with the fuel. More oxygen means a faster flame front, at least to the natural limits of the fuel, and vice versa.

Another confusing concept about making power with gasoline is its energy or heat content. We've already talked about the BTU content of gasolines so we won't rehash it here. What we need to talk about is releasing all the energy in a specific amount of gas. Actually we're already talking about this concept, since the primary method of releasing the BTU content of gasoline is to vaporize it first.

But here's a key tuning concept: Use a gasoline with the highest calorie or BTU content per unit of measure that will vaporize in your engine in the ambient temperatures on race day. You don't necessarily want the most dense gas or fuel with the highest BTU content. Straight toluene is loaded with BTUs, but getting it to vaporize and react with oxygen is another story.

7.7.3-1
ENERGY DENSITY AND A/F RATIO

A tuning aid you'll hear about around the pits is jetting, or setting injector pulse widths in accordance with the specific gravity of the fuel. Specific gravity is a measure of the density of the fuel at a certain temperature. As the temperature of the fuel rises, it becomes less dense. If it's less dense, then for given pulse width or jet size you're introducing less BTUs and assuming the air density is unchanged, the engine will run lean. This is a valid tuning concept.

An invalid tuning concept is using the most dense fuel thinking that that will have the highest BTU content. The specific gravity of a fuel and its energy density don't have a direct correlation. When choosing a fuel to tune your engine to, you need to look at its BTU content per pound or gallon. Most of this information comes with the fuel's literature. In addition, as we've said earlier, select a fuel with a realistic distillation curve. Once again, if the fuel will not vaporize, it will not oxidize. It will not burn to make heat.

It's important to compensate for the energy density and the specific gravity of a fuel. If you're running a finely tuned engine just on the edge of detonation and you get a substantial decrease in the specific gravity of your fuel, you'll go lean and quickly get detonation. On the other hand, if the specific gravity increases, you'll run rich. A slightly rich condition does not result in a substantial loss of power, so almost always this is not a concern.

Essentially the same relationship holds true for the energy density or BTU/lb. of gasoline. The MechTech "Man" in Escondido, Calif., told us a great example of this effect. He had an engine finely tuned to run on 100 octane racing fuel. One time he put in a different fuel, one with a slightly higher octane rating so he wasn't worried. What he didn't expect was for it to run absolutely pig rich. All he did was substitute fuel, he didn't change pulse width or injectors. When he emptied the tank and used the original fuel, the engine ran crisp and sharp.

SECTION 7.8.0
HOW TO USE THE RATIO & FLOW EQUIVALENT TABLES

The ratio & equivalent flow tables display fuel flow and corresponding nitrous flow rates of 5:1 and 6:1 at a Brake Specific Fuel Consumption rate (BSFC) of 1/2 pound of fuel per hour for each hp. We express this in decimal form as .5, i.e. 5/10ths; 50/100ths which are simply other ways of expressing 1/2. For example, to make 100 hp at a .5 BSFC means that the engine uses 50 lbs of fuel per hour to generate 100 horsepower.

Why do we use .5 BSFC? This value has been found to be a good average number of fuel consumption in gasoline fueled internal combustion engines. An engine doesn't really operate at .5BSFC all the time. It will vary how much power it produces per unit of fuel consumed as it sweeps through its engine speed, or rpm range. This observation is displayed graphically in Figure 7.8-2. As you can see in the figure, the BSFC varies a great deal, but the average consumption is right near .5 lbs of gasoline per hour per horserpower. It's just a convenient number that lets you calculate safe fuel needs for a given power output.

It may not be obvious, but you need a dynomometer to get BSFC numbers. We use them here mostly out of convenience, since we'll have to assume a power output level. For nitrous oxide user's this is ok since most kits are rated at a specific power output and using that number gives us a starting point.

Another concept we need to discuss is the relationship of air/fuel ratios to BSFC. The BSFC value is not the air fuel ratio but its magnitude is influenced by air/fuel ratios. Figure 7.8-1 shows the relationship of air/fuel ratio to BSFC. Engine tuner's have found through experience that for gasoline fueled engines, air/fuel ratios in the range of 12.5:1 to 13.3:1 make the most power but not the lowest BSFC. The dyno data in figure 7.8-2 show this relationship relative to the torque curve and BSFC. Notice the the highest torque output occurs at the lowest BSFC value. This is fair-

ly typical of gasoline fueled engines.

Essentially this curve and the power/fuel consumption relationships hold true for each individual cylinder. The goal of an engine builder/tuner is to construct a combination that gives each cylinder the same air/fuel ratio. In pratic however, this is almost impossible. Port fuel injected cars get very close, because the computer regulates the fuel injectors at each cylinder to deliver precise amounts of fuel. Any unequal fuel distribution is usually the result of varying flow rates between indvidual injectors.

Carbureted engines, especially ones with centrally located carburetors can have quite poor distribution. In fact one of the reasons a dual plane manifold doesn't respond to a plate as well as a single plane is the dual plane manifold generally gives less equal distribution than a single plane manifold.

What happens then, with unequal fuel distribution, is that instead of each cylinder performing at the point in the illustration, each cylinder gets a different air/fuel ratio and so produces more or less power as it consumes more or less fuel. So you can have one, two or more cylinders getting the proper 12:5:1 to 13.3:1 ratio; two or three slightly rich and two or three slightly lean.

The cylinders on the rich side aren't as great a problem as the lean cylinders, and here's why. If you look at the mean effective pressure curve, you'll notice that it doesn't drop off as quickly on the rich side as it does on the lean side. This means that a slightly rich cylinder still makes good power but at a cost of consuming extra fuel. The lean cylinder on the other hand produces much less power, a trend that is aggravated as the cylinder gets leaner. On a port fuel injected engine, you can just increase fuel deliver to that cylinder to bring it up to power. But on a carbureted system, you have to enrich *all* the cylinders to get the individual cylinder to perform properly. That scenario usually puts more of the cylinders on the way-rich side, which increases fuel consumption and reduces power output. Still you have to do it because the lean cylinder is most likely to experience detonation before the richer cylinders. Remember, with a multi-cylinder engine the sum of each cylinder's output is what moves the flywheel.

It's interesting to see how interdependent all of these measurements are. The air/fuel ratio directly influences mean effective pressure which determines the torque for a given engine displacement which influences how much horsepower is produced, which in turn influences BSFC which is dependent on the air/fuel ratio. It's what tuning is all about.

These tables are here to help you dial in your nitrous combination. If you get totally lost then you can use these tables as a map to get back to where you want to be; or you can use them to figure your next tuning move or in designing your next stage or nitrous system.

The table is keyed from the horsepower level in the far-left column. The next column is a theoretical BSFC of .50 at that horsepower level. BSFC is calculated as the mass of the fuel flow divided by the horsepower. So if you're flowing 50 lbs/hr of fuel and making 100 hp you have a BSFC of .50. To convert that figure into lbs/min we divide it by 60.

Next we get the nitrous mass flow per minute at a 6:1 nitrous to fuel ratio by multiplying the BSFC/min figure by 6. In the next column we list the oxygen content, by weight, of the nitrous flow rate. This is done by multiplying the mass flow number in the preceding column by .36. (Nitrous is 36% oxygen by weight.) To convert our nitrous mass flow into a CFM rate, we use the specific volume of the gas at 70°F@sea level or 8.726 cubic ft/lb. Multiplying the lbs/min figure by 8.726 gives an approximate expanded volume of that flow rate.

To get equivalent atmoshere flow rates we chose an oxygen content slightly less than that most commonly presumed. If you take the basic encylopedic listing that the atmosphere is 23—something % oxygen you tend to over estimate the actual oxygen in the air the engine injests. We chose 19% because Ken Dutweiller told us that's a more relistic number. The great average oxygen content of the atmsphere may be almost 24 percent but under most

conditions it only contains around 19% oxygen. So multiplying the lb/min@6:1 figure by .19 gives us an approximate equivalent rate. Then we take this figure and divide it by .0762 to convert the lbs/min rate to CFM.

That's how we arrrived at the values chosen for the tables. The reason we chose them can best be explained by an example.

Assume you have a nitrous kit that's calibrated to make 100HP. The jetting guide says use X nitrous jet and Y fuel jet, each at a specified

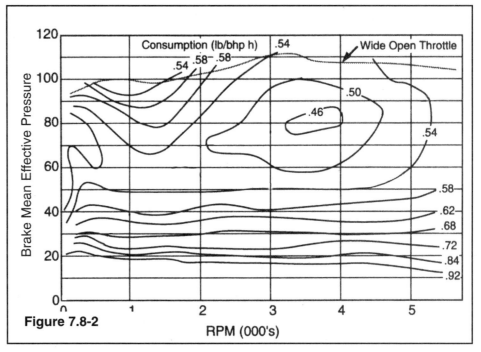

Figure 7.8-2

pressure. You can take the suggested jetting on faith, which for the most part you can do, the manufacturers are pretty accurate. But what if the combination doesn't perform as expected. What do you do then? What changes should you make in order to tune th system?

These tables are designed to give you reference points. Continuing our example, we know the kit is jetted to make 100hp. That means at a BSFC of .5 it needs to deliver 50 lbs/hr of fuel; or .83 lbs/min of fuel. Right here you have something you can test that will varify if in fact the nitrous kits fuel side is deliverying the requires fuel. You know X-jet at 7 psi doesn't tell you that. The same is true of the nitrous flow rate. You can wieght the bottle, verify bottle pressure, turn on the system for a specific length of

time and calculate the nitrous flow. If the system isn't delivering the required amount of nitrous you'll know that too.

The atmosphere equivalents were included to show the relationship between air and nitrous. Because when you get to the core, fuel makes the power not the nitrous. It also lets you establish an approximately equivalent air/fuel ratio. Just divide the equivalent atmosphere in lbs/min by the BSFC in lbs/min. For example at 100 hp the BSFC /min is .83 and the equivalent atmosphere is 9.47

lbs/min.: 9.47/.83 =11.40:1 equivalent air/fuel ratio. This puts the tuning in a more familiar format. From this you know you can put in a little more nitrous or take away some fuel if the plugs look like they need it.

Any way, that's the strategy behind the ratio tables. We hope they work for you.

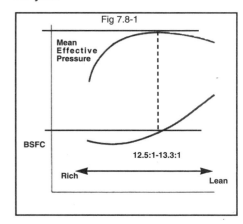

Fig 7.8-1

Nitrous Oxide Flow rates at 5:1 Nitrous to Fuel Ratio With a .5 BSFC Equivalent air/fuel ratio= 9.45:1

Horse power	Gasoline lbs./hr @ BSFC=.50 HP*.5	Gasoline lbs./min @ BSFC=.50 BSFC/60	Nitrous lbs/min @5/1 BSFC*5	Oxygen lbs/min @ 5/1 *Nitrous lbs/min * .36*	CFM @ 70°F *Nitrous lbs/min * 8.726*	Equivalent Atmosphere lbs/min *Oxygen lbs/min / .19*	Equivalent Atmosphere CFM *Atmosphere lbs/min / .0762*
50	25.00	0.42	2.08	0.75	18.18	3.95	51.80
45	22.50	0.38	1.88	0.67	16.36	3.55	46.62
40	20.00	0.33	1.67	0.60	14.54	3.16	41.44
35	17.50	0.29	1.46	0.52	12.73	2.76	36.26
30	15.00	0.25	1.25	0.45	10.91	2.37	31.08
25	12.50	0.21	1.04	0.38	9.09	1.97	25.90
20	10.00	0.17	0.83	0.30	7.27	1.58	20.72
15	7.50	0.12	0.62	0.22	5.45	1.18	15.54
10	5.00	0.08	0.42	0.15	3.64	0.79	10.36
5	2.50	0.04	0.21	0.07	1.82	0.39	5.18

Nitrous Oxide Flow rates at 6:1 Nitrous to Fuel Ratio With a .5 BSFC Equivalent air/fuel ratio= 11.40:1

Horse power	Gasoline lbs./hr @ BSFC=.50 HP*.5	Gasoline lbs./min @ BSFC=.50 BSFC/60	Nitrous lbs/min @ 6/1 BSFC*6	Oxygen lbs/min @ 6/1 *Nitrous lbs/min * .36*	CFM @ 70°F *Nitrous lbs/min * 8.726*	Equivalent Atmosphere lbs/min *Oxygen lbs/min / .19*	Equivalent Atmosphere CFM *Atmosphere lbs/min / .0762*
50	25.00	0.42	2.50	0.90	21.82	4.74	62.16
45	22.50	0.38	2.25	0.81	19.63	4.26	55.95
40	20.00	0.33	2.00	0.72	17.45	3.79	49.73
35	17.50	0.29	1.75	0.63	15.27	3.32	43.51
30	15.00	0.25	1.50	0.54	13.09	2.84	37.30
25	12.50	0.21	1.25	0.45	10.91	2.37	31.08
20	10.00	0.17	1.00	0.36	8.73	1.89	24.87
15	7.50	0.12	0.75	0.27	6.54	1.42	18.65
10	5.00	0.08	0.50	0.18	4.36	0.95	12.43
5	2.50	0.04	0.25	0.09	2.18	0.47	6.22

Nitrous Oxide Flow rates at 6:1 Nitrous to Fuel Ratio With a .7 BSFC Equivalent air/fuel ratio= 11.36:1

Horse power	Gasoline lbs./hr @ BSFC=.7 HP*.7	Gasoline lbs./min @ BSFC=.7 BSFC/60	Nitrous lbs/min @ 6/1 BSFC*6	Oxygen lbs/min @ 6/1 *Nitrous lbs/min * .36*	CFM @ 70°F *Nitrous lbs/min * 8.726*	Equivalent Atmosphere lbs/min *Oxygen lbs/min / .19*	Equivalent Atmosphere CFM *Atmosphere lbs/min / .0762*
50	35.00	0.58	3.50	1.26	30.54	6.63	87.03
45	31.50	0.52	3.15	1.13	27.49	5.97	78.33
40	28.00	0.47	2.80	1.01	24.43	5.31	69.62
35	24.50	0.41	2.45	0.88	21.38	4.64	60.92
30	21.00	0.35	2.10	0.76	18.32	3.98	52.22
25	17.50	0.29	1.75	0.63	15.27	3.32	43.51
20	14.00	0.23	1.40	0.50	12.22	2.65	34.81
15	10.50	0.17	1.05	0.38	9.16	1.99	26.11
10	7.00	0.12	0.70	0.25	6.11	1.33	17.41
5	3.50	0.06	0.35	0.13	3.05	0.66	8.70

Nitrous Oxide Flow rates at 6:1 Nitrous to Fuel Ratio With a .7 BSFC Equivalent air/fuel ratio= 13.25:1

Horse power	Gasoline lbs./hr @ BSFC=.50 HP*.5	Gasoline lbs./min @ BSFC=.50 BSFC/60	Nitrous lbs/min @ 7/1 BSFC*6	Oxygen lbs/min @ 7/1 *Nitrous lbs/min * .36*	CFM @ 70°F *Nitrous lbs/min * 8.726*	Equivalent Atmosphere lbs/min *Oxygen lbs/min / .19*	Equivalent Atmosphere CFM *Atmosphere lbs/min / .0762*
50	25.00	0.42	2.92	1.05	25.45	5.53	72.52
45	22.50	0.38	2.62	0.94	22.91	4.97	65.27
40	20.00	0.33	2.33	0.84	20.36	4.42	58.02
35	17.50	0.29	2.04	0.74	17.82	3.87	50.77
30	15.00	0.25	1.75	0.63	15.27	3.32	43.51
25	12.50	0.21	1.46	0.53	12.73	2.76	36.26
20	10.00	0.17	1.17	0.42	10.18	2.21	29.01
15	7.50	0.12	0.88	0.32	7.64	1.66	21.76
10	5.00	0.08	0.58	0.21	5.09	1.11	14.50
5	2.50	0.04	0.29	0.10	2.55	0.55	7.25

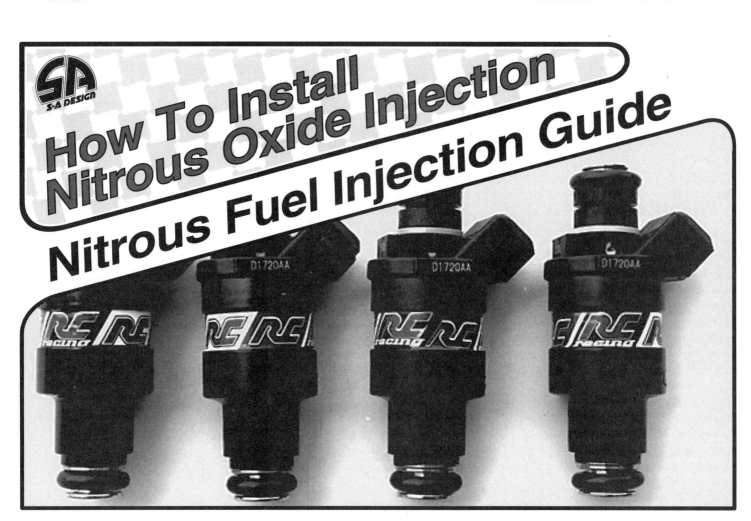

How To Install Nitrous Oxide Injection

Nitrous Fuel Injection Guide

8.1.0
FUEL INJECTION FUNDAMENTALS

When you combine the precision control of fuel injection with the latest high-flowing top end components and nitrous oxide, you have the potential to make your fuel-injected engine a monster killer. Anytime you increase airflow, which is essentially what a nitrous system does, you also have to introduce more fuel to keep the air/fuel ratio at optimum levels. This means you have to do two things: tune the fuel curve by programming the computer and install a set of injectors that will deliver the fuel required by the engine. Deciding how to select the appropriate size and style of injector is the focus of this story. But first a little background on electronic port fuel injection.

Port fuel injection, as the name implies, injects fuel directly into each port just upstream of the intake valve. This type of injection uses at least one injector per cylinder. One of the main advantages is that fuel can be introduced near the valve, leaving most of the intake manifold dry. This allows near-perfect cylinder-to-cylinder fuel distribution. A dry-flow intake manifold is much easier to design since fuel distribution isn't a problem. Port injection also promotes superior fuel atomization and subsequently more efficient combustion because fuel is injected at high pressure through a small hole directly in the high-speed airflow.

Two different types of airflow calibration are used with port fuel injection: speed density and mass flow. It's further characterized by two types of injection: batch, or group fire, and sequential fire.

Sequential injection means that the injection of fuel is timed to coincide with the valve opening. Group fire triggers a bank of injectors with each ignition cycle. Sequential injection is the current state-of-the-art in electronic fuel management.

Speed density fuel injection uses the speed of the engine and the density of the air, along with a sensor to measure manifold vacuum, to calculate engine airflow. Most aftermarket EFI systems also use speed density.

Mass flow fuel-injection systems use a Mass Air Sensor (MAS) to measure the mass of the air being inducted into the engine. Intake air is ducted past the MAS, which measures total airflow in one of several different ways depending on the type of MAS. The most prevalent type is the hot wire sensor pioneered by Bosch. The hot wire sensor routes airflow past a heated wire (hot wire). This wire is part of an electronic circuit that measure electrical current in milliamps. Current flowing through the wire heats it to a temperature that's always above the inlet air temperature by a fixed amount.

Air flowing across the wire draws away some of the heat, so an increase in current flow is required for it to maintain its fixed temperature. When air flow is low (idle), little current is required to heat the wire to temperature. At high airflow (WOT), it takes a lot of current to heat the wire because heat is being removed from it more quickly. The current necessary to heat the wire is proportional to the mass of air flowing across the wire. A temperature sensor in the MAS provides a correction for intake air temperature so that the output signal is not affected by it. A circuit in the MAS converts the current reading into a voltage signal for the Electronic Control Module (ECM), which converts it to grams per second (gps). The output of this sensor is not linear with respect to airflow; it's sensitive to low air flow and less sensitive at high air flows. Idle speed air flow is typically about 4 to 7 gps, increasing with rpm. The hot wire is made of platinum and is sensitive to contaminants or deposits; therefore, it is super-heated after engine shutdown to burn off any deposits.

Mass flow fuel systems measure the mass of the air directly, so there's no need for the ECM to correct for air density. Other inputs to the ECM include a throttle position sensor and an O_2 sensor for closed-loop air/fuel ratio control. Once the ECM knows the amount of air entering the engine, it looks at the other sensors to determine the engine's current state of operation (idle, acceleration, cruise, deceleration); then it refers to an electronic table or map to find the appropriate air/fuel ratio and select the fuel injector pulse width required to match the input signals. Finally, the ECM energizes the fuel injector for the appropriate number of milliseconds to inject the fuel.

A Mass Flow fuel system adapts easily to changes in the engine as well as hardware because airflow is measured directly. In other words, a Mass flow system is self-compensating for most reasonable changes to the engine and is extremely accurate under low-speed, part-throttle operation. The downside is that the sensors are expensive and sometimes unreliable. Many MAS also provide a considerable restriction to airflow in high-horsepower engines, limiting their power.

A speed density system calculates the airflow of the engine since it has no sensor to measure it directly. If you simplify the engine as an air pump, theoretically, it will move half of its displacement in air for every rotation of the crankshaft (half because it's a four-stroke engine). Thus the engine itself is an air meter. Engines, however, rarely flow the theoretical airflow due to restrictions in the inlet, the cylinder head, and the exhaust.

The volumetric efficiency (VE) of an engine is defined as the ratio of the actual mass airflow to the theoretical mass airflow. If an engine flows its theoretical airflow, then the VE would be 100 percent . At WOT, high-performance engines can approach a VE value of 100 percent and racing engines can exceed 100 percent within a specific rpm range because of more efficient inlet and exhaust tuning. All engines will have low VE values at part throttle (except for engines equipped with a turbocharger or supercharger, where the inlet manifold is often pressurized under part-throttle conditions.). The volumetric efficiency of an engine changes for every throttle position and engine speed. A large table or map of these values can be generated on an engine dynamometer by measuring the actual airflow at all the speed load points and calculating the VEs. This procedure is called mapping an engine.

Speed density systems use this map of engine volumetric efficiency to calculate the air flow of the engine under any operating condition. These systems measure engine vacuum via a Manifold Absolute Pressure (MAP) sensor. This sensor reads absolute pressure in KPA (Kilopascals) and supplies a voltage signal to the ECM proportional to manifold vacuum. All of the VE maps are referenced by manifold vacuum and rpm; the computer reads engine speed (rpm) and manifold vacuum (KPA) and looks in the reference table to find the volumetric efficiency at this speed load point. Once the computer finds the VE value, it computes the airflow directly. As most racers know, air density changes with temperature; therefore, the computer must then correct the calculated airflow value based on a sensor reading of the air temperature in the manifold.

The computer's calculations are all based on the map of VEs. Production variations and wear and tear are not compensated for when a test engine is mapped. If the intake or exhaust manifolds were changed, this would seriously affect the volumetric efficiency of the engine and throw the computer's calculations into error. A racing engine would be remapped to incorporate any changes, but this is obvi-

ously not feasible for car manufacturers. Production cars compensate for wear and production variation through the closed-loop control provided by the exhaust gas oxygen (EGO) sensor. This sensor supports calculation of the air/fuel ratio based on the oxygen content of the exhaust. The ECM looks at the air/fuel ratio from the EGO sensor (also known as the O_2 sensor) and corrects fuel delivery for any errors. This works fine when the engine is in closed-loop control mode (all part-throttle driving conditions), but when the engine is at WOT, it's not under closed-loop control and correction factors are not that accurate. Obviously, the ECM is doing a lot of number crunching with a speed density system.

N Alpha fuel systems are a simple design for engines that operate primarily at WOT and are thus used extensively in racing. N Alpha uses only the speed of the engine (N) and the throttle angle (alpha) to calculate the required amount of fuel delivery. These are simple speed-density systems that use throttle angle to approximate load instead of a MAP sensor. This approach is logical for racing engines with aggressive camshaft profiles that generate weak manifold vacuum signals and spend little time at part-throttle. N Alpha systems are just as accurate as speed density systems at WOT, but have much less accuracy at part throttle due to the reduced size of the engine map.

That's the basic run down on how electronic fuel-injection systems work. The point for all this is to give you some background so you can see just how delicately balanced your engine's fuel management system is. All the components have to work together to make power while retaining good driveability. Selecting the proper fuel injectors is just one piece, though a critical one, of the electronic fuel-injection puzzle.

Choosing the proper injector is always a compromise, especially for a car that needs part-throttle response. In other words ,if you still have to drive the car on the street or around the pit, you can't necessarily install the injector that will deliver the most fuel. Installing over-sized injectors is somewhat analogous to over-carbureting an engine. And in extreme cases you can pump so much fuel into the combustion chambers there isn't a chance in Hades that it'll fire or idle.

That said, here are some useful formulas to guide you in selecting the proper injector for your combination. The two main criteria are injector size, or the amount of fuel it will deliver, and injector compatibility with the electronics that control the injector.

8.1.1
HOW TO CALCULATE THE PROPER SIZE INJECTOR FOR YOUR COMBINATION

An injector consists of a solenoid that moves an internal plunger when the magnetic windings are energized by the application of voltage. A sized orifice is opened when the plunger is activated, allowing pressurized fuel to flow through the created opening. The critical element is the injector's ability to maintain linear fuel flow from narrow pulse widths to wide pulse widths, so that the dynamic range of fuel delivery remains accurate for any given rpm and load requirement. The injector's metering orifice is designed to spray the fuel in a cone-shaped pattern of 15 to 30 degrees for optimum fuel atomization.

Fuel flow is controlled by varying the pulse width or duty cycle of the injectors. Pulse width is the time in milliseconds that the injector is open, while duty cycle is the injector's overall percentage of open time. A 70-percent duty cycle means that the injector is open 70 percent of the injector's maximum cycling time.

Ultimately, to find the optimum injector size for a given application, you have to test it. You can map it out on a dyno sizing the injector based on observed maximum brake horsepower (BHP) and brake specific fuel consumption (BSFC) at peak power. You can also use a wide band oxygen sensor that tells you the a/f ratio at the load points for which you're tuning. The following formulas will get you close to the correct size injector for WOT performance. Driveability and idle require a little more finesse, which we'll cover later.

$$\frac{(BHP \times BSFC)}{Number\ of\ injectors \times 0.8} = Injector\ size\ (flow\ rate)$$

The scaler 0.8 adjusts the calculated injector size to produce the fuel necessary for peak power at an 80-percent duty cycle. An accurate BHP figure is critical for proper injector sizing, but not all dynamometers have fuel flow instrumentation, so BSFC is often estimated at approximately 0.5 lb./bhp-hr. for normally aspirated engines.

Take an engine with a known BSFC of 0.49 making 300 horsepower. Applying the formula, we derive:

$$\frac{(300 \times 0.49)}{(4 \times 0.8)} = 45.9\ lb./hr.\ (required\ injector\ flow\ rate)$$

You also can calculate the maximum horsepower a given injector size can support by plugging a known injector size into the formula using either the measured or estimated BSFC.

$$\frac{Flow\ Rate \times Number\ of\ Injectors \times 0.8}{BSFC} = HP$$

or:

$$\frac{50\ lb../hr. \times 4 \times 0.8}{0.49} = 326.5\ HP$$

Running an engine on a dynamometer to determine its performance statistics isn't practical for most of us, so BHP is often estimated by using quarter-mile performance and one of the performance slide rules, or "dream wheels." You also can calculate the CFM flow of the engine using assumptions about volumetric efficiency. (See the section on sizing a carburetor for the formula to find the CFM of your engine at max rpm.)

Then use the following formula to convert CFM to estimated injector size.

$$\frac{CFM \times 0.44298}{\#\ of\ cylinders} = estimated\ injector\ size$$

This formula only gives an estimat-

ed injector size and assumes one injector per cylinder on a normally aspirated engine.

Fuel Flow vs. Fuel Pressure

A fuel injector is a precision-calibrated orifice. All injectors are rated for flow at a specific fuel pressure, typically 43.5 lb. (3 bar). The injector flow rate will change if the supply pressure is varied. The equation to convert the static flow of an injector to that of a higher pressure is:

$$F_2 = \sqrt{P_2 / P_1} \times F_1$$

For Example: Calculate the static flow rate of a 24 lb./hr. injector when the fuel pressure is raised from 30 to 40 psi.

F2= Sqrt of 40 psi/30 psi x 24 lb./hr.
F2=1.1547 x 24
F2=27.71lb./hr.

Higher fuel pressure generally means better fuel atomization, but it also makes the injector works harder when opening. Increasing fuel pressure also slows down an injector's response time. Typical response time is 1.5 to 2.0 milliseconds. When pressure is raised significantly—from 43.5 lb. (3 bar) to 72.5 lb. (5 bar)—the injectors may have to work so hard that their useful life is drastically shortened. Generally it's safe to raise the fuel pressure no more than 10 to 15 percent. Raising the fuel pressure of a stock injection system changes the specific fuel flow calibration of the injector. The computer bases all its calculations on the known calibration of the injector. When the calibration changes due to an increase in fuel pressure, the computer cannot know this without a calibration change (PROM change). Since the injector's flow rate changes, all the computer's original calculations are in error and the fuel curve will experience a shift that may be harmful across most of the engine's operating range. On a turbocharged engine, or with the appropriate NOS system installed, with a linear pressure regulator, extra high pressure exists under boost conditions where fuel pressure rises in proportion to boost. This situation is different from trying to run a normally aspirated engine with the idle pressure cranked up to 50-plus psi. If you do, you're idle air/fuel ratio will be way too rich and it will bog and stumble coming up off idle.

8.1.2
INJECTOR COMPATIBILITY

In addition to selecting the correct injector size, the chosen injector must be electronically compatible with the computer that controls it. There are two kinds of injector-control circuits (drivers): 1) saturated (high impedance or voltage mode-type); and 2) peak and hold (low impedance or current mode type).

Depending on the type of driver, an injector is referred to as either a saturated injector or a peak-and-hold injector. Saturated injectors have a higher electrical resistance (12 to 16 ohms) than peak-and-hold injectors (2 to 5 ohms). An injector's resistance may be measured with an ohmmeter across its two terminals. Resistance dictates the compatibility of injectors and ECM drivers.

A 12-volt saturated injector uses 12 volts to open and close the injectors. These are high-resistance injectors that maintain low current flow in the injectors and drivers to keep them cool and promote longer life. Saturated circuits generally have slightly slower response time, which limits their operating range.

Peak-and-hold injectors are more exotic and have a greater dynamic range, but require more amperage to operate. It's important not to replace a saturated injector with a peak-and-hold injector because the additional amperage required to operate the peak-and-hold can destroy the ECM's drivers. The higher (peak) current level generates more force for opening the injector and the lower (hold) current improves closing response by reducing the hold force. It's possible to replace a peak-and-hold with a saturated injector since the amperage required to operate a saturated injector is lower and within the range of the peak-and-hold injector's drivers.

Most racing injection systems use a peak-and-hold injector. These low-resistance drivers are also known as current limiting. Twelve volts are still delivered to the injector, but because the resistance is low, current in the driver circuit is high. The peak current is used to kick the injector off its seat quickly, then the lower current holds it open until the ECM closes it. There are two basic drivers for peak-and-hold systems: 4 amp peak/1 amp hold, and 2 amp peak/0.5 amp hold. Although this type of driver is rated up to five amps, it will not draw that amount. A lower current limit is deliberately set to protect the circuitry.

Use Ohm's Law to determine the cur-

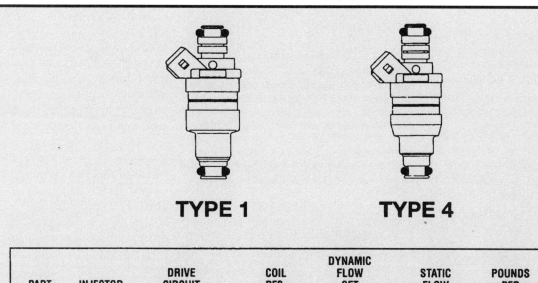

TYPE 1   **TYPE 4**

PART NO.	INJECTOR TYPE	DRIVE CIRCUIT TYPE	COIL RES. (OHMS)	DYNAMIC FLOW SET *	STATIC FLOW **	POUNDS PER HOUR	PRESSURE ***
62 1002	4	SATURATED	15.9	4.58	150.00	19.82	3.0 BAR
62 1030	1	SATURATED	16.2	8.13	271.00	35.81	2.7 BAR
62 1031	4	SATURATED	15.9	9.96	320.00	42.29	3.0 BAR
62 1032	1	PEAK & HOLD	2.4	11.80	394.00	52.07	3.0 BAR
62 1033	4	SATURATED	15.9	3.28	150.00	19.82	3.0 BAR
62 1034	4	SATURATED	15.9	5.28	162.00	21.41	3.5 BAR
62 1035	4	SATURATED	15.9	6.10	200.00	26.43	3.0 BAR
62 1036	4	SATURATED	15.9	4.50	161.00	21.28	3.0 BAR
62 1037	4	SATURATED	15.9	8.42	282.00	37.27	3.0 BAR

```
  *   MILLIGRAMS FUEL/PULSE
 **   GRAMS FUEL/MINUTE
***   BAR × 14.5 = P.S.I.
```

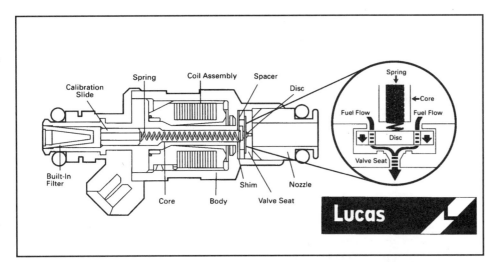

Lucas

rent in a given injector and driver. Ohm's Law states that current is equal to voltage divided by the resistance in ohms:

If I=V ÷ R then V=I x R

where:
V=Voltage
I=Current (amps)
R=Resistance (ohms)

A saturated 12-volt injector with a resistance of 12 ohms has a current of one amp. A peak-and-hold injector with two ohms resistance and 12 volts supplied will draw a current of six amps. Compared to a peak-and-hold

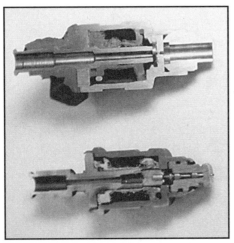

The injector on the bottom is a stock Honda unit. It's a pintle type in which fuel is metered by moving a pintle in and out of a sized orifice to regulate fuel delivery. The injector on top is a Lucas disc type. RC Engineering advocates using rotary disc fuel injectors for high-performance street applications. They can operate at 85 to 95 percent duty cycle and have as little as 0.8-0.9 millisecond opening time to deliver small amounts of fuel to improve idle quality.

The standard GM-style Multec injector built by Rochester Products uses a stainless steel ball-and-seat valve with a special director plate designed to deliver a more precise spray pattern and remain insensitive to poor fuel properties that cause clogging. These are the same type of injectors offered by MSD for performance applications.

injector, a saturated design runs cool. The peak-and-hold's six amps creates considerable heat, making them more vulnerable. However, this current is precisely what allows the racing fuel system to flow large amounts of fuel and still have exceptional response.

MSD Racing Injectors

Part #	Resis. (ohms)	Injector Driver Type	Fuel Flow
2012	2.0	2/0.5 peak & hold	34 lb./hr. @ 43.5 psi
2013	12.0	12v saturated	50 lb./hr. @ 43.5 psi
2014	2.0	4/1 peak & hold	72 lb./hr. @ 43.5 psi
2015	2.0	4/1 peak & hold	96 lb./hr. @ 43.5 psi
2018	12.0	12v saturated	38 lb./hr. @ 43.5 psi

8.1.3
Injector Duty Cycle: What is it?

We stated earlier that fuel flow is controlled by varying the pulse width or duty cycle of the injectors. Pulse width is the time in milliseconds that the injector is open, while duty cycle is the injector's overall percentage of open time. A 70-percent duty cycle means that the injector is open 70 percent of the injectors maximum cycling time. But what does "maximum cycling time" mean?

You could call that the injector's redline. Its maximum cycling time is how quickly it can open, fire a pulse of fuel, close, and be ready to open and fire another pulse of fuel. The limiting factor here is the injector's response time. As we said earlier, typical response times are in the 00.0015 to 0.002 second range. That means in order for an injector to fire every 0.010-second, i.e., 10 milliseconds the duty cycle, the actual pulse width of the injector, can only be 0.008 or 0.0085-seconds (8.0 or 8.5 milliseconds) depending on the response time of the injector. (Some injectors have quicker response times making them more useful to high-performance tuners. See Russ Collins on fuel injection for more info.) This is the reasoning behind using a scale factor when you calculate fuel-injector sizes for your engine combination.

This whole injector sizing thing gets a little misleading at this point. It probably does so because it's easy to assume that 0.010-second is all the time an injector can hang open. It isn't. If it were, you wouldn't be able to get the raw flow number in lb./hr. from a flow bench. In these tests the injector is simply locked open. So the injector will stay open as long as the computer tells it. Of course we run into the question of whether or not the computer and injector drivers on the fuel management system are up to the task, but that's a different question.

HOW TO GET MORE POWER FROM YOUR FUEL-INJECTED ENGINE

8.2.1
BALANCED INJECTOR FLOW FOR MAXIMUM PERFORMANCE

Having a balanced set of injectors in your engine combination does two things. First, it lets you know the actual fuel flow to the cylinders. Second, it ensures that each cylinder is getting the same amount of fuel as the others. Assuming the rail pressure is the same at each injector. When you start super tuning your engine, both parameters are critical.

Since it takes a certain amount of fuel to support a certain amount of horsepower, you have to know the total fuel flow capacity of your injectors. Brake Specific Fuel Consumption (BSFC) is a value derived by dividing the amount of fuel an engine consumes by the horsepower it's generating. BSFC=fuel pound per hour/horsepower. A modern, efficient, fuel injected, normally aspirated engine usually has a BSFC of 0.50 or slightly less at the torque peak. So as you saw in the section on fuel injection basics, you can use this fuel consumption-to-horsepower ratio to determine how much fuel you'll need from your injectors to support a certain amount of horsepower.

The second issue of making sure each cylinder receives the same amount of fuel is important when you're trying to get the last bit of power from your engine. If an engine has uneven distribution of the air/fuel mixture between cylinders, the leaner cylinders are more prone to detonate. That means you have to, or the computer has to, retard the timing for the mixture of the leanest cylinder. This most often occurs on carbureted cars, but it also happens to fuel-injected cars as the injectors get clogged or just weren't built right at the factory. Basically, if one cylinder is down on power, the rest of the cylinder are brought to that level by the computer retarding timing. So you're losing a lot more power than you should.

Russ Collins has a sensational fuel-injection lab. He built a flow bench that has much greater resolution than commercial flow benches. His flow bench will catch smaller variations in flow capacity between injectors. If you really want to run your engine on the edge, RC's flow bench will give you the numbers.

8.2.2
INJECTOR DUTY CYCLE PERFORMANCE WINDOW

Another test bench Collins built is what he calls an injector dyno. This test bench lets him observe the behavior of an injector under different fuel pressures, duty cycles, pulse widths, and frequencies. This test bench has led him to some interesting conclusions about injector performance and selection. He's found that at 85-percent duty cycle, most injectors freeze in between opening and closing; they sort of flutter and reduce fuel flow by half. "The Lucas disc injector," says Collins, "will stay stable to about 90- to 95-percent duty cycle; that's why I use them and sell them to my customers."

This is good information to have if you're pushing your combination right to the limit. If you step over it and get to the point where the injectors flutter you can lean out and get into detonation right at the worst possible time—full-throttle high rpm.

When Collins sells you a set of bigger flow-balanced injectors, he'll clean and balance your old set for free to keep as a backup—a nice customer service. You can call and give him the serial number on your computer print out and he'll be able to locate your data, run the program, and tell you exactly what you need to do to get exactly where you want to go at various fuel pressures and injector sizes. If you have a stand-alone computer, you can say you want to run your injectors at 70-percent duty cycle and 10 psi boost, and you want a little reserve for a safety for overboost conditions. Or perhaps you want to run a specific brake-specific fuel number—you can get there with Collins' computer program. If you know exactly what your making now, you can reverse engineer it.

An injector works by turning off and on quickly to deliver pulses of fuel. The length of time the injector is on or open, allowing fuel to be sprayed into the port, is known as the duty cycle. Duty cycle is measured in milliseconds—one-thousandth of a second.

The percent of duty cycle is exactly like jet sizes. But jet size is area; a lot of guys don't understand that a 100 jet isn't twice as large as a 50 jet. Whereas percent of duty cycle is linear, i.e., 25-percent duty cycle is exactly half of 50-percent duty cycle, because time is time. You're not changing the area of the orifice, you're change the amount of time the orifice is open, making it wonderfully easy to do.

Most injectors don't operate much slower than 2 milliseconds, maybe 1.8 milliseconds. The Lucas plate-type injector will operate down to 0.8, 0.9, or 1 millisecond because the plate has much less mass than the pintle in pintle-style injectors. In an idle situation, you can run a larger Lucas injector than a pintle-style injector because the Lucas operates at substantially shorter duty cycles and so delivers less fuel to keep the engine idling.

What happens when you put a big 550 Bosch or Nippodenso injector (any pintle style) in an engine, even with an aftermarket computer, is you can't get the big injectors to operate at a short enough duty cycle to lean the mixture to the point where the engine idles.

The Lucas has a larger surface area and uses a plate, so it won't operate at as high of pressures as the pintle type. But what we're talking about is that the Lucas will only operate up to about 90 psi, where the others will operate at 110 psi. The Lucas will run fine in the 80- to 90-psi window, but you shouldn't operate injectors higher than 65 psi anyway, no matter who makes them, unless the injector is designed to operate at high pressures. Most car injectors are designed to operate at around 55 to 65 psi. Figure that you can exceed manufacturers' recommendations by about a max of 30 percent. Once you try to put 50, 75, or 100 percent more pressure on an injector, you're setting up a failure scenario.

On our injector dyno you can hear the injector groan under increasing pressure; you can see and measure the fuel flow dropping off, and you can see the spray pattern dissipate. On the oscilloscope you can see the duty cycle become irregular. Our advice is don't run high fuel rail pressure, unless you're willing to replace your injectors often.

Here's a pintle style injector. It has a small pintle. It's made by Keihin, and is nice looking, with a light weight pintle and a minimum duty cycle of the usual 1.8 or 1.9 milliseconds. It's much lighter than the Nippondenso or Bosch units. Nippondenso has some of the heaviest pintles.

If you look at a Bosch or Nippon-

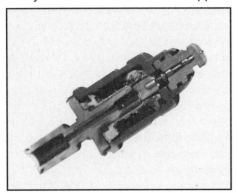

denso standard pintle injector, they put the fuel orifice pretty deep into the intake manifold so it's close to the intake valve. Every time you shut the motor off at least one or two intake valves are open, depending on how many cylinders the engine has, and sometimes the exhaust and the intake

valves will be open. On turbo motors, the glowing-pink hot turbo is dissipating a lot of heat that doesn't go down the exhaust pipe, but up through the engine to the intake where it's cooler. The heat goes through the intake tract and just boils the fuel in the injector around the pintle. With the Lucas injector, the operating mechanism is buried in a stainless steel heat sink. It's so much further away from the hot air that it stays cleaner longer in a turbo car.

The injectors that need service most often are on turbo-engined cars. Ford, Toyota, and especially V-6 turbo engines are high on the list because they just boil the injectors to death in the intake. They've jumped through a lot of hoops to get the injectors to live on the V-6—peak-and-hold, saturated, side flow, top flow, rail feed, galley feed, and they finally got a galley feed injector to work; it stays cool probably because there's enough fuel passing around it. But it took the engineers a long time trying to find something that would stay alive.

The rotating, self-cleaning disc on the Lucas injector doesn't use an O-ring anywhere on the injector. This means it's more resistant to fuel additives. Fuel additives dissolve the laminates and glues that hold most injectors together, and they don't like O-rings.

Let's compare a Keihin to a Lucas. The Lucas injector operates by lifting a disc 0.004-inch off the seat, letting fuel pass. It tends to be consistent because a heavy pintle isn't beating

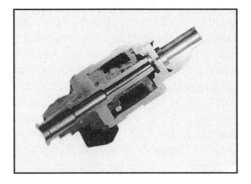

against the seat. Flow is controlled by the size of the orifice and the fuel pressure. A pintle type uses a needle and seat arrangement, and is more subject to changing spray pattern and atomization because of wear.

We recommend replacing the stock

injectors with high performance units. Russ Collins runs performance injectors on any high-performance car that he services. This recommendation comes from doing extensive research to find the right part numbers that work well for stock and modified engines.

8.3.1
TUNING FACTORS IN NOZZLE PLACEMENT

On dry systems (port fuel injection), you want the nozzle as far away from the throttle body as possible. That gives the nitrous that's coming out of the nozzle at minus 190 degrees F time to cool the intake charge. We've found that a three-foot distance from the throttle body with a 60-horsepower kit dropped the intake air temperature from 120 to 60 degrees F before the car got into third gear. If you place the nozzle right at the throttle body, which most people do out of a misunderstanding of the needs of a dry system versus a wet system, you're loosing power. In a wet system, nitrous and fuel are injected together into a carbureted or throttle-body-injected engine. Since the whole intake runner is filled with explosives, you need to keep that volume down. Then if the motor backfires, you won't have as powerful an explosion as you would if the intake runner were filled with gas combined with the nitrous, and filling up the cold air ducting as well. If you're running a wet system, you want to introduce the nitrous and fuel as close to the valve as possible, mainly for backfiring damage control. Dry systems don't have that problem, so you can take advantage of cooling the air. Place the nitrous nozzle right after the air cleaner. The more you cool the intake charge, the more free horsepower you get. Ideally, if you didn't have the backfire concern, injecting the cold nitrous away from the throttle would be advantageous; however, you have to deal with fuel distribution problems, such as fuel falling out of suspension.

8.3.2
CHOOSING FUEL INJECTORS FOR A NITROUS SYSTEM

The best nitrous system is a dry system that lets the computer deliver more fuel to the mix and even control the timing. When you get into to serious nitrous amounts, though, you must install higher-capacity injectors. It gets a little tricky when you're trying to keep good idle quality and naturally aspirated throttle response. Re-program the computer for normal driving so all the drivability and full power is good—without injecting nitrous. If an injector is sized correctly for a naturally aspirated engine, at 6000 rpm you'll see a 10-millisecond duty cycle for each injector. Obviously, at 7000 rpm it'll be less than 10 milliseconds, and so on, but at 5000 rpm, you'll have more than 10 milliseconds. It's an easy number to remember.

A properly sized injector shouldn't pull a duty cycle any longer than 7.5 milliseconds, which means it's at 75 percent of the duty cycle. When running a bigger injector to compensate for nitrous injection, that number can go as low as 5 milliseconds without a nitrous injection. When you inject nitrous, depending on how much you're injecting, the duty cycle will proportionally add up to 7.5 milliseconds. Now instead of 180 it's producing 260 horsepower. To support 260 horsepower you need more fuel, but if it's already at 7.5 milliseconds, there isn't much time to give more fuel, which means you have to give it a bigger injector. As a result, with the nitrous off, you only have 5 milliseconds of fuel; you're naturally aspirated at WOT, which is fine, and the injector's loafing. The injector is too big for the application until you add another 80 or 100 horsepower of nitrous on top of the system, which bumps you up to 7.5 milliseconds. At WOT with maximum nitrous injection, you can see on the DFI data logger that the injectors show 7.5 milliseconds at the desired rpm level. As long as that corresponds to the plug readings, you know you're getting the mixture you desired.

Russ Collins is the injector guy. He's a good source of advice on which injectors will run and behave at 90

percent and which won't. When you see an injector working hard at 85 percent then freak out at 90, you just about die. However, this seems to explain why some holes go lean on port-injected engines. At 90 percent, the injected fuel starts fluttering, the nice fuel pattern goes away, and then the flow goes away, which kills the atomization and flow of the fuel. That knowledge is important. We've had success choosing injectors with lots of reserve. We don't run more than 80 percent duty cycle, and at 6000 r.p.m., we don't want to see more than 8 milliseconds.

We won't tell the DFI to open the injector more than 8 milliseconds. Looking at our air/fuel meter, we want a 12.5 ratio when we've got the injector at 80 percent (8 milliseconds). However, if we're at a 13 ratio, the injectors are too small. We can go to 8.5 milliseconds, but at 7000 rpm the injector is in the 90-percent range, and a lot of these engines run in the 7000- to 8000-rpm range. When you're trying to feed an engine at high rpm, you need a bigger injector that feeds the motor more fuel more quickly. The idle times are all in the 1.2- to 1.6-milliseconds range, at which most injectors will idle. With a plate-type injector, you can run it to 90- or 95-percent duty cycle with consistent fuel delivery and spray pattern.

Another thing to consider in fuel injectors for a nitrous system is idle quality. For instance, take an Integra non-VTEC engine that makes 160 horsepower naturally aspirated. Quick calculation gives us 40 horsepower per hole with a 0.5 BSFC. That calls for a 20 lb./hr. injector. Divide by 0.8 to factor in duty cycle and move the value up a little bit. You're in the 20 lb./hr. range. Let's say we're running a 140-horsepower shot of nitrous. That's 300 horsepower divided by 4, which is equal to 70 horsepower per hole. Divide by 0.5 BSFC and 0.8 duty cycle, and you'll need a 40- to 45-lb./hr. injector. Now you've got a motor that wants a 20-lb./hr. injector in naturally aspirated mode, but wants a 44-lb./hr. injector to support the nitrous shot. At idle, the 20-lb./hr. injector wants a 1.4- or 1.6-milliseconds duty cycle. However, if you run the 44-lb./hr. injector at a 1.4- or 1.6-millisec-

ond duty cycle, you've got almost twice the fuel you need to idle. You have to slow it down as much as possible to maybe a 0.8 or 0.9 cycle—less than a millisecond. A Rochester won't go that slow; the pintle is too heavy. Bosch injectors are pretty good, and the Bosch will go that slow, but the Lucas plate-type are about the best.

You've got a problem on the other side, too—a reasonably expensive DFI unit with a 50-cent injector driver. (Motec and some of the other higher-dollar boxes have better injector drivers.) The injector driver won't go lower than a 1.4 milliseconds cycle. According to the DFI manual, it won't run that slow, but we've run that injector driver down to a 0.9-millisecond duty cycle and it seemed okay. We didn't, though, put these injectors on the test bench and let the DFI run it, which would be interesting. We'd like to let the DFI idle and lower the pulse width to a 0.9 to see what the spray pattern looks like.

All the DFI boxes, except the high-end sequential units, batch fire. The back of the valve is squirted four times before it opens to let the air/fuel mix in. You need a small pulse width, depending on the size of the injector, to get a big horsepower engine to idle; however, the high-end sequential unit's firing scheme fixes this problem. Ken Duttweiler builds Mustang motors that produce 200 horsepower per cylinder, and he uses 96-lb./hr. injectors. The only way he gets these engines to idle is with the sequential box, but it costs more than $2000. For less than half that price we do pretty well with the batch fire system.

8.4.0
FUEL-INJECTED ENGINE TUNING STRATEGY

8.4.1
How to Tune a Fuel Curve

Editor's note: RC Engineering markets an air/fuel ratio meter to help you tune its RSR fuel-injection system. The manual for the meter is instructive and extremely accurate about facts surrounding the art of tuning your engine's fuel curve. We liked it so much we decided to reprint it (with permission, of course), and encourage you to give Russ Collins a call or stop by his shop and see if either one of these systems is right for you.

Computer or no computer, developing a fuel curve for a motor is a difficult process. There are many points to calibrate in a "digitized" system, which, when totaled, comprise the base fuel map. This mapping process must be approached systematically with an understanding of the engine's fuel needs. This manual was written primarily to aid in the calibration of our RSR Fuel Injection Systems, but the use of the RSR Digital Air/Fuel Ratio Meter has equal validity in carburetor jetting. Whether you are tapping computer keys or changing needles and jets, you're after the same thing...the correct air/fuel ratio.

Air/Fuel Ratios

The mixture of the air and fuel can be expressed in three ways, all based on a common point called stoichiometry. Stoichiometry is the chemically "correct" point at which the most complete combustion takes place, which is 14.7 parts of air to one part of fuel by weight. Expressed in three ratios, we offer the following correlations:

Air/Fuel Ratio	Fuel/Air Ratio	Fuel Ratio Actual/ Stoichiometry
9.80:1	.1020	1.5
10.50:1	.0952	1.4
11.30:1	.0885	1.3
12.25:1	.0816	1.2
13.36:1	.0748	1.1
14.70:1	.0680	1.0
16.33:1	.0612	0.9
18.37:1	.0544	0.8
21.00:1	.0476	0.7
24.50:1	.0408	0.6

8.4.2
Mixture Requirements

The proper air/fuel ratio for each particular set of operating conditions is most conveniently broken down into two categories: steady-state running and transient operation. Steady-state running is taken to mean continuous operation at a given speed and power output with normal engine temperatures. Transient operation includes starting, warming up, and the process of changing from one speed or load to another.

8.4.3
STEADY-STATE FUEL REQUIREMENTS

Idle

Due to the low port velocity and frictional losses, idle mixtures are typically set at a fuel ratio of 1.2 or, expressed differently, 12.25:1 air/fuel ratio.

Your motor will idle at stoichiometry (14.7:1) or less than stoichiometry, but this is near misfiring, and if operating temperatures are not stabilized at a high level, the motor will die. For example, operational fluid temperatures can vary from 150 to 250 degrees F, and inlet air temperatures can easily vary 100 degrees F. These variations in temperature all necessitate different mixture requirements, so it's far better to keep the fuel ratio in the 1.2 region to preserve idle quality and off-idle responsiveness.

Steady-State Throttle

At a given rpm under steady-state load conditions your mixture strength should be a 1.1 fuel ratio or 13.2:1 air/fuel ratio. At this point you'll have your peak cylinder or Brake Mean Effective Pressure (BMEP) figures. The development of a base fuel map is generally done around this figure as it's 11 percent richer than stoichiometry but within the correction range of a closed-loop oxygen sensing system. This allows the base map to be calibrated for maximum power without excessive fuel consumption and still allows the closed-loop operation to self-adjust to 14.7:1 for normal, steady-state operation.

8.4.4
Transient Fuel Requirements

The principal transient conditions are starting, warming up, acceleration (increase of load), and deceleration (decrease of load).

Starting and Warming Up

Abnormal or rich mixtures are required to start a cold engine. The air/fuel ratios must be progressively reduced from this point during the warm-up period until the engine will run satisfactorily with the normal, steady-running air/fuel ratios. Starting or cranking fuel is also a temperature-dependent variable, with more cranking fuel required for lower temperatures. Air/fuel ratios on initial start-up in cold weather can easily be 50 percent greater than stoichiometry i.e., in the 11.0:1 to 10.3:1 air/fuel ratio range.
1. Steady-State Running
2. Starting and Warm-up Cycles
3. Acceleration Fueling
4. Deceleration Fueling
5. Full-Throttle Operation

Using the RSR Digital Air/Fuel Ratio Meter

You should be aware of the following limitations:

1. Your O-sensor must reach 600 degrees F for the display to become active so it will not "read" any exhaust gases until it reaches this temperature. This takes one to two minutes.

2. Your O-sensor will become contaminated if you run leaded racing gas, and the display will not give true readings. Using unleaded pump gas, the O-sensor is easily reliable for 50,000 miles.

3. Nitrous oxide will confuse the sensor because the Lambda O-sensor reads free oxygen content and the nitrous will add oxygen molecules to the system, giving false readings on your meter.

There's no magical, absolute, digitized answer to developing your application's fuel requirements. You must drive your machine, and a considerable amount of judgement must be placed in such areas as cold start, warm-up, acceleration fueling, idle quality, and driveability. Each motor is different and the calibration will be only as good as the effort you put into it. Much subjective decision making will take place and the air/fuel ratio meter will

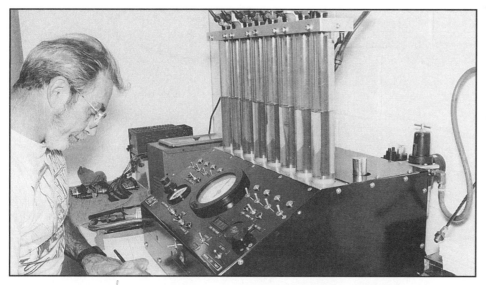

Russ Collins hard at work flow-testing a batch of injectors. He tests all injectors at 43 psi fuel pressure for either 30 seconds or a full minute to establish a baseline. His flow bench can raise fuel pressures much higher for special testing, but 43 psi is right at or close to where most injectors should operate.

This machine has larger, graduated tubes than most commercial flow benches. Its divisions are 1 cc, but you can be reasonably accurate down to the half cc per minute. You easily can see an imbalance in the flow capacity between these two injectors.

If Collins notices a slight discrepancy in flow rates, he can let it run longer to get a more accurate reading on the imbalance. Running the flow test for a longer time period gives you a more accurate measure of the total flow.

By firing the injector into a clear chamber and synchronizing it with a strobe, Collins freezes the spray pattern. It's a convincing demonstration to see the spray pattern collapse when the injector starts fluttering. This is how he determines the quality of the spray pattern on the injector sets he sells.

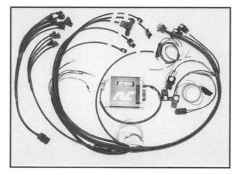

RC Engineering also markets a trick, stand-alone fuel-injection system. It doesn't control timing, but it's user friendly when it comes to mapping fuel curves. For more information, contact RC Engineering.

Here's the RC Engineering injector dyno in operation. Collins tests the injector at various fuel pressures, duty cycles, and frequencies to mimic what actually occurs in a normally aspirated engine. His usual procedure is checking to see the real pulse width durations supported by the injector. Critical areas are the shortest duration the injector can cycle because this determines idle quality. Another is how the injector behaves when pushed past an 80-percent duty cycle. He's found that, with the exception of the Lucas disc style injector, which seems to operate well at 90 percent of duty cycle, most others freeze between opening and closing at 80-percent duty cycle, where they begin to flutter and reduce fuel flow by half.

Using electronic test equipment Collins can control the frequency and the duty cycle of the injector. The oscilloscope lets him track the rise and fall time of the voltage, which is somewhat analogous to the behavior of the injector.

not provide you all the answers. Stopwatches, ETs, lap times, and your own opinions as a tester are equally as valid.

How To Install Nitrous Oxide Injection
Dyno Sessions

9.1.0
TEST PROCEDURES

The test procedures follow the same principles and sequence you should use when testing and tuning your own system. We're presenting the procedure we used in detail to show, first of all, it works; and second, that tuning is a process and procedure that harmonizes the multiple systems that combine to produce power from an engine.

To get meaningful data from a test session, either on the dyno or at the track, you have get your engine running right without the nitrous system first. For dyno testing purposes you need to do this because you need a reliable base line from which to compare increasing or diminishing performance. For a street car you need to because 90% of the time you'll be running on the motor alone. You don't want to jet the carburetor to add fuel or anything like that. You want all the additional fuel to come through the nitrous system.

Next you start tuning the nitrous system with the fuel jets to bring it to an optimum state of tune.

Typically you should start with a conservative jetting combination and tune toward higher output. You don't want to start at the leanest jetting and break your engine right at the gate. If you don't have a reference point, then you're much better off starting conservative. It's just much more fun installing larger jets than sweeping up your engine.

Just keep putting in larger jet sizes, fuel and nitrous, or alternate between the two until the plugs read about like they would naturally aspirated. If you have the jetting correct the plugs should read almost exactly like a naturally aspirated engine only your running nitrous so you're using a lot more fuel. You don't have to run a nitrous system so rich the plugs are black.

While it is true that it is safer to run the mixture rich and some engines will make more power on the rich side than on the lean side, these observations come about from distribution problems not so much from the characteristics of the chemical reaction of fuel and nitrous. You'll see what we mean when you read the section where we test a street Chevy Small Block.

In addition to establishing a baseline naturally aspirated performance at the beginning of each of the three test days, we weighed an empty bottle with the test pressure gauge to make sure we knew when the bottle was getting close to the end. The empty bottle weight, is stamped on the bottle but we had to find the weight of the gauge and adapter in order to correct our reading.

9.1.1
TESTING A
STREET SMALL BLOCK

The first dyno test data we'll look at is from a typical Chevy small block-street combination. In keeping with the spirit of the street, the nitrous system is an NOS Super Powershot plate system. This is system is one of the more popular choices for high performance street cars. It's an adjustable unit that makes an advertised 100 to 150 hp. We found that the advertised power rating is very dependent on engine combination, mostly in the choice of manifolds.

9.1.2
STREET ENGINE COMBINATION

The Summit Racing kit engine combination is as follows:

Camshaft part number: 12- 555-4
Designation: NX256H-13
Duration @ 0.006: 256/268
Duration @0.050: 212/222
Max lift w/1.5RR: 0.447/0.468
Lobe Separation: 113
Lobe ID numbers: 5441/5212
Intake Centerline: 108
Engine Type: Chevrolet 350
Bore: 4.030
Stroke: 3.480
Displacement: 355
Compression: 9.25: 1
Heads: Dart SR/Torquer
Intake: Edelbrock Performer
Carburetor: Edelbrock Q-Jet
Exhaust: 1.75 Hooker #2360
Nitrous system:Single-stage adjustable street plate system
Plugs: UR4-V-power NGK

Results:
Torque @ 3200 rpm: 371 ft./lb.
Power @ 5100 rpm: 326 hp
With N_2O: 600 ft./lb.
With N_2O: 439 hp
Manifold Vacuum: 16.5-in. Hg @ 800 rpm and 18.5-in. Hg @ 1000 rpm, no load

9.1.3
TEST RESULTS
AND INTERPRETATIONS

Test 1

Our first test, actually three pulls right at 295hp and slightly above, established a baseline power curve without using nitrous. With 30° ignition timing and 9 psi fuel pressure the engine made almost 300 hp and 361 ft/lbs of torque. It's a darn good street combo, though it lacks the rpm range to see low 12 or high 11 e.t.'s.

Test 2

This was our first shot of nitrous so we just put the suggested jets for 100 HP worth of fuel and nitrous from the Powershot kit. A .047 nitrous jet with a .053 fuel jet should yield 100hp. We

Our Summit Racing kit engine was assembled with some minor modifications to accomodate our nitrous intentions. The short block is all Summit while Dart SR/Torquer iron heads were used to emulate a budget street engine. A Comp Cams Nitrous HP camshaft was selected for all the nitrous tests on this engine.

Federal Mogul L2417F forged pistons were substituted because they have a full height top ring land, and the single, full length valve notch promotes better combustion because it doesn't inhibit inlet mixture flow across the piston top. They are a structurally superior piston.

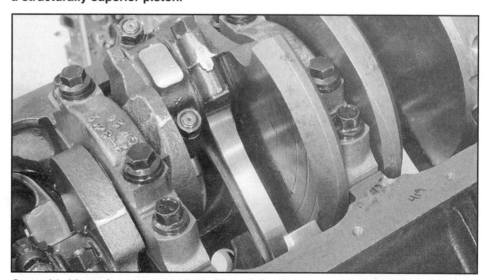

Summit's kit engines are supplied with polished beam connecting rods, a standard cast crankshaft and a 4-bolt main block.

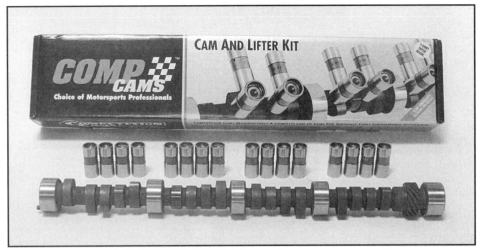

Comp Cams Nitrous HP cam kit was selected because it is specifically designed for use with nitrous oxide injection systems. It features more aggressive exhaust timing to complement the increased exhaust pressure generated by the nitrous oxide.

The Summit Racing kit engine is a good way to keep costs down. It incorporates such basic components as a low buck Summit roller chain, GM chrome timing cover and pointer and a factory GM balancer. We added a Moroso deep sump oil pan and a low buck engine gasket set, but we didn't scrimp on the head and intake gaskets. We went with Fel Pro all the way.

kept the 30° timing and 9-psi fuel pressure and had 850-psi bottle pressure. As you can see by the dyno sheet we have some tuning to do. The engine made about 450 ft-lbs of torque at 3700 rpm, after falling a quick 50 ft-lbs from when we hit the nitrous; horsepower peaked between 4600 and 4700 rpm with a 355 ponies.

Because the power dropped off as almost directly proportional to the amount of enrichment fuel, it seemed to indicate an overly rich condition. The jetting was correct according to the NOS instructions; however, we were running a little too much fuel pressure. Notice that 9 psi didn't affect the Edlebrock Q-jet carburetor. The baseline pull looked good. But when we hit the nitrous, it didn't respond as well as it should.

Test 3

We kept the 47/53 jetting with 9-psi fuel pressure but with 900-psi bottle pressure with 36° timing. This was a 4500 rpm steady state dyno pull that lasted for 6-secs using around .5-lb nitrous or about 5 lbs/minute. That's right where it should be to support a 100hp worth of fuel. We ran the steady state test to let the fuel system stablize. In Test 2 we noticed the sudden rise in fuel flow and a corresponding power loss. This was a way to isolate the problem. If it was in the fuel system we'd be able to see it after the fuel flow rates stabilized. If it was a timing problem, we'd see that, too.

The engine made appoximately 420

ft-lbs of torque and 360 HP on this pull. Since the only change we made was an increase of timing lead, with a resultant drop in torque of 30 ft-lbs and a slight 5 hp increase, we figured this combination responed better to 30° lead instead of 36°. But we weren't sure where to go from here.

Test 4

We still didn't know if the engine was overly rich, so after looking at the fuel flows, we knew we had enough to make more power than we observed on the dyno, so it was probably safe to step up on the nitrous jetting.

The next jetting combination was a .055/.053 with 9 psi fuel and 900 psi bottle pressure. The dyno pull was at the torque peak bwteeen 3700-3800 rpm. This bumped the torque up to 436 ft-lbs. better, but not as good as the 450 ft-lbs we observerd in the first pull.

On the air/fuel question, it didn't appear to be overly rich. The brake specific fuel consumption ranged from the high .4's to the low .6's about what we expect with this engine combination.

Test 5

Okay. The last jetting combination wasn't that much better. We decided to go back to the suggested jetting and reduce the fuel pressure. So this run, near the hp peak is with

An Edelbrock Performer EGR intake and Quadrajet comprised the street induction system, and a MSD Billet HEI with MSD wires lights the fire. NOS plate is seen under the carb with 125 HP kit solenoids rigged for action.

47/53 jets, 900-psi bottle pressure and 5-psi fuel pressure with 36° timing. We found about 10 more HP, observing 370 HP at 4500 rpm. Still not the 100 hp advertised.

Test 6

Because we saw a power increase in the last test, we thought we might have been too rich. So let's keep the same fuel jet and pressure and step up to a .053 nitrous jet. The next combination was a 53/53 with 825 psi bottle; 5-psi fuel pressure with 36° timing. This combination lost ground with a peak torque of 415 ft-lbs and peak power of 356 HP.

Test 7

At the begining of this second day of testing we ran a baseline without nitrous and 36° timing. The engine was still making around 360 ft-lbs at 3700 rpm and 294 HP at 4800 rpm. Thus began a marathon session of trying as many jetting combinations and fuel pressure combinations as time allowed. In Test 8 we drilled a .052 nitrous jet and put it with a .053 (undrilled) fuel jet with 850-psi bottle and 5-psi fuel pressure. Even with that we still only saw 370 HP at the power peak. That seemed about the limits, and perhaps we were up against the limits of the engine combination. This is something you need to know. There are limits to the amount of power you can make with certain engine and nitrous combinations unless you're willing to make the power purely from the nitrous system, which would require an awful lot of nitrous and enrichment fuel.

The next test with .055/.061 fuel jet drill out to .064; 850 bottle pressure/ 5-psi fuel; 36° timing only gave us 369 HP, again it seemed like we hit a ceiling. Stepping up to .055/.073 jets with 850 psi bottle; 5 psi fuel; 36° timing brought only 365 HP. The next combo of .055/.072 jettting with 850 psi bottle; 7 psi fuel; 32° timing set us back to 350 HP.

With Test 13 we found more power with a fresh bottle and .064/.073 jetting, 36° timing; and 850 bottle and 7 psi fuel pressure. We saw 378 hp at 4800 rpm with a reasonably stout 440 ft-lbs at 4800 rpm.

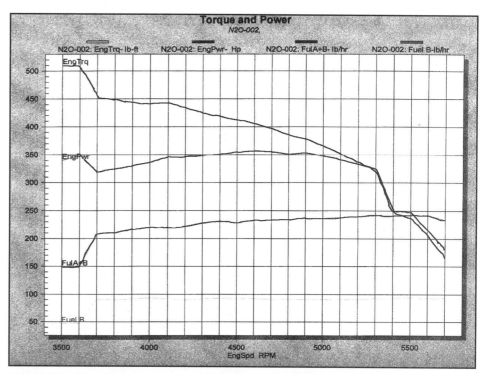

Test 2: The first nitrous test using NOS's suggested tuning for 100 hp. Obiviously we've got some tuning to do before we get close to making an extra 100hp. If you look at the fuel curve, you'll see a big clue standing on its head trying to be noticed.

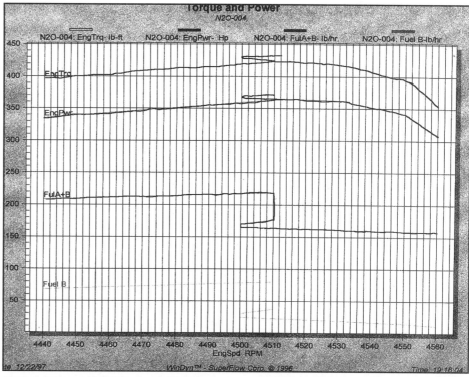

Test 4. The next jetting combination was a .055/.053 with 9 psi fuel and 900 psi bottle pressure. The dyno pull was at the torque peak 3700-3800 rpm. This bumped the torque up to 436 ft-lbs., but not as good as the 450 ft-lbs we observed in the first pull.

That was about the best we could expect so we ran it again as an acceleration test of 300/sec 4100 to 5100 rpm 64/73 850 psi/7 psi. That gave us 395 hp at 4800 rpm and 480 ft-lbs of torque at 4100 rpm, right at the 100 hp advertised rating for the kit. However, the jetting it took to get there was substantially larger than advertised. But there is a good reason for this.

Almost all the advertised power levels are from engine combinations with

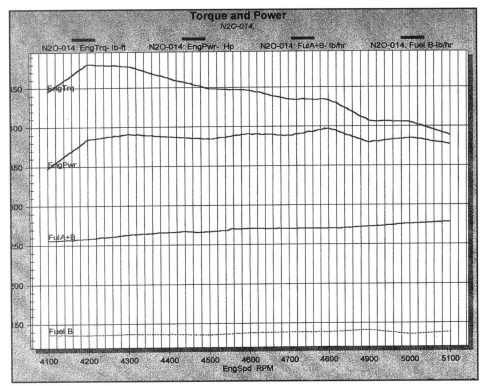

Test 14. Our best effort came with a .064/.073 jetting combo with 850 psi in the bottle and 7-psi at the carb. That gave us 395 HP at 4800 rpm and 480 ft-lbs of torque at 4100 rpm, right at the 100 HP advertised rating for the kit, though we did have to use the 125 HP jetting. Nitrous plates don't respond as well to dual plane manifolds as they do to single plane manifolds.

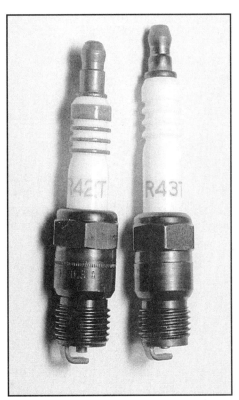

What you really need is a plug with a short, wide and thick ground strap such as these.

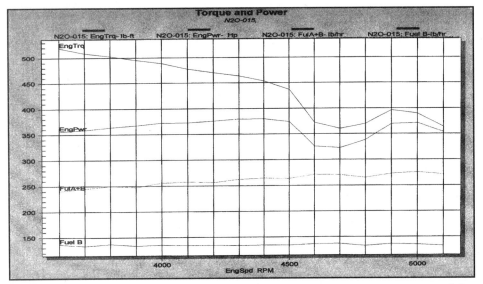

Here's a dyno sheet that shows the effect of detonation on the power output of the engine. Notice how quickly power drops off then comes back slightly as we ease off the throttle. The moral of the story is to have forged pistons and don't try to drive through the detonation. Back off as quickly as possible. We saved this

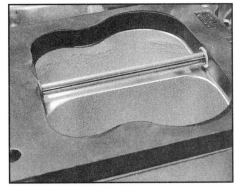

Raising the spray bar 1/2-inch with a couple of spacers increased the torque curve slightly from 3500 to 4000 rpm. We found 10 ft-lbs at 3500 rpm which then tapered back to the previous test level at 4000 rpm.

single plane manifolds. The engine responds much better to nitrous with a single plane manifold as opposed to a dual plane manifold. This is due to the relatively poor fuel distribution as well as the restricted air flow of a dual plane manifold compared to a single plane unit.

We inadvertently proved this point by pushing the limits of our combina-

tion. We pushed it right into a severe detonation; not intentionally, but our misfortune is your, as well as our, learning experience.

In our next test we kept all adjustments the same but with .055/.064 jetting. The fuel jet was drilled. This is displayed as Test 15 and shows the dyno traces of detonation. The power drops way off right away. So if you feel

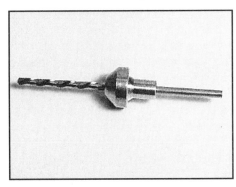

It's easy to check jet sizes, just fit them with a drill of known (i.e. checked) diameter. You also can drill out a smaller diameter jet to fine tune the jetting.

When your mixture is right, the plugs run clean, even though you do get a fuel ring. You don't have to run so rich that you carbon up the plugs.

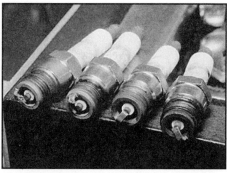

When we tried to lean our most powerful tune we stepped over the line into detonation. Actually these plugs weren't the best nitrous plugs. They have relatively thin electrodes that trap heat and can prematurely force detonation.

These plugs are from the passenger side cylinder bank. The plugs from the photo to the left are from the driver's side. You can see that some cylinders detonated and others didn't. That's the effect of unequal fuel distribution.

this you know to get out of the throttle as quickly as you can. Fortunately we have good forged pistons so we didn't damage the engine, we just toasted a few electrodes. But these toasted electrodes let you see the disparity of fuel distribution. When we tried to find that last bit of power by leaning out the combination, we got detonation.

If you look at the plugs, though you'll notice that not all the electrodes melted. This is because not all the cylinders were detonating. Just about half of them were, and that showed up on the dyno in a big, although negative way.

9.1.4
SPARK PLUG CHOICE
AND FUEL DISTRIBUTION

Regarding spark plugs: the ground strap on spark plugs is usually longer on stock engines because the combustion temperatures aren't that hot. The problem with running these types of plugs with nitrous is that the heat path is so long that the ground strap becomes red hot, the plug turns into a glow plug, and then you get detonation. Even if you use a plug a few steps cooler like the nitrous kit manufacturers tell you to, you can still run into this problem. Again, it is the style of plug, one with a long ground strap that causes the problem, not necessarily the heat range.

What you really need is a plug with a short and wide thick ground strap. Louis Hammel says he even cuts the ground strap so it isn't over the electrode so they spark can jump from the corner of the electrode. He keeps the same gap

because this shortens the strap. You'll find this same approach on racing plugs that have a very short ground strap mounted to the side of the electrode. On these plugs the ground strap is short, thick and wide so it more effectively transfers the heat to the cylinder head.

You choose the heat range of the plug for the type of duty the engine sees. If you go too cold then the plug won't clean itself and the cylinder won't fire. If you go too hot then you can get into detonation and even melt and crack the plug. With nitrous you don't have to use a non-projected style plug, such as a racing plug, but you do have to change the style of ground strap.

9.2.0
SEEKING A 1000 HP
SMALL BLOCK

9.3.1
Piston/Ring Design Tips

The engine component most impacted by nitrous is the piston/ring assembly. The piston and rings, among other things, have to seal cylinder pressure in *and* keep oil out. If you get oil in the combustion chamber it lowers the octane of the fuel mixture leading to detonation. Even though this is a concern, you don't need to order special oil rings. We merely present it for your education.

However, while we are on the subject of rings and by association pistons, we have a few tips from the engineers at Federal-Mogul.

With high horsepower engines you need to be concerned with sinking the heat out of the crown of the piston. If you're using a high flow of nitrous and not a lot of rpm, then you shouldn't need to go to a real thin ring. If you do, you are asking for trouble because a thin ring holds the heat in the crown. The heat in the piston crown has to go somewhere, and the only place it goes is out the side of the piston, through the rings into the cylinder case. Most people think the piston is cooled by oil splashing on the bottom of it. It is true this provides some cooling, but not nearly as much as is commonly supposed, except in cases where supplemental piston oilers have been installed on a racing engine to spray oil on the bottom of the piston crowns. In fact, most cooling of the piston top comes from the heat path through the rings into the cylinder case. This is why when you start losing ring seal you start losing pistons.

Unfortunately, this tends to be a common problem for nitrous users. When you get into detonation with nitrous, it easily bends the ring over the ring lands, and since the piston is really hot the pressure in the combustion chamber will bend the ring land down and start pinching the ring.

One of the more common solutions to this problem is to move the top ring down away from the crown of the piston. But a better solution is putting more space between the rings. Moving the second ring down puts more land material between the top and second ring and provides more support for the top ring. This is important because the top ring is under

This 355-cubic-inch nitrous test engine is used to evaluate heavy nitrous oxide use. This engine was built with expensive but basically off-the-shelf components to make it typical of many nitrous applications in use today. We have seen engines of this displacement make well over 1000 horsepower on nitrous.

tremendous pressure which tries to bend it down over the land. In severe cases you can see a shiny ring on the bottom of the top ring that develops from the distortion. You can tell that the ring has been bent over from the pressure and has ridden on the sharp edge of the ring land. When this happens the ring loses its seal because the ring face is at an angle to the cylinder wall instead of sitting flush.

The ring is still sealing, but what it is not doing is transferring the heat from the piston crown to the cylinder case as effectively as before. The reason is less surface area is now available to transfer heat. This causes the piston to heat to a point that it softens and the pressure forces the ring land to collapse on the second ring. What's weird is that as the second ring binds, the top ring remains free with apparently no problem.

If you are not spinning your motor past 7000 rpm, use a wide ring. Even as wide as 5 \ 64-inch ring would not be detrimental to performance. With nitrous you don't have to run thin

rings in an effort to get that last few horsepower. So why keep wasting pistons and rings; go wide and build reliability.

A nitrous motor and a pro stock engine are two different animals. In an nitrous motor you don't have the

cooling cycle that you do with a naturally aspirated pro stock engine. Nitrous motors have a longer burn time and more thermal loading of the pistons.

This same concept may apply to the technique of moving the whole ring

Callies Stealth crankshaft is a non-twisted forging designed for maximum abuse with nitrous oxide or turbocharging. An ATI Super Damper keeps errant harmonics in check under the heavy stresses imposed by high-horsepower nitrous oxide useage.

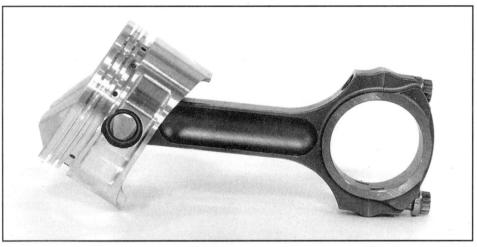

Heavy nitrous useage demands the highest quality pistons and connecting rods available. These JE forged pistons and Oliver 6.0-inch connecting rods are the best insurace you can get for nitrous oxide applications.

JE piston dome is contoured and fitted to the AFR combustion chambers. With modern ignitions, only a moderate fire slot is needed for optimum combustion.

High-quality hardware is essential for nitrous. These ARP cylinder head studs and Fel Pro gaskets are manditory for this application.

pack down. Here's the theory: The cylinder pressure acts hydrostatically, i.e., the pressure will still be as great no matter how far down the piston you put the ring pack. It isn't necessarily a pressure problem, it is a heat problem.

If you were to design a stronger piston design one of the things to request is more material behind the rings because as you move the ring package down you get into an area of the piston that is thinner. When that hap-

pens, the heat has then to flow out of the small cross section of piston skirt and through the rings. The small areas of the piston really take a high thermal load, which tends to soften these areas allowing them to bend. It's like a bottle neck, and pretty soon, as these areas soften, the whole top of the piston wants to come off.

Yet another tip the engineers from Federal-Mogul told us is they want to see a little larger ring gap on the second ring than on the top ring. They say they find a better seal with this gap configuration in hot running conditions. Just how hot is hard to say, but you know the engine is too hot when the rings butt together. What happens in this case is the top ring closes more than the second ring, so even if you set both ring's end-gaps at .025, the top ring gap will be smaller than the second ring gap.

It is important for the gaps to be this way because you want the pressure between the top ring and the second ring to go out the gap of the second ring faster and easier than it gets past the top ring gap. The Federal-Mogul engineers assert you do not want the pressure to equalize before and after the top ring. If that happens there is no pressure to force it against the cylinder wall and seal the bore. If the pressure is equal here then all that's sealing the cylinder is the ring tension, which isn't nearly enough. You have to have a pressure difference above and below the top ring for it to work properly.

This happens far too often to guys

Moroso three-stage dry sump pump and oil pan offer maximum oil control. The full length oil stripper screen keeps oil off the crankshaft, and the three-stage pump keeps the pan empty while providing optimum oil pressure.

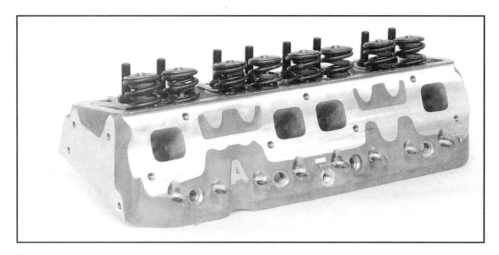

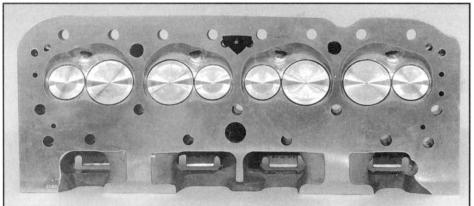

Air Flow Research heads have 2.05-inch intake valves and 1.600-inch exhaust valves. Raised exhaust ports assist quick scavenging of the nitrous charged exhaust flow. Comp Cams' Pacaloy valve springs with titanium retainers ensure high-rpm stability.

CNC-ported Air Flow Research cylinder heads feature high-flow 220cc intake ports with contoured valve guides.

running zero gap rings on nitrous engines. Zero gap rings, especially the second ring, are fine for pro stock engines where you want zero leak. But it just doesn't make any sense because that takes the pressure off the top ring and you lose cylinder pressure. What's going on when you observe horsepower gains with zero gap rings is the friction of the top ring is eliminated, which shows up on the dyno as more power at the flywheel. But the top ring is no longer sealing so you better hope the second ring is good because it now has to do all the sealing and heat transfer work.

9.3.2
Should You Use Hypereutectic Pistons In Your Nitrous Engine?

You don't want to use hyperuetectic pistons in a nitrous engine. They'll take a lot of pressure, you can stand a mountain on them, and they won't break under the weight, but the minute you ring them with the frequency that nitrous causes when it detonates they shatter like glass. They break, they don't melt. In other words, in a nitrous engine, they're all they're cracked up to be.

9.3.3
Bottom End Design tactics

As for the bottom-end, build for strength and reliability and choose rod ratios to make power at some efficient point, somewhere between 6000 and 7000 rpm. Most engines breathe well at these speeds, and with nitrous there is no reason to twist it real tight and tear up the valvetrain. With nitrous you don't have to rely on high rpm to do more work in less time, just put more nitrous and fuel into the engine and it will make as much power as your bottom end will take. Even the Pro Mod creatures don't spend much time past 7000 rpm. They've found they don't have to. Just put more nitrous and fuel, choose the

right gear, put as many gears in the transmission as you can, and go racing. Keep the engine in a narrow power band and you can go insanely fast.

9.3.4
AIMING AND POSITIONING THE NOZZLES AND THEIR INFLUENCE ON AIRFLOW THROUGH THE MANIFOLD.

You want to point the nozzle so the nitrous and fuel are aimed at the port, but the precision with which this is done is not going to help or hinder power that much. Whether the nozzle is angled 45 degrees off the flow path or shooting straight down the port, it probably won't make much difference in a direct port system. If you look at the air flow through the runner at any particular time, it is starting and stopping, pulsing as the valve opens and closes. So there is always going to be a period of time in which the nozzle is flowing with the valve close and no air going down the runners.

HIGH HORSEPOWER
RACE ENGINE COMBINATION

The Westech Racing engine combination is as follows:

**Block: Chevy Bowtie CNC
Crankshaft: Callies lightweight
Rods: Oliver 6.0-inch
Pistons: JE
Rings: Speed Pro
Hardware: ARP Racing Products
Ignition: MSD 6AL w/Crab Cap dist. and crank trigger system
Camshaft part number: 12-000-9
Designation: 300-8/323-7 R1315**

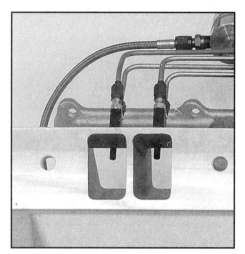

Port Fogger systems viewed through the intake ports. Fogger nozzles introduce nitrous oxide and fuel directly into the high speed airstream.

Duration @0.050: 272/287
Max lift w/1.5RR: 0.660/0.690
Lobe Separation: 113
Intake Centerline: 108
Engine Type: Chevrolet 350
Bore: 4.030
Stroke: 3.480
Displacement: 355
Compression: 13:1
Heads: Air Flow Research 220
Intake: Edelbrock Victor Ram
Carburetor: 2 Holley 830 CFM HP
Exhaust: Hooker 2360 Sprint Car
Nitrous system: Adjustable Port Fogger System
Plugs: NGK 5671-9

Results:
Torque @ 6000 rpm: 489 ft./lb.
Power @ 7600 rpm: 568 hp
With N$_2$O: 844 ft./lb.
With N$_2$O: 969 hp
Manifold Vacuum: 10-in. Hg @ 1000 rpm

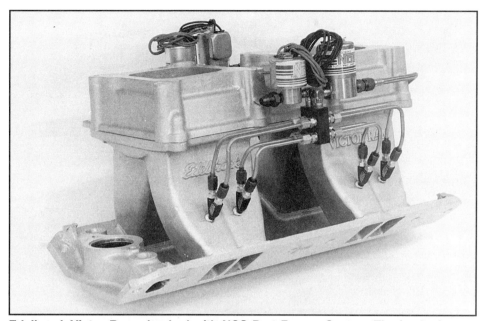

Edelbrock Victor Ram plumbed with NOS Port Fogger System. The intake is port matched to the Air Flow Research aluminum heads. This type of plumbing requires special consideration for throttle linkage and fuel lines.

MSD crank trigger system is used to ensure rock steady ignition timing at all engine speeds. MSD pulleys and crank mandrel provide accurate alignment for the water pump and dry sump pump belt drives.

This view shows the Moroso dry sump drive system with pump mounting and plumbing details. An Edelbrock oval track aluminum water pump is plumbed with separate water lines to introduce water between the center exhaust ports.

POWERFUL PROTECTION

In the race for speed, once the engine is properly tuned, engine builders have to look long and hard for a few extra HP. One of the areas that offers substantial power increases is the lubrication system. We know the quickest and fastest cars waste as little power as possible pumping oil, but finding the right pump combination to deliver just enough oil and not waste power pumping too much oil or pressure is tricky. However, that doesn't mean you

can't take advantage of an efficient oiling system if you're not the most skilled lubrication engineer. The crew at Dyson Oil, makers of Synergyn racing oils and lubricants, make sure of that. This firm offers some of the most sophisticated and effective synthetic racing oils and lubricants on the market. We can say that after seeing the result for ourselves during the dyno testing of this rev happy NOS'd Chevy small block.

To make a long testing-story short, we ran-in the engine with mineral-based oils. You need to do that to get

the clearances right and loosen up the engine. After that we filled the sump with a name-brand synthetic and continued the tuning in preparation of tuning the nitrous shot. After tuning the nitrous system to deliver approximately 375hp consistenly in addition to the engine's 586, hp we felt we topped out this combination at 961 hp. After talking to Ken Duttweiler of Duttweiler Performance we decided to test with Synergyn racing oils in the sump. We were pleasantly surprized by the additional power. With

Low-profile MSD Crab Cap style distributor for use with crank trigger systems and tunnel ram intakes keeps the plug wires routed cleanly.

Moroso dry sump tank is supported by a Moroso dry sump tank stand made specifically for engine dyno testing.

TEST RESULTS

Our test engine was built to be representative of 80 percent of the nitrous motors being used in racing applications. There are outer limits classes where nitrous engines are built to the last degree of technological innovation. We felt this engine represented about as good a piece as the average guy could build at home, given a pretty substantial budget.

With the Nitrous HP camshaft it made about 585 HP and ran easily through 8000 rpm. The design of this cam is such that it takes about 50 horsepower out of the engine in normally aspirated mode. The valve events are timed specifically for nitrous oxide, and they bleed off too much cylinder pressure when nitrous is not being used. Under nitrous conditions, this cam makes big power below 8000 rpm. Using the same principles we just discussed, this 350 approaches the 1000 HP mark. No doubt, there are nitrous smallblocks already exceeding 1000 HP and we think this one will achieve that distinction as well once we get it fully dialed in.

The optional high speed camshaft is designed to spin the motor to very high speeds, which to our way of thinking defeats the primary purpose of nitrous oxide, which is to help the motor makes a ton of

Hooker's #2360 sprint car headers with spread port flanges and stepped primarys are ideal for high-horsepower dyno testing. Because ignition quality is so critical with nitrous oxide, extra care was taken to route the MSD plug wires away from header heat. MSD wire separators are used to prevent crossfiring.

the LTS15W50 we found that when we put some heat into the oil, i.e., the second or third pull, it showed a power increase of around 2% at 960hp. (Reportedly the oil is good to 300°F and is best when it's very hot, above 190°F. With the LTS3W30 we saw almost 10 HP more to push the total to 989hp—almost, but not quite a 1000hp. With performance like that it's no wonder racers like Warren Johnson and Jimmy Shmidt are filling their sumps with the Latest Trick Stuff from Dyson Oil.

Dyson Oil lubricants include Synergen Racing Oil, LTS 3W30, 15W50, SAE 50, and the latest and greatest: LTS-00000 as used in many current Pro Stock motors.

Comp Cams Pacaloy valve springs and titanium retainers teamed with Comp's Hi Tech stainless rockers ensure valve train stability at 8000 rpm plus engine speeds.

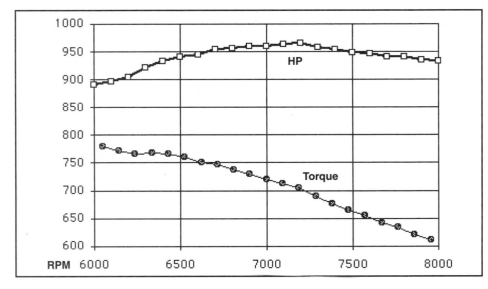

Cam PN	12-000-9
Grind No.	300-8/323-7 R1315
Duration @ .050	278°/287°
Lift	.660/.690
Lobe Separation	113°

Valve Timing @ .050-inch lift	Open	Close
	28° BTDC	66° ABDC
	82° BBDC	25°ATDC
Valve Lash	.026 Int.	.028 Exh.

Optional High Speed Cam for 7500 to 9000 rpm operation

Duration @ .050	272°/283°
Lift	.660/.630
Lobe Separation	110°

Valve Timing @ .050-inch lift	Open	Close
	26° BTDC	66° ABDC
	72° BBDC	31°ATDC
Valve Lash	.026 Int.	.028 Exh.

The camshaft affords significant opportunity to influence the power curve to suit your specific performance requirements. Depending on engine content, the camshaft can make or break your combination. Cams designed specifically for use with nitrous oxide injection, such as Comp Cams Nitrous HP series, can deliver more horsepower by allowing you to run a higher load of nitrous than that possible with more conventional cam timing.

power at reasonable rpm levels so you don't have to abuse it with engine speed. If, however, this is your thing, there is probably some serious high speed power available by using the optional high speed grind.

Your own nitrous application can reach power levels far in excess of what the rest of your drivetrain can probably handle, but hey, that's another book right? If you adhere to the principles set forth in this book you will be assured of getting the maximum power available from whatever nitrous system you happen to be using.

FUEL PROPERTIES

Our big horsepower nitrous engine requires high-quality fuel to make big horsepower. We chose Trick Racing Products' Turbo Racing gasoline. It is specially formulated for the unique needs of high cylinder pressures.

			Distilation °f	
Research Octane	119			
Motor Octane	109		Initial Boiling Pt.	93
R + M/2	114			
Reid Vapor Pressure	6.1		10%	155
Tetra Ethyl Lead gr./gal.	4.19		50%	205
Specific Gravity	.73		90%	235
Color	Mean Green		End Pt.	241

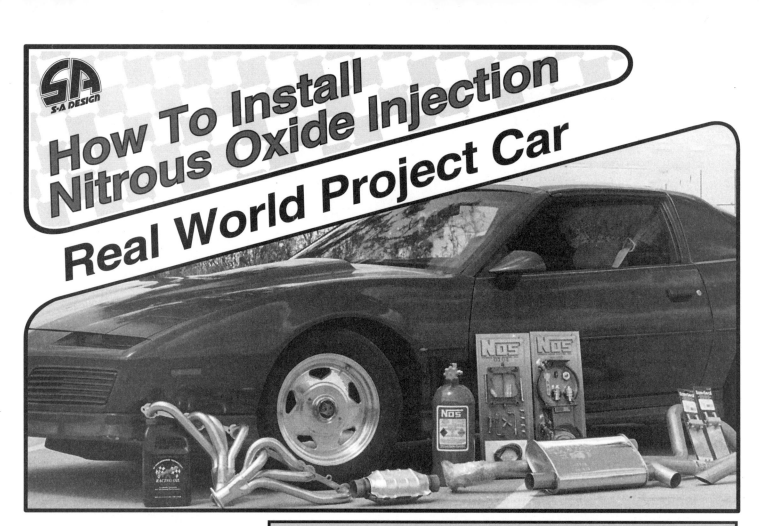

How To Install Nitrous Oxide Injection
Real World Project Car

**BUDGET BULLET:
BUILDING AN 12-SECOND
STREET CAR**

Where do You Start?

Now that you're at least reasonably comfortable using nitrous oxide, you probably want to build a car to take advantage of all your new knowledge. The question is, "Where's the best place to start?" The answer, of course, is at the beginning.

Exactly where you should begin is impossible to say with any certainty. In lieu of that, we'll analyze the process of building a real 12-second street car. One that looks good, sounds good, and is quick as well as reliable. That way, you can just pick up the story at your particular skill level.

When you're planning a project like this, you have to know what you're up against. Ultimately, your adversary is the power of your engine relative to the weight of your car.

Even though you may already have a car and want to build it into a real

What's it take to run 12s? 11s?

The following chart displays the horsepower required to achieve a 12.90 e.t. and an 11.90 e.t. for several vehicle weights. These are the barriers you have to crack and it's not as easy as you think. The formula (shown), developed by Chrysler's drag racing program in the early '70s, assumes an optimized car and an optimized run down the strip. In other words, the shift points, gearing, engine combination, and driveline components were properly chosen and matched and the car had perfect amount of tire slip at the start.

Horsepower to Weight chart:

E.T.	MPH	HP	WT	E.T.	MPH	HP	WT
12.92	100	231	3000	11.95	109	299	3000
12.92	100	239	3100	11.95	109	309	3100
12.92	100	247	3200	11.95	109	319	3200
12.92	100	255	3300	11.95	109	329	3300
12.92	100	262	3400	11.95	109	339	3400
12.92	100	270	3500	11.95	109	349	3500
12.92	100	278	3600	11.95	109	359	3600
12.92	100	286	3700	11.95	109	369	3700
12.92	100	293	3800	11.95	109	379	3800
12.92	100	301	3900	11.95	109	389	3900
12.92	100	309	4000	11.95	109	399	4000

$$E.T. = (5.5) * \sqrt[3]{\left(\frac{wt}{hp}\right) * \left(\frac{(mph - 100)}{400} + 1\right)}$$

We used the Centerforce Dual-Friction clutch and pressure plate assembly because of its superior performance. The weights on the pressure plate increase torque capacity by applying more clamping force to the clutch disc as the engine speed climbs higher.

The Dual Friction clutch plate uses thermal resin compounds which offer more friction at higher temperatures; the other side uses a non-asbestos compound that produces max friction at lower temperatures.

12-second or 11-second street car, you can't get around the power to weight requirements, so beginning here is the most logical. You have to have a specific amount of power for each pound your car weighs to run a specific e.t.

If you look at chart 10.1.0 you can see that, as the weight of the vehicle increases, so does the power needed to maintain the e.t. The obvious conclusion is that lighter is better.

Since we're talking about street cars, most of us mortals on a budget have to chose from the street steel that weights in the 3300- to 3500-lbs range. Don't use the manufacturer's curb weight, which is almost always, undervalued. You have to use the actual weight of the car as you plan to run it down the dragstrip, meaning with fuel and driver factored in.

The vehicle we chose to build, a

1984 Pontiac Trans Am, weighs in at 3400 lbs. At 3400 lbs, the car will need 262 hp to break into the 12s and around 340 hp to move into the 11s. Remember these e.t.'s can only be generated with an optimized combination and a perfect run down the strip. We need a reality check, then, to adjust our model closer to the realities of a production platform.

Patrick Hale, a drag racer/engineer and computer programmer, has marketed a couple of programs, Quarter and Quarter jr., that have detailed mathematical models of the physics behind drag racing. These programs let you make changes to your combination on your computer and show you the results before you start wrenching. These programs are quite accurate, within a few percent of the actual dragstrip performance, or, as a scientist would say, "the empirical data."

Hale uses a slightly different constant with his equations. Instead of the 5.5 constant used with the formula developed for pure, fully optimized, racing vehicles, he uses 5.825, a factor that scales the formula to take into account such things in production cars such as the higher average mass of the flywheels, driveline, and tires and wheels.

Applying Hale's constant to our car we find it will take around 306 HP to drive to a 12.99 e.t. at 105 mph. (see chart 10.1.0.1)

At this point in the process we can't say exactly how accurate Hale's constant will be. But since this is a street car with a torque limitation in the transmission, we'll have to make up time on the top end because we're sacrificing time getting to the 60 foot light. If we altered the suspension to give the hardest launches, we'd lose the transmission and we'd sacrifice street handling performance, which is something you really can't afford to lose in a street-driven car. It becomes a safety issue when you can't avoid obstacles when you are driving on the street.

Back to our reality check. The power we need to reach our e.t. targets calculates out to just over 300 HP instead of 262 HP to turn a 12.90 e.t. and 410 HP instead of 339 HP for an 11.95 e.t. These power levels are well

Chart 10.1.0.1			
E.T.	MPH	HP	WT
12.99	104.93	270	3000
12.99	104.93	279	3100
12.99	104.93	288	3200
12.99	104.93	297	3300
12.99	104.93	306	3400
12.99	104.93	315	3500
12.99	104.93	324	3600
12.99	104.93	333	3700
12.99	104.93	342	3800
12.99	104.93	351	3900
12.99	104.93	360	4000

Chart 10.1.0.2			
E.T.	MPH	HP	WT.
12.06	114.82	350	3000
12.18	113.58	350	3100
12.30	112.38	350	3200
12.42	111.23	350	3300
12.53	110.13	350	3400
12.64	109.07	350	3500
12.75	108.05	350	3600
12.85	107.07	350	3700
12.96	106.12	350	3800
13.06	105.21	350	3900
13.16	104.32	350	4000

within the range of a streetable small block Chevy V8—naturally aspirated, let alone one injected with nitrous oxide—and it is fortunate the vehicle weighs what it does.

The Trans Am's reasonable weight and therefore potentially advantageous power to weight ratio, isn't the over riding reason we chose it, however. That's just a happy coincidence.

10.1.1
PRICE-TO-PERFORMANCE POTENTIAL RATIO

The fundamental reasons we chose the car is a combination of cost, cosmetics, and performance potential.

Prices for 3rd generation F-body cars, Camaro/Firebirds, have fallen sharply. Unlike Mustangs of similar vintage, F bodies are a real bargain. Street Machiners don't seem to be interested in this generation car. That just makes them less expensive to enthusiasts that still like the style and performance potential and are more concerned with performance than being chic.

We paid around $1000 for this machine. The transmission and rearend were toast, but the body and interior were in good shape. Plus, we got a TransAm with good things like 4-wheel disc brakes, a good suspension design, and good styling elements in addition to the lowest Cd of any production car of its time, and is still slightly more slippery than most cars today. Read that as free horsepower on the top end.

10.1.2
EVALUATING THE DRIVELINE

As difficult as it is to make horsepower, it does you no good if the driveline won't deliver the power to the pavement. The driveline includes the clutch, transmission, the driveshaft (for rear drive), and the rearend and axles. We'll go over each of these components separately to show you how we dealt with them on this project.

The transmissions in the '84 Trans Am were weak to begin with, so it was not surprising to find that the previous owner had slam-shifted its insides into mush. That being the case, we had no choice but to get a new or at least a used trans. We opted for a used one, from an '87 TransAm that cost about $600. The '87 and newer T5 five-speeds are stronger than those previously built, and can take about 300 ft/lbs of torque. That gets us close to being able to put 300 hp through the trans. This is just a quick guide, and based on the fact that torque equals hp at 5252 rpm. It's not technically accurate but it's easy to remember and it puts you in the ball park.

The transmission then, is the main limitation of the car, at least as far as e.t.'s are concerned. The trans can only take around 300 ft-lbs, so we have to limit the engine output to around 300 hp. That means we'll have to settle for high 12s at best if we want a car we can still drive somewhat reliably to and from the track. That's okay because a legit, high-12 second street machine is quicker than 90 percent of the posers revving their engines at you at the stoplight.

While we were installing the trans, it made sense to upgrade the clutch and the U-joints. Concerning the U-joints, we simply replaced them with the factory part. At the power levels we're dealing with, the stock units should be heavy-duty enough. We did however install an aftermarket clutch—opting for a Centerforce unit with the firm's exclusive Dual Friction clutch disc. These clutch assemblies operate very smoothly, the design of the mechanism make it so.

10.2.3
INSTALLING A CENTERFORCE DUAL FRICTION CLUTCH AND PRESSURE PLATE

The friction compounds on each side of the clutch plate are optimized for the specific conditions. The flywheel side tends to see more heat and force than the pressure plate side, so the compounds are engineered accordingly. The unique design of the pressure plate increases clamping force at higher rpm, where an engine tends to make power. This is accomplished by using the centrifugal force acting on a series of tiny weights positioned around the end of the pressure plate diaphram spring to increase clamping force. This also provides a side benefit of low pedal pressure which is extremely important for a street driven vehicle. Unless of course you're designing the clutch system as a means to workout and build thigh muscle mass.

Perhaps best of all, installing a Centerforce clutch and pressure plate is a basic remove and replace operation. It's essentially a replacement part that gives high performance.

The next component in the power flow is the rearend. Most enthusiasts assume that the stock 10-bolt rearend is a weak unit. From what we've found it isn't exactly weak, it's just a matter of application. We talked to a couple of drag racers that used to run the 10-bolts in a stock class and they said they'd run the rearends successfully down to low-12 e.t.'s. The spider gears, and posi units tend to break first on these rearends. And since the Performance Locker unit doesn't use the spider gears, we're optimistic about the performance potential. We'll probably have problems with the transmission before we start reaching the edges of the rearend's performance envelope.

That about covers the modifications and the reasoning behind the choices made regarding the driveline. The next step is to evaluate the engine to decide if it is capable or not of using nitrous.

10.1.4
HOW TO EVALUATE A USED ENGINE BEFORE YOU INJECT NITROUS OXIDE

The $1200 price-tag included a fairly tired though still running 305 high output small Chevy V8. Before you install a nitrous system on a used engine, you need to evaluate the engine's health. You can install and use successfully 50 or 60 extra hp from an nitrous system. This is a judgment call; so learn as much as you can about the engine before you squeeze it.

Though it's difficult to tell you all the conditions and observations of when to squeeze and when not to, there are a few common ones you should be aware of. The following assumes that these symptoms aren't caused by incorrect parts, failing fuel system, or malfunctioning ignition system.

Oil Consumption

Of prime concern is oil consumption. Oil in the combustion chambers leads to detonation rather quickly, though it's not completely intolerant. Normally, oil gets into the combustion chamber either through the rings or through the valve guides.

• If it smokes just a little on start up, the most likely cause is oil seeping through the valve guides. Take this as a warning and don't hit the engine hard with nitrous. You can get away with it, but the guides need to be replaced and a rebuild can't be that far behind.

• If the engine smokes under load, you've got oil pushing past the rings and this will definitely cause detonation. *do not* use nitrous on such an engine. It's time to rebuild or buy a remanufactured engine. See the Bonded Motors Product Listing in the reference section.

Timing Variations

If, when you use a timing light and as you are observing the timing mark in the strobe, it jumps around more than about 4° or 5° take that as a sign the timing chain is loose, indicating a high-mileage engine. Apply nitrous cautiously in low doses and count on a rebuild shortly.

Intermittent Misfire

This indicates problems with the ignition system. You probably need to replace the ignition cables and rebuild the distributor. At the very least you need a tune up. These symptom indicate a high-mileage engine and increase the odds of detonation occurring.

Unusual Performance

If you notice any type of unusual performance, such as a rythmic miss, assume you need to rebuild and don't put any nitrous through it. A consistent rhythm to the miss indicates a mechanical problem, for example a flat or worn cam, which only can be repaired by replacing it.

10 .2.0
BUILDING A STRONG STREET SMALL BLOCK CHEVY

After evaluating the engine that came with the car it became clear it would need to be rebuilt. And since that was the case, it seemed a waste to simply rebuild the stock 305 Chevy. If you're going to the trouble of rebuilding the engine, why not rebuild a 350 small block instead ?

That's the direction we took. We found a four-bolt 350 block, crank, and rods in the classified ads for $100, scrounged up a set of stock heads (casting numbers ending 441 and 882 are good for performance) that flowed pretty well, then took them to the machine shop.

The machinist bored the cylinders .030 inch over, align-honed, and decked the block. Just the usual prep before a rebuild. For more information on rebuilding and hot rodding a small block Chevy read John Baechtel's SA design books on the subject.

The only departure from stock was a little head work and the use of Federal-Mogul bearings, gaskets, and forged pistons. Federal-Mogul makes excellent quality components, and since we planned on beating on the engine with nitrous, we wanted to make sure we had heavy duty bearings, rings, pistons— everything to be as reliable as possible. Federal-Mogul makes the right stuff, so we use it.

10.2.1
PRO TIPS FOR BUILDING A NITROUS ENGINE

Of particular importance were the forged pistons. When you're tuning an engine to run lean and mean, you're almost guaranteed to get into detonation at some point. As we said elsewhere in this book detonation is particularly hard on pistons. It's far too easy to break a stock piston under detonation, and hypereutectic pistons are even more sensitive to detonation. The most durable choice for a high-performance engine, running nitrous or not, is a good forged piston.

10.2.2
PISTON DESIGN FOR NITROUS

The engine component most affected by nitrous is the piston. By design this includes the ring pack that controls the amount of oil that gets into the combustion chamber as well as sealing the cylinder bore so the piston can compress the air/fuel mixture, thereby heating it up preparing it for combustion. For more information on this subject, particularly if you're building an engine to make over 700 HP, checkout Chapter 9 The Dyno Sessions, for a detailed look at piston/ring design and how nitrous users can benefit from subtle changes.

10.2.3
BOTTOM END DESIGN TACTICS

As for the bottom-end build for strength and reliability and choose rod ratios to make power at some efficient point, somewhere between 6000 and 7000 rpm. Most engines breathe well at these engine speeds, and with

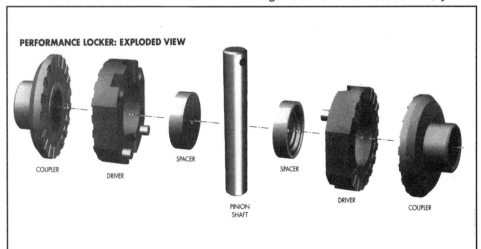

PERFORMANCE LOCKER: EXPLODED VIEW

COUPLER · DRIVER · SPACER · PINION SHAFT · SPACER · DRIVER · COUPLER

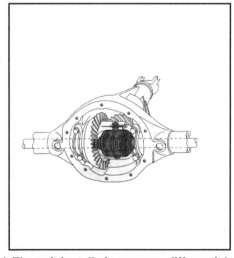

The Performance Locker from Powertrax is a relatively low-cost alternative differential. The unit installs in an open differential, so if your car, like ours, has a posi differential, you'll have to source an open diff. Operation is positive under power. Both rear wheels dig hard to give you good acceleration off the line. On the street you have to turn corners, and you can tell you've got a locker behind you. Ours made a ratcheting sound around corners with an occasional loud "adjustment" as the diff slipped detents between the coupler and driver. From what we've been told from racers that have used the 10-bolt rearends, we should be able to push this unit deep into the 12s. If we get a good deal on a T56 trans, we may test that theory out.

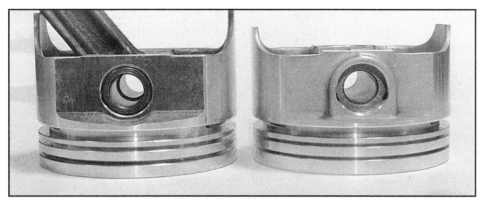

New version of the L2256F piston features a shorter skirt, lighter weight, and revised oil control openings in the oil ring groove.

Speed Pro's new L2256F piston and high-performance ring package are the perfect complement for a nitrous-assisted street engine combination.

nitrous, there is no reason to twist it real tight and tear up the valvetrain.

With nitrous you don't have to rely on high rpm to do more work in less time; just put more nitrous and fuel into the engine and it will make as much power as your bottom end will take. Even the Pro Mod creatures don't spend much time past 7000 rpm. They have found they don't have to. Just put more nitrous and fuel and choose the right gear and put as many gears in the transmission as you can and go racing. Keep the engine in a narrow power band and you can go very very quick.

In this regard the 350's rod ratio (5.7 rod length / 3.48 stroke) of 1.63 puts it right in the 6000 rpm window. If you wanted to make power higher in the rpm window you could go to the expense of a 6.0 inch rod for a ratio of 1.72. This ratio is virtually the same as that used in the Honda 1.6-L VTEC del Sol, one of the world's highest specific output emissions-legal production engines with 1.6 HP/cubic inch. It makes 160 HP near 7000 rpm from 97 cubic inches. Think about that for a second. If a smog legal 350 made 1.6 hp /inch you'd have a 560 HP street legal machine.

The next item to consider is the quality of the rods and rod bolts.

Rod bolts break from the inertial loading at overlap. That is the highest loading the rod bolts ever see. On the compression stroke they see pressure, helping to slow the rod down. On the power stroke, the rod sees compression, the rod bolts aren't stressed, the load on the big end is on the rod side of the bearing. The rod bolt could fall out here and it wouldn't make a difference. When the piston comes up

on the exhaust stroke, there's still a little pressure as it pushes the exhaust gas out until it gets to top dead center. Then the intake valves open, the exhaust valves are just closing, releasing cylinder pressure that was cushioning the piston by absorbing some of the inertial energy. Now the only thing holding the rod and piston to the crank is, you guessed it, the rod bolts. And when you snap off the power at the end of a long straight or the quarter-mile, the butterfly is closed so there is no pressure coming in through the intake; in fact, there's a slight vacuum on a naturally-aspirated car. So in addition to the piston and rod wanting to continue in a straight line through the head, as the crankshaft starts pulling the rod and piston back down the bore the inertia of the rod and piston combine with the opposing force of the crank rotation and can stretch the rod bolt. A few cycles of this and—crunch—there goes your motor. If you're going to stretch a rod bolt, you can only stretch it at overlap. When else can you stretch it?

The problem is accentuated by a motor with a short rod ratio. The shorter the rod, the faster the piston has to slow down and the faster the crank throw will re-accelerate it. On a real long rod ratio motor, the piston hangs around top dead center forever. So the inertial energy of the piston and rod can disipate a little before changing directions.

The structural integrity of the rod is more important in handling compressive loads. If a rod breaks in the middle of beam just under the pin, that is a sign of too much power. So is a bent rod, however severe detonation can also bend rods.

We'll be sticking with the standard 5.7-inch rod with a stock 350 stroke because we don't want to spend money on components needed to keep the engine alive at higher engine speeds. This engine will make its power below 6000 rpm, so the stock Chevy crank and rods will do just fine.

10.2.4
CAM AND VALVETRAIN

While the performance emphasis of the bottom end is on reliability, the emphasis of the top-end is on power. Sure your top-end combinations have to be reliable, but you have far more choices of top-end components compared to the bottom end. Your choices not only affect the reliability of the engine, but directly bear on the shape of the power curve and how much total power the combination is able to produce.

For our purposes, we were looking for a cam that would make the most horsepower higher in the rpm range of the engine. A reasonable rpm range for a street motor is, as we've said, around 6000 to 6500 rpm. At this rpm you can run a good hydraulic lifter cam without having to use expensive components such as titanium spring retainers and locks, or extremely high valve spring rates. We want the engine and the valvetrain to be reliable and perform well for quite a long time.

Cutting right to the chase, we consulted the Comp Cams crew. After explaining our performance goals and the size and type of engine, the tech guy suggested a combination.

He recommended using one of Comp Cams new Nitrous HP camshafts. For our purposes he felt we should use a cam a little larger than what he'd ordinarily suggest. That way we'd get a little more power on top and less torque on the bottom. With nitrous, torque is not the problem, managing it is.

His call was for the Nitrous HP camshaft part number NX268H-13 with 224/236 degrees duration at .050 lift; .477/.490 lift at the valve with 1.5 ratios rockers and a 113° lobe separation angle. This is a hydraulic flat tappet cam that makes power from 2000 to 6200 rpm. Cool. That's right where we'll need it, a fact that'll crystallize when we analyze shift points.

A cam is only part of the valvetrain, so ordinarily we'd have to come up with a balanced set of valve train components. Fortunately Comp Cams makes that easy with matched component kits. A K-kit, part number K12-560-4, includes cams, lifters, springs, retainers, locks, valve seals, a timing set, assembly lube and even Comp Cams decals (you never know when a contingency award opportunity may show itself.) In addition an RP-kit, part number RPM1412-16, puts together a set of Magnum rocker arms and matched push rods.

10.2.5
HEAD PREPARATION

Even though we're trying to keep this project as budget-minded as possible by staying with a stock head, the economic reality is that the cost of stepping up to an aftermarket head, particularly iron, is so minor that it's almost a wash. If you stay with the stock head and pay for the required machining, you're only a few hundred dollars under the price of a new high performance head with much more performance potential. That's the word from D.J. Chemello, of Cylinder Head Specialist in Fullerton, California. It's always tempting, but if you're on a tight budget, you may need to put the $200 somewhere else, especially if you already have a good flowing set of heads.

For us we had a set of casting # 041 heads, so we decided to stay stock and let the crew at Cylinder Head Specialist show us the right way to prepare a set of high-performance heads.

The first thing they do is tag the

head and all the components. They don't want to lose any of your parts, so if your restoring a piece or just need your performance head freshened up, they make sure you get your parts back. The valvetrain components are tumbled in a media mix to clean them, then they oven-cook the heads for several hours to remove most of the grease and oil before putting them through a pressure wash for a final degreasing. After that the heads are Magnafluxed and pressure checked for defects. Then they are quickly painted with a special cast iron paint to keep the heads from rusting. Raw cast iron oxidizes fast. If you're keeping your valves, they bead blast the valve head, clean it, and recut the angles. Or if you like they have a complete line of valves from which to choose.

For performance-oriented or stock heads, they like to use bronze guides. They don't use the inserts, but rather full guides.

Since these heads were to see nitrous, we had them install larger 1.600 exhaust seats and valves. This meant they has to machine the old seat out and put a new hardened seat in. When you have a shop do this make sure they machine away the lip from the smaller valve seat. If you don't, you won't get much more flow than the old seat. You have to remove the head material behind the seat.

Once all the machining is done, the heads are checked and trued on a flat belt sander. After the face is cleaned up, the head is again painted with cast iron paint and sent to the assembler.

The assembler double checks the machining and installs valves and springs. The basic performance package includes a set of swirl polished valves and stock small block springs. The stock springs should be good to 6000 rpm with cams under .50-inch lift.

However, since we needed to spin the engine up to 6500 rpm, we went with the spring package from Comp Cams. We set the spring pressures to 120 lbs/in. on the seat; 320 lb/in. over the nose of the cam. This is approximately the pressure limit for a flat tappet cam and will keep stainless steel valves from floating up to about 6500 rpm. If you install lighter valves, you

can opt for less spring pressure or keep the spring pressure and rev the engine higher.

10.2.6
INTAKE AND EXHAUST

The intake and exhaust systems control and direct the air flow. The intake has the added burden of flowing fuel, at least in this "wet-flow" intake. Port fuel injection intake systems are dry flow, since they don't have to be designed to carry fuel along the port walls to the combustion chamber. How well the engine performs is directly related to how well the intake and the exhaust match the flowing capacities of the head and cam.

10.2.6.1
INTAKE

For our purposes, the Edelbrock Performer RPM intake matched our combination perfectly. The manifold supports enough air flow to let the 350-inch engine make good power up to around 6500 rpm. The #7104 Performer RPM fits spreadbore carbs such as Rochester and Spreadbore Holleys, plus its carb pad accepts square-bore carbs without adapters. (Part number 7101 fits square bore carbs only.)

We had to go with the Performer RPM instead of the standard Performer because we needed the additional rpm to reach our performance goals. The Performer RPM is designed for maximum horsepower with a broad torque curve so it's a good middle-ground choice between the power of a single-plane and the throttle response of a dual-plane. The Performer RPM is .700-inch taller than Performer (#2101) and has provisions to add an oil fill tube but not for exhaust heated or stock-style choke. It accepts the late-model waterneck, air-conditioning, alternator and H.E.I units. It fits cast iron Bowtie heads but not 1987 and later cast-iron heads. Designed especially for spread-bore carburetors such as the Performer RPM Q-Jet #1910.

The additional height was some concern, but after checking the dimensions under the hood, we found that it would fit with very little persuasion.

10.2.6.2
EXHAUST

For the exhaust, we chose to install Dynomax headers with a Dynomax Ultraflow catback system.

The Dynomax ceramic coated headers feature a superior flange-to-engine seal. Any distortion in the plane of a flange surface can cause exhaust gas leakage. DynoMax's computer-controlled, high precision machining means flatter, truer flanges for a better seal.

Headers tune where the power peak occurs. The primary tube diameter affects flow rate, flow rate affects where torque peaks occur in relation to engine speed. Smaller diameter tubes result in the torque peak occurring at lower rpms. Larger-diameter tubes deliver peak torque at higher rpms for racing. Primary tube length affects torque curve. Adding length adds torque below the peak and reduces it above the peak, Shortening primary tubes adds torque above-the-peak, at the expense of below-the-peak torque. Any constriction at bends results in restriction of flow. DynoMax primary tubes have mandrel bends for up to 35% better flow than ordinary, serrated bent tubes. DynoMax's high luster ceramic coated headers are covered 100% inside and out with a long life protective surface. This exclusive coating actually enhances header performance by retaining heat inside the header. The result is easier gas flow and an increase in horsepower. Plus the ceramic coating won't discolor, chip or rust.

The short design of our headers with 1-½ inch diameter primaries flowing into a 2-½ inch collector give it a broad power band. If all we were doing is racing, tuning the headers for more top-end would have been an option, but since the engine will see more street duty than racing action ,the compromise was well worth it.

At the end of the exhaust pipe, an Ultraflow stainless steel muffler with a straight through design for maximum flow mellows the tone without too much restriction. It's all-stainless street construction gives high temperature durability up to 1900° F. It uses continuous roving fiberglass so it won't blow out and produces mellow, yet authoritative, performance sound.

We get maximum flow with mandrel bent 2-½ inch tubing because it maintains a constant cross-section for the smoothest possible, unrestricted exhaust flow. Plus it uses heavy-duty all-aluminized tubing for durability and corrosion resistance and, it's easy to install because DynoMax Systems follow O.E. routing and attach directly to the existing mountings.

10.2.6.2.1
CATALYTIC CONVERTER

We had to replace the converter on this car, which, as it turns out, works to our advantage. Dynomax markets a complete line of replacement converters with more frontal area so they flow more air. The catalytic converter element was melted on this car, probably because the previous owner ran the engine in a state of extremely poor tune. A carbureted engine will put raw fuel into the converter very quickly which, raises the internal temperature to the melting point. It's sort of curious, but you can't just change your catalytic converter. The original must be defective. The following highlights the current EPA regs on the subject:

CATALYTIC CONVERTER INSTALLATION GUIDE

In August 1986, the U.S. Environmental Protection Agency (EPA) issued new proposed guidelines for the construction, efficiency, and installation of aftermarket converters. The EPA guidelines state that replacement converters may be installed only in the following situations:

1. The vehicle is missing a catalytic-converter.

2. A state or local inspection program has determined that the existing converter needs replacement.

3. The vehicle is more than five years old or has more than 50,000 miles and a legitimate need for replacement has been established and documented.

The installer must include the customer's name, address, and the make, model, year, and mileage of the vehicle on the service invoice, along with a stated reason for replacement. Where a state or local government has determined that a converter is damaged or needs replacement, the service or repair facility must retain a copy of the written statement or order by a proper government representative which indicated that the converter should be replaced and attach it to the invoice. Where the replacement need has not been verified by a proper state or local government representative, the customer and a representative of the service or repair facility must sign a statement verifying that replacement is justified. That statement is included in every Walker converter carton.

Furthermore, the EPA has issued the following installation requirements:

1. The converter be installed in one of the three situations outlined above.

2. The converter be installed in the same location as the original catalytic-converter.

3. The converter be the same type as the original converter (i.e. oxidation, three-way or three-way plus oxidation).

4. The converter be the proper one for the vehicle application as determined and specified by the manufacturer.

5. The converter be connected properly to any existing air injection components on the vehicle.

6. The converter be installed with any other required converters for a particular application.

7. The converter be accompanied by a warranty information card to be filled in the installer.

8. Federal law prohibits removal or replacement of properly functioning O.E catalytic converters.

10.2.7
IGNITION SYSTEM/ REV CONTROL

Choosing an ignition wasn't easy. There are so many good products on the market but, to keep the system from getting way too complex, we decided to go with an MSD Super HEI Kit II (pn 8500) with the MSD6AL. The MSD6AL has a built-in soft-touch rev

Comp Cams' Nitrous HP camshaft, part number NX268H-13 has 224/236 degrees duration at .050 lift; .477/.490 lift at the valve using 1.5 ratios rockers. This is a hydraulic flat tappet cam that makes power from 2000 to 6200 rpm. The cam's 113° lobe separation angle reduces overlap a few degrees to improve idle and throttle response when not using nitrous. But it has the duration to handle the additional exhaust of nitrous, allowing your engine combination to take full advantage of a shot of nitrous. Comp Cams makes completing your valvetrain easy with matched component kits. Our cam called for a K-kit (p/n K12-560-4) that includes the cam, lifters, springs, retainers, locks, valve seals, a timing set, assembly lube and even Comp Cams decals. In addition, an RP-kit (part number RPM1412-16) puts together a set of Magnum rocker arms and matched push rods.

control, a feature that takes some of the wiring hassle out of installing the system. This let us keep the stock HEI distributor since this is a computer-controlled car, and get the advantages of the Multiple Spark discharge of the so-named MSD capacitive discharge ignition amplifier.

With the engine safely rpm limited by the ignition system, it also let us wire in the new MSD rpm window switch to limit the window in which the nitrous system will be active. The plan for ignition-based rev control is to set the limit the engine can rev naturally aspirated, then have a slight margin from that to the rpm limit of the nitrous system. It probably limits the engine to 6500 rpm with a nitrous window of 3500 rpm to 6200 rpm. We'll also use a switch on the clutch in addition to the micro switch on the throttle to trigger/deactivate the system. We need the clutch switch to make sure the system is deactivated if your's truly gets his clutch foot and throttle foot slightly out of sync. (See wiring schematic for details.)

That the MSD ignition is such a versatile component certainly factors into our choice, but equally important is that it keeps up with the engine above 4500 rpm where the stock unit typically

causes the engine lose some of its power.

That's a very good thing for performance because you need the rpm to make power to post a good e.t. and mph in the quarter-mile.

For the record the engine combination made around 300 HP as installed in the car. We were hoping for 350 hp, but the single exhaust, though a quite good single exhaust is well, still a single pipe and it just doesn't have the flow to allow much more power through the engine. But remember we're trying to have fun, build a reliable street machine that'll pull consistent 12 second e.t.'s. We're not trying to build the world's quickest street car. Sure, there are plenty of 8-second streeters, but not daily drivers. Don't let anyone tell you lies; the quicker the car, the more it costs. Not only to build, but to maintain.

The engine may only make 300 HP unassisted, but it makes a cool 400 hp on the nitrous. Granted we had to run a little more than advertised to get it, but the cause of that is the dual plane manifold. The Edlebrock Performer RPM is the best dual plane ,but it still makes the air turn and the fuel drops out, so you don't get each cylinder pulling like it could. So it

goes. For more info on this subject checkout the chapter on engine dyno sessions.

10.3
DRAG STRIP TESTING

This has been a long-winded exercise, but please bear with us a little longer. We're finally getting to the fun part–drag strip testing.

Okay, almost. First we're going to model the quarter-mile performance of this combination using Patrick Hale's Quarter Jr. program. He markets a complete line of performance software. The entry-level Quarter Jr. uses the same sophisticated mathematical modeling as the Quarter professional program, but with less intricate input data. Quarter Jr. retails for $95; the Quarter professional program fetches $265. He also has Engine Jr. and Engine Professional, a pair of power simulators with the same pricing structure as The Quarter programs. For the very serious racer, Hale offers a clutch program, a four-

If you have larger exhaust seats installed, make sure the shop removes the excess material behind the seat. If it doesn't, the larger valve and three-angle valve job are all for naught.

Cylinder Head Specialist recommends screw in studs for all high performance heads. Don't try this at home, you need to make sure the head is level and all the angles are perfect.

This shot shows the guide before Cylinder Head Specialist installed the new ones. The older guide castings were taller posing a potential interference problem.

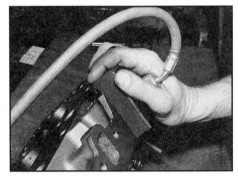

After assembly, the heads are vacuum checked for proper sealing. From this station the heads go to a final visual inspection before being shipped.

Mr. Hale offers a clutch program, a four-link program and a density altitude program. For more information you can contact Racing Systems Analysis, P.O. Box 7676, Phoenix, AZ 85011 (602) 241-1301.

The reason simulating the run is a better idea than just blasting down the track, is you can try as many leave scenarios as you want. The leave, or launch or whatever you like to call it is the most critical segment of a drag race. It's also the hardest to control, most certainly this is so when applying nitrous.

Check out figures 10.3 a, b. These charts show the best theoretical quarter mile performance with and without nitrous on Goodyear 255/50-16 Eagle Formula 1 street tires. As you can see the leave rpm is quite different

between the two runs but the 60 ft time is almost identical. That's a clue to managing the leave. It'd be almost impossible to have the full dose of

nitrous hit and be able to manage the clutch slip as demanded by our model. So we need a different activation tactic.

Given enough time to experiment, you could probably come up with a few dozen or more schemes with which to tackle this problem. However, why re-invent the wheel, or the nitrous activation scheme when NOS already has two good solutions in the box.

The first one is a low bucks approach, using off the shelf components. This tactic involves waiting until second gear to activate the full dose of nitrous. By installing a micro switch to respond to the position of the shift lever, one can quickly design a system that wont activate while in first gear. With this design we'll probably spin the tires a little but the torque multiplication is less than in first gear so it should hook up better. We probably won't reach the 12.35 e.t. because driving errors will occur. The most we expect is to get into the 12.70s. We'll most likely take more time between shifts and not get as good of a launch but you never know.

Perhaps the best solution is to use NOS's progressive time based controller. It's more expensive because you have buy the controller and with a wet manifold system you have to get an installation kit (PN00050) which consists of an additional nitrous solenoid, adaptors and relay to operate the second unit. NOS's Time Based Progressive Nitrous controller gives you the most control over the dynamics at the starting line but a trade-off of

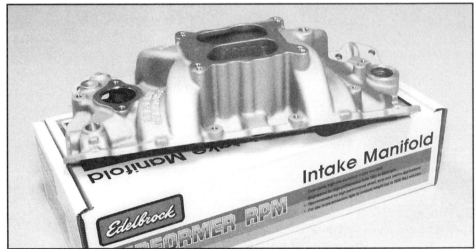

The Edelbrock Performer RPM intake manifold in concert with the cam, a reasonably good set of head and exhaust system let the engine pull to 6000 rpm.

schedule. Because this system pulses the solenoid, just like a fuel injector only much slower, you have to check the solenoids frequently and on a regular basis.

Using this nitrous oxide controller allows you to control the power from your NOS nitrous oxide injection kit to maximize traction and minimize et. It makes compensating for changes in starting line and track conditions as easy as turning a knob.

By only applying as much power as your vehicle can handle at the starting line, you will be able to prevent excess wheel slippage This is accomplished by adjusting the "initial power" knob to the point where maximum acceleration on launch is achieved, just prior to excess tire slippage.

The knob that adjusts the rate at which maximum power is attained can then be adjusted to bring power in as aggressively as traction limitations will allow.

Figure 10.3-E shows representative rates of how power can be adjusted to fit your situation. In example 'A" 20% power is engaged when the system is activated. Power is increased linearly over the next five seconds until full power is reached.

This unit can also be used to delay the flow of nitrous into your engine. The delay feature is engaged by setting the "initial power" knob in the area marked "delay".

Setting the knob all the way counterclockwise will delay the start of nitrous and fuel flow 20% of the time that the "time to full power" knob is set at. Setting the knob halfway between power = 0 and all the way counterclockwise, will delay the start of nitrous and fuel flow 10% of the time at which the "time to full power" is set at.

Example "B" shows use of the delay feature. The plot shown is accomplished by setting the initial power knob all the way counterclockwise and the time to full power setting at 5 seconds.

- 20% of 5 seconds is 1 second.
- 20% of 4 seconds is .8 second.
- 20% of 3 seconds is .6 second.
- 20% of 2 seconds is .4 second.
- 20% of 1 second is .2 second.

This combination presents another hurdle, in so far as successfully using the time-based controller. Since the car is a manual transmission, we'll be activating and deactivating the system several times during the run. So we can't, nor is it necessary, given the modest power increase, use the delay feature nor can we set the time to full power much more than a second or so. To compromise, we'll start with 20% initial power and quickly ramp up to full power with a second or less. That way when we shift, we won't be wasting time to get to full power. On the leave, one-second should put us around the 30 ft mark with all the weight that's going to be transferred to the rear wheels, so we have more grip to grab the additional horsepower.

That's the street tire strategy. And it worked almost exactly as planned. We found after getting the timing on the clutch release down we could start with a little more initial power, at least on the day we tested, though this will change with track conditions. And by extending the time to full power to about 1.5 seconds, we were getting a good pull off the line, stopping the 60-ft clocks with a best of 2.10. With more time in the car we could probably find the tenth-second on the start to improve the e.t., but all in all we are very happy to get a street tire equipped car to run 12.65 @114 mph without breaking any parts.

We also wanted to simulate how the car would perform with a set of Goodyear Stock and Super Stock class slicks. Again, this car offers limited space in the wheel wells so we can't put a huge tire under it. It's a very tight fit to get the 28.0 x 9.0-15s under it. We had to go back to the stock springs and a few other tricks to get the tires in the wheel wells.

As you can see in Figures 10.3 C and D a taller, stickier tire gives you lots of traction and a slower-revving engine through the course. The big tire hurts the naturally aspirated performance slightly, but more than made up for that when we put the squeeze on.

With a big reserve in traction, we could get very aggressive with the nitrous controller. Actually, we could

hit it with full power instantly but to save the transmission, we delayed full power about .25-.5 second with an initial setting of 80%. This helped the transmission, driveshaft, and rearend absorb the shock. The slicks wrap up also cushions the application of force.

With the slicks and nitrous we were predicting a best possible run of 11.99 at 114 mph. Well, we didn't quite get that, but a 12.20 at 113 mph wasn't all that bad. The slicks give the car the potential to run in the high 11s. In this territory you have to start worrying about the rearend and the T-5 transmission.

Bob Hanlon of Hanlon Motorsports (3621 St. Peter's Rd, Eleverson, PA 19520; 610/469-2695; fax 2994) says a World Class T5 in good condition should be able to pull low 12s in these cars. He says what really hurts these transmissions is constant speed shifting and abuse. But if you do a good rebuild on a wrecking yard '87 and later World Class T5 trans you should be safe to at least low 12s and even to the high 11s if you watch it and rebuild it often. He has trick parts for the T5 that lets some of his more experienced customers run low 10 second e.t.'s with a T5 in a Mustang, so don't believe everything you hear or read about the T5 transmission. Just call Hanlon Motorsports for the full scoop on these transmissions and his upgrades.

Here's a few of his tips to keep you T5 alive:

Don't power shift it constantly. Save that for the track.

Don't install the most aggressive clutch you can find; you don't need more than a 10.5-inch heavy duty clutch. That's about it.

You can run low 12s and if you don't abuse it, it can live a reasonably long and happy life.

To give you an idea, he says he had a Mustang with a dynotested 462 hp with a Proshifted (one of his build levels) T5 that ran low 11s without breaking. He couldn't run them forever but they hung in there for several race days before he rebuilt them.

The bottom line, says Hanlon, is that low 12s in a T5 tranny'd pony car is no problem. We agree.

MSD 6AL ignition box was installed to complement the HEI II distributor kit which is designed specifically for computer controlled ignition systems.

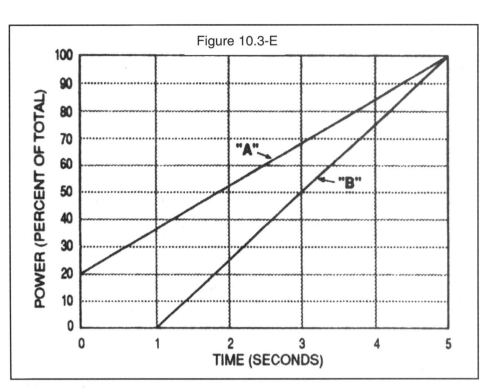

Figure 10.3-E

A Fluidampr harmonmic balancer ensure smoothe engine operation, especially when the nitrous starts adding tones of cylinder pressure.

Synergyn racing oil offers a little more power once your street engine has been well broken in. After extensive drag testing we cut open the oil filter and found no metal flakes or contaminants.

Fig 10.3. A QUARTER jr 2.02
No NOS 300hp 5000rpm leave street tires

Time	Dist	MPH	Accel	Gear	RPM
0.00	0	0.0	0.71 (s)	1	5,000
.275/0.00	Rollout	4.7	0.70 (s)	1	5,000
1.32	30	25.1	0.69 (s)	1	5,000
2.00	60	34.6	0.52	1	5,430
2.35	79	38.3	0.45	1	6,000
2.55	90	40.9	0.57	2	4,230
4.65	246	59.1	0.33	2	5,990
4.77	256	60.0	0.36	3	4,660
4.85	263	60.7	0.38	3	4,230
5.57	330	65.4	0.30	3	4,520
8.58	660	83.4	0.26	3	5,610
9.94	833	90.1	0.21	3	6,000
10.00	841	90.4	0.23	4	5,210
10.15	860	91.2	0.24	4	4,530
11.17	1,000	95.5	0.19	4	4,710
12.26	1,157	100.0	0.18	4	4,900
13.35	1,320	104.3	0.18	4	5,100

ELAPSED TIME:13.35 SEC   SPEED 103.4 MPH

Fig 10.3. B QUARTER jr 2.02
NOS-400hp 3000rpm leave- street tires

Time	Dist	MPH	Accel	Gear	RPM
0.00	0	0.0	0.71 (s)	1	3,000
.267/0.00	Rollout	4.8	0.71 (s)	1	3,000
1.31	30	25.1	0.70 (s)	1	3,910
1.99	60	35.2	0.69	1	5,460
2.24	74	38.7	0.60	1	6,000
2.44	85	41.9	0.69 (s)	2	4,290
3.96	199	59.5	0.45	2	6,000
4.01	203	60.0	0.46	3	5,160
4.16	217	61.7	0.48	3	4,270
5.32	330	71.8	0.39	3	4,910
7.66	608	89.6	0.30	3	5,990
7.86	635	91.0	0.32	4	4,540
8.04	660	92.1	0.27	4	4,590
9.38	848	100.0	0.26	4	4,930
10.00	941	103.5	0.26	4	5,070
10.38	1,000	105.6	0.25	4	5,170
12.35	1,320	115.7	0.22	4	5,610

ELAPSED TIME:12.35 SEC   SPEED 114.8MPH

Fig 10.3-C
QUARTER jr 2.02
No NOS-slicks 4400 rpm launch

Time	Dist	MPH	Accel	Gear	RPM
0.00	0	0.0	0.67	1	4,400
.304/0.00	Rollout	4.9	0.66	1	4,400
1.33	30	24.5	0.66	1	4,400
2.03	60	34.1	0.53	1	4,650
2.98	115	44.2	0.42	1	6,000
3.18	128	46.5	0.51	2	4,170
4.81	256	60.0	0.40	2	5,320
5.61	330	65.8	0.31	2	5,810
5.96	364	68.1	0.29	2	6,000
6.16	384	69.5	0.33	3	4,200
8.62	660	83.1	0.25	3	4,950
10.00	835	90.1	0.22	3	5,330
11.21	1,000	95.7	0.22	3	5,630
12.24	1,148	100.0	0.18	3	5,860
12.84	1,238	102.3	0.17	3	5,990
12.95	1,254	102.8	0.19	4	4,890
13.04	1,267	103.2	0.20	4	4,510
13.38	1,320	104.4	0.16	4	4,550

ELAPSED TIME:13.38 SEC   SPEED 103.7 MPH

Fig 10.3-D
QUARTER jr 2.02
NOS Slicks-4500 rpm launch

Time	Dist	MPH	Accel	Gear	RPM
0.00	0	0.0	0.88	1	4,500
.264/0.00	Rollout	5.7	0.88	1	4,500
1.16	30	28.1	0.87	1	4,500
1.77	60	38.3	0.67	1	5,270
2.23	88	44.5	0.54	1	6,100
2.43	102	47.4	0.65	2	4,290
3.56	191	60.0	0.48	2	5,370
4.47	277	68.6	0.39	2	6,090
4.68	298	70.5	0.42	3	4,300
4.98	330	72.8	0.36	3	4,430
7.69	660	92.6	0.30	3	5,510
8.90	831	100.0	0.26	3	5,900
9.63	939	103.9	0.24	3	6,100
9.83	971	105.1	0.26	4	4,600
10.00	996	105.9	0.23	4	4,630
10.02	1,000	106.0	0.23	4	4,630
11.99	1,320	115.4	0.21	4	5,010

ELAPSED TIME: 11.99 SEC   SPEED 114.6 MPH

The NOS powershot is the system of choice for our real world project Firebird.

A Progressive Nitrous Controller and RPM Window Switch.

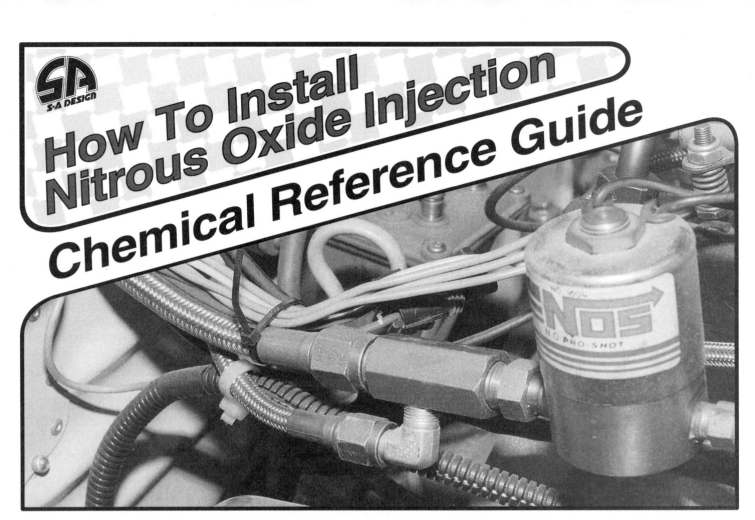

How To Install Nitrous Oxide Injection
Chemical Reference Guide

CHEMICAL REFERENCE DESCRIPTION

Nitrous oxide at room temperature and atmospheric pressure is a colorless gas with a barely perceptible sweet odor and taste. It is nonflammable but will support combustion. At elevated temperatures, nitrous oxide decomposes into nitrogen and oxygen. Decomposition in the absence of catalysts is negligible at temperatures below 1200°F (649°C). Nitrous oxide is moderately soluble in water, alcohol, and oils. Unlike some higher oxides of nitrogen, nitrous oxide does not affect the acidity of water solutions.

GRADES AVAILABLE

Nitrous oxide is available in medical, commercial, and high-purity grades. The medical (USP) grade is the most widely used. Manufacturers typically produce nitrous oxide for this use to the specification published in the United States Pharmacopoeia/National Formulary. [1]CGA G-8.2, Commodity Specification for Nitrous Oxide, describes the requirements for particular grades of nitrous oxide. [2] Other specifications to meet

particular requirements are available from suppliers. Table I, from CGA G-8.2, presents the component maxima, in parts per million (mole/mole) unless otherwise shown, for specific grades of nitrous oxide, also known as quality verification levels. The absence of a value in a listed quality verification level does not mean to imply that the limiting characteristic is or is not present, but merely indicates that the test is not required for compliance with the specification.

USES

The major use of nitrous oxide is for anesthesia and analgesia. It is also used for cryosurgery. Nitrous oxide also finds use as an oxidizing gas for atomic absorption spectro photometry, a propellant for pressure or aerosol products (whipped cream is most prevalent), and a fuel oxidant for racing vehicles. Some product for this latter application 1. supplied with an additive to deter abuse of the product. Nitrous oxide is also used in the manufacture of semiconductors.

PHYSIOLOGICAL EFFECTS

Nitrous oxide's primary physiological effect is central nervous system (CNS) depression. At high concentrations, anesthetic levels can be obtained, but the low potency of nitrous oxide necessitates concomitant administration of other depressant drugs. Nitrous oxide has been associated with several side effects from long-term exposure. The most strongly substantiated effect is neuropathy. Epidemiological studies also suggest leto-toxic effects and higher incidents of spontaneous abortion in exposed personnel. Although no cause-and-effect relationship has been firmly established, exposure to the gas should be minimized.

Inhalation of nitrous oxide without the provision of a sufficient oxygen supply may be fatal or cause brain damage. Due to the concern over long-term exposure effects, release of the product into general work areas should be minimized. The National Institute for Occupational Safety and Health (NIOSH) has recommended limits of 25 ppm for hospital operating rooms and 50 ppm for dental offices measured on an eight-hour time-weight-

NITROUS OXIDE AT A GLANCE

CHEMICAL SYMBOL: N20

Synonyms: Nitrogen monoxide, dinitrogen monoxide, laughing gas
CAS Registry Number: 10024-97-2
DOT Classification: Nonflammable gas
DOT Label: Nonflammable gas
Transport Canada Classification: 2.2
UN Number: UN 1070 (liquefied gas); UN 2201 (refrigerated liquid)

PHYSICAL CONSTANTS

	U.S. Units	SI Units
Chemical formula	N2O	N2O
Molecular weight	44.0128	44.0128
Specific volume		
at 59°F (15°C) and 1 atm	8.538 ft3/lb	0.533 m3/kg
at 70°F (21-1°C) and 1 atm	8.726 ft3/lb	0.5447 m3/kg
Specific gravity of		
the gas (air= 1)	1.5297	1.5297
Density of the gas		
at 59°F (15°C) and 1 atm	0.1172 lb/ft3	1.877 kg/m3
at 70°F (21.1°C) and 1 atm	0.1146 lb/ft3	1.947 kg/m3
Critical density	28.15 lb/ft3	450.4 kg/m3
Boiling point at 1 atm	-127.4°F	- 88.5°C
Latent heat of vaporization		
at boiling point	161.8 Btu/lb	376.1 kJ/kg
at 32°F (0°C)	107.5 Btu/lb	249.9 kJ/kg
at 70°F (21-1°C)	77.7 Btu/lb	180.6 kJ/kg
Latent heat of fusion		
at triple point	63.9 Btu/lb	148.5 kJ/kg
Specific heat of the gas		
at 59°F (15°C) and 1 atm Cp	0.207 Btu/(lb)(°F)	0.866 kJ/(kg)(°C)
at 59°F (150°C) and 1 Cv.	0.158 Btu/(lb)(°F)	0.665 kJ/(kg)(°C)

	U.S. Units	SI Units
Ratio of specific heats		
at 59°F (15°C) and 1 atm Cp/Cv	1.303	1.303
Solubility in water, vol.and 1 atm		
at 32°F (0°C)	1.3	1.3
at 68°F (20°C)	0.68	0.68
at 77°F (25°C)	0.59	0.59
Viscosity of the gas		
at 32°F (0°C)	0.326 lb/(ft)(hr)	0.135 x 10-3 Pa(s)
at 80°F (27°C)	0.359 lb/(ft)(hr)	0.149 x 10-3 Pa(s)
Thermal conductivity of the		
gas at 32°F (0°C)	0.0083 Btu (ft)/h(ft2)(°F)	0.0144 W/m(°C)
at 212°F (100°C)	0.0135 Btu (ft)/h(ft2)(°F)	0.0233 W/m(°C)

ed average basis. Contact with liquid nitrous oxide can freeze skin tissue and must be avoided. The American Conference of Governmental Industrial Hygienists has adopted a time-weighted average threshold limit value of 50 ppm (90 mg/m3) for an eight-hour workday exposure to nitrous oxide.

Warning: Misuse of nitrous oxide can cause death by reducing the oxygen necessary to support life. Nitrous oxide abuse can impair an individual's ability to make and implement life-sustaining decisions.

MATERIALS OF CONSTRUCTION

Nitrous oxide is non-corrosive and may therefore be used with any of the common, commercially available metals. Because of its oxidizing action, however, all equipment being prepared to handle nitrous oxide, particularly at high pressures, must be free of oil, grease, and other readily combustible materials. Nitrous oxide may cause swelling of some elastomers.

SAFE STORAGE, HANDLING, AND USE

Nitrous oxide will support combustion. It must be kept away from oil, grease, and other combustible materials. Never permit oil, grease or any other readily combustible substance to come in contact with cylinders or other equipment containing nitrous oxide.

Store and use nitrous oxide with adequate ventilation. Containers that become exposed to fire, including bulk storage tanks, could rupture violently if subject to localized heating.

See Chapter 5 for general guidelines concerning the safe storage and handling of compressed gases, including nitrous oxide. Detailed recommendations for nitrous oxide storage locations are given in CGA G-8.1, Standard for Nitrous Oxide Systems at Consumer Sites. [4] Requirements for nitrous oxide systems in hospitals and other health care facilities are found in NFPA 99, Standard for Health Care Facilities. [5]

DISPOSAL

Nitrous oxide is not harmful to the environment and can be released to the atmosphere, provided ventilation is adequate for protection of personnel in the immediate vicinity of the release point. Do not release in the vicinity of building air intakes.

HANDLING LEAKS AND EMERGENCIES

Turn off ignition sources in the general area of the leak if possible. Nitrous oxide is nonflammable but is an oxidizer which can cause or intensify fires. Evacuate the area to prevent asphyxiation. Use self-contained breathing apparatus to enter the area. Provide as much ventilation as possible. Avoid contact with liquid spills. Contact supplier for assistance.

FIRST AID

People acutely exposed to high levels of nitrous oxide should be immediately removed from exposure, after which symptoms should rapidly reverse. If obtundation (dulling or blunting of sensitivity, such as to pain) is present, oxygen should be administered. Mechanical ventilation should be instituted in the event of respiratory arrest. Vomiting may occur as the person awakes. In order to prevent aspiration, exposed individuals should be placed on their side with their head at the level of or slightly lower than their body.

Editor's note: The following was extracted from the 1996 Grollier's Encyclopedia CD for Macintosh

OXYGEN

Oxygen is a gaseous chemical element in Group VA of the periodic table. The chemical symbol for atomic oxygen is O, its atomic number is 8, and its atomic weight is 15.9994. Elemental oxygen is known principally in the gaseous form as the diatomic molecule, which makes up 20.95% of the volume of dry air. Diatomic oxygen is colorless, odorless, and tasteless.

PHYSICAL AND CHEMICAL PROPERTIES

Three naturally occurring isotopes of oxygen have been found: one with mass 16 (99. 759% of all oxygen), one with mass 17 (0.037%); and one with mass 18 (0.204%). The rarer isotopes, principally the latter, find their major use in labeling experiments used by scientists to follow the steps of chemical reactions.

If oxygen at a pressure of one atmosphere is cooled, it will liquefy at 90.18 K (-182.97 deg C; -297.35 deg F), the normal boiling point of oxygen, and it will solidify at 54.39 K (-218.76 deg C; -361.77 deg F), the normal melting point of oxygen. The liquid and solid forms of oxygen have a pale blue color. Several different structures are known for solid oxygen: solid type III, from the lowest

temperatures achievable to 23.66 K; type II, from 23.66 to 43.76 K; and type I, from 43.76 to 54.39 K. The critical temperature for oxygen, the temperature above which it is impossible to liquefy the gas no matter how much pressure is applied, is 154.3 K (-118.9 deg C; -181.9 deg F). The pressure of liquid and gaseous oxygen coexisting in equilibrium at the critical temperature is 49.7 atmospheres.

Molecular diatomic oxygen is a fairly stable molecule requiring a dissociation energy (the energy required to dissociate one mole of molecular oxygen in its ground state into two moles of atomic oxygen in its ground state) of 493.6 kilojoules per mole. The molecule is dissociated by ultraviolet radiation of any wavelength shorter than 193 nm. Solar radiation striking stratospheric oxygen dissociates it into atomic oxygen for this reason. The atomic oxygen formed in this fashion is capable of reacting with oxygen to form OZONE.

CORROSION

Many direct, uncatalyzed reactions of oxygen do not occur rapidly at room temperature. This fact has a number of important consequences. One of these consequences has to do with the use of metals as structural materials. Metals that are used in construction, such as iron (principally as steel) and aluminum, form highly stable oxides. For example, the oxidation of aluminum has a significant tendency to occur. However, in spite of this tendency, the reaction occurs so slowly at room temperature that it can be said for most practical purposes not to occur at all, and for this reason aluminum is an appropriate and widely used structural material. The slowness of this reaction is due in part to the stability of the oxygen-oxygen bond and in part because of a very thin, protective layer of oxide that forms on the surface of the aluminum. The oxidation of iron is a complex process involving impurities in the iron, as well as water and carbon dioxide. This oxidative destruction, or rusting, of iron and steel—which are among our most important structural materials—is extremely costly to modern societies.

REACTIVITY

There is a marked difference between the rates of reactions with oxygen at

room temperature and the rates at elevated temperatures. Many substances that do not react rapidly with oxygen in air at temperatures below 100 deg C will do so at 1000 deg C with a strong evolution of heat (exothermically). For example, coal and petroleum can be stored indefinitely at the temperatures encountered under normal climatic conditions, but they readily oxidize, exothermically, at elevated temperatures.

The most common compounds of oxygen are those in which the element exhibits a valence of two. This fact is associated with the electronic structure of atomic oxygen; this atom requires two additional electrons to fill its outermost energy level. Examples of divalent oxides are numerous among well-known substances such as water; carbon dioxide; aluminum oxide; silicon dioxide; the silicates, calcium carbonate or limestone; and sulfur dioxide. Oxygen is also known to have other valences, such as in the PEROXIDES, of which hydrogen peroxide is an example.

The direct reaction of oxygen with another element frequently follows the pattern discussed above; that is, it does not occur rapidly or at all at room temperature but is strongly exothermic, and once oxidation is initiated the evolved heat raises the temperature of the reactants such that the reaction is self-sustaining. Examples of such reactions are with the elements magnesium, carbon, and hydrogen. Magnesium and carbon burn in air once the reaction is initiated, and a hydrogen-oxygen mixture can react explosively when the reaction is initiated by a flame or spark. The explosion of a hydrogen-oxygen mixture is an extremely fast reaction and occurs because of the formation of atomic oxygen in the exploding mixture.

USES

Pure oxygen is used extensively in technological processes. It is used in the welding, cutting, and forming of metals, as in oxyacetylene welding, in which oxygen reacts with acetylene to form an extremely hot flame. Oxygen is added to the inlet air (3 to 5%) in modern blast furnaces to increase the temperature in the furnace; it is also used in the basic oxygen converter for steel production, in the manufacture of chemicals, and for rocket propulsion.

Oxygen is also used in the partial combustion of methane (natural gas) or coal (taken here to be carbon) to make mixtures of carbon monoxide and hydrogen called synthesis gas, which is in turn used for the manufacture of methanol. Processes in which combustible liquids are produced from coal will become increasingly important as petroleum resources become further depleted.

PRODUCTION

Oxygen is conveniently produced in the laboratory by heating mercuric oxide or potassium chlorate to moderately high temperatures. The production from mercuric oxide is the method that was employed by Joseph Priestley, and the production from the potassium chlorate method commonly used by students in today's laboratories. Oxygen is liberated when solid potassium chlorate is heated to 400 deg C or, when manganese dioxide is added as a catalyst, to 200 degrees C. The liberated oxygen can be collected by water displacement because of the low solubility of oxygen in water.

Oxygen can also be produced in the laboratory by the electrolysis of water, a process that reverses the violent hydrogen-oxygen reaction discussed previously. When a current is passed through water the liquid is decomposed at the electrodes. This method is also used to produce oxygen on a commercial scale when a high-purity product is desired.

The more economical, and therefore preferred, method for the commercial production of oxygen is the liquefaction and distillation of air. The air is cooled until it liquefies, principally by being made to do work in a rotating expansion turbine, and the resulting liquid air is fractionated by a complex distillation process. The gaseous oxygen produced in this fashion is shipped in pressurized cylinders or, as is often the case when large amounts are involved, through pipelines to nearby industrial plants.

–Hugo F. Franzen

Bibliography: Asimov, Isaac, Building Blocks of the Universe, rev. ed. (1974); Bannister, J. V., ed., The Biology and Chemistry of Active Oxygen (1984); Brown, T. L., and LeMay, H. J., Jr., Chemistry, 3d ed. (1988); DeLeo, J. D., Fundamentals of Chemistry (1988); Ebbing, D. D., General Chemistry, 2d ed. (1987); Gilleland, M. J., Introduction to Chemistry (1986); Greenwood, N. N., and Earnshaw, A., Chemistry of the Elements (1984); Rodgers, M. A., and Powers, E. L., eds., Oxygen and Oxy-Radicals in Chemistry and Biology (1981); Seese, W. S., and Daub, G. W., Basic Chemistry, 5th ed. (1988).

TRANSFER PUMP INSTRUCTIONS P/N 14251

Your NOS nitrous oxide transfer pump is designed for high-speed filling of NOS nitrous oxide bottles. For proper performance, it is necessary that all instructions be followed carefully. Please read through the instructions and safety tips thoroughly before attempting to use your transfer pump. If you have any questions about its operation or components, call the NOS Technical Department.

SAFETY TIPS

• Never directly inhale nitrous oxide. When inhaled in large quantities, nitrous oxide can cause respiratory ailments or in extreme cases, death via suffocation.
• Never allow escaping nitrous oxide to contact skin. Nitrous oxide discharges at - 130 degrees Fahrenheit. If allowed to contact skin, it will cause severe frostbite.
• Never overfill any compressed gas cylinder. Maximum weight that any NOS cylinder should weigh is clearly labeled on the side of the cylinder.
• Always wear hand and eye protection when performing nitrous oxide transfer operations.
• Always use an airline water trap.
• Never permit oil, grease, or any other readily combustable substances to come in contact with cylinders, valves, solenoids, hoses and fittings. Oil and certain gases (such as oxygen and nitrous oxide) may combine to produce a flammable condition.
• Never deface or remove any markings which are used for content identification on compressed gas cylinders.
• Nitrous bottle valves should be closed when transfer pump is not in use.
• Keep valves closed on all empty bottles to prevent accidental contamination.
• After storage, open nitrous bottle valve for an instant to clear opening of any possible dust or dirt.
• Notify supplier of any condition which might have permitted any foreign matter to enter valve or bottle.

• Never drop or violently strike bottle.
• Do not use an air line oiler with this pump.
• Do not over tighten AN style fittings. They can easily be damaged.

SYSTEM REQUIREMENTS

The transfer pump is driven by compressed air. Your air compressor must be capable of producing a working line pressure of at least 50 psi. In general, the higher the line pressure, the more effective the pump. Maximum operating pressure should be limited to about 125 psi.

The air supply must be clean and free of oil and water contaminants. A high-quality water trap should be used upstream of the transfer pump. Do not use an air line oiler.

Air lines and filters should be a minimum of 1/4-inch NPT.

Use Teflon paste on pipe threads. Avoid Teflon tape. If used incorrectly, Teflon tape residue can lodge in the transfer pump or your nitrous system.

KIT COMPONENTS

Before assembling and attempting to use your transfer pump, compare the components you received with those shown in Figure 1 and listed in Table 1. If any components are missing or damaged, contact NOS technical department at 714/821-0592 for assistance.

Item	Description	Quantity	NOS P/N
(1)	Transfer Pump	1	14251 -S
(2)	Bottle Stand	1	14230-S
(3)	6AN Bottle Nut Filter	1	14231-S
(4)	Bottle Washer	2	16210-S
(5)	6-ft 6AN Hose	1	15430-S
(6)	1/4 NPT X 6AN 90° Fitting	1	17680-S
(7)	3/8 NPT X 6AN Fitting	1	17987-S
(8)	1/4 NPT X 1/8 NPT Fitting	1	17000-S
(9)	6AN Nitrous Filter	1	15552-S
(10)	2-ft 6AN Hose	1	15410-S
(11)	Compressed Air On/Oil Valve	1	16149-S
(12)	N20 Control Valve Assembly		
(13)	4-ft 6AN Hose	1	15420-S
(14)	6AN Bottle Nut	1	16230-S
(15)	"326" to 6AN Adaptor	1	16235-S
(16)	4AN X 6AN adaptor	1	17060
(17)	1-ft 6AN Hose	1	15401
(18)	1-lt 4AN Hose	1	15210

Consists of On/Off TEE Valve P/N 16148-S (1), Nitrous Gauge P/N 15910-S (1), Brass TEE P/N 16777-S (1), 1/4 NPT X 1/8 NPT adaptor P/N 16784, and 6AN X 1/4 NPT adaptor P/N 17980-S (2).

TRANSFER PUMP

INSTALLATION

1. Select mounting location for transfer pump (1). Lowest point of transfer pump should be located above highest point of the tallest NOS nitrous bottle you intend to fill. Bolt pump securely in place.

2. Install bottle stand (2) on your nitrous oxide source bottle.

The bottle stand supplied is designed to work with #65 source bottles produced by Puritan-Bennett, which are commonly used for this operation. It is possible to use smaller nitrous oxide source bottles. To do so you must first determine if your source bottle has a siphon tube. If so, the bottle must remain upright to transfer properly. If it does not have a siphon tube, it must be inverted for proper transfer operation (the #65 Puritan-Bennet bottle does not have a siphon tube).

3. Install bottle nut (3) and washer (4) on the nitrous oxide source bottle.

4. Invert the nitrous oxide source bottle and place near the transfer pump.

Bottle must be near enough to the transfer pump for the 6-ft 6AN hose (5) to reach from the source bottles valve to the transfer pump.

5. Install the blue 1/4-inch NPT X 6AN 90°fitting(6) in the Transfer Pump N20 outlet port (labeled OUT).

6. Install the blue 3/8-inch NPT x 6AN fitting (7) in the Transfer Pump N20 inlet port (labeled "IN").

7. Install the blue 1/4-inch NPT x 1/8-inch NPT fitting (8) in the compressed air inlet port.

8. Connect the 6AN Nitrous Filter (9) outlet port to the 2-ft 6AN hose (10). Connect the open end of the 2-ft 6 AN 2 hose to the blue 3/8-inch NPT X 6AN fitting at the Transfer Pump inlet port.

9. Connect inlet port of the N20 filter to the nitrous oxide source bottle with the 6-lt 8AN hose (5).

10. Install compressed air on/off valve (11) in the 1/4-inch NPT X 1/8-inch NPT fitting at the compressed air inlet port.

11. Connect N20 control valve assembly (12) to the 1/4 NPT X 6AN 90°fitting at the Transfer Pump outlet port using 4-it 6AN hose (13).

If you desire to mount the compressed air on/off valve assembly remotely, or in a different orientation, 1/8-inch NPT adapters can be purchased at most local hardware or parts stores.

12. Connect 1-ft 6AN hose (17) to N_2O control valve (12) outlet.

TRANSFER PUMP OPERATION

1. Place the NOS cylinder you intend to fill on an accurate scale. Determine how much nitrous oxide is left in the cylinder. If there is only a small percentage left in the cylinder, open the valve and relieve all the pressure in the cylinder. If a cylinder-is more than 1/3 full is going to be 'topped off', it may be necessary in hot climates to place it in a refrigerator or freezer for a short period of time to cool it off to approximately 45° F. Lowering the temperature will also lower the bottle pressure and allow a complete fill. In areas where daytime temperatures exceed 80 degrees F, this method of cooling cylinders before filling may be necessary for all cylinders. regardless of whether they are full or empty.

2. Connect N_2O control valve assembly to the NOS cylinder to be refilled, using a 6AN Bottle Nut (14). Be sure to use a Teflon washer (4) between the NOS cylinder and the Bottle Nut.

If the cylinder being refilled is equipped with a 4AN fitting, use 4AN X 6AN adaptor fitting (16) and 1-ft 4AN hose (18).

If the cylinder being refilled is equipped with an old style valve, use the standard valve adaptor (15).

3, Place the NOS cylinder on the scale and note weight. There will be a slight weight increase due to the N_2O control valve assembly. This additional 'tare' weight must be added to the filled weight of the cylinder as stated on the cylinder label.

4. Close the shuff-off valve on the N_2O control valve assembly.

5. Fully open the valve on the nitrous oxide source bottle.

6. Fully open the valve on the N_2O cylinder to the filled.

7. Open the shut-off valve on the N_2O control valve assembly. Wait for the pressure in the source bottle and the NOS cylinder to equalize.

8. Slowly open the air pressure control valve on the compressed air on/off valve assembly. Watch the scale reading and close the air pressure control valve when the NOS cylinder reaches its full weight.

If the cylinder being refilled reaches 1100 psi before the full weight of the bottle is reached, stop the pump by turning off the compressed air valve. Invert, then fight the NOS cylinder, Repeat several times until you feel the bottle temperature drop. You can then turn the pump back

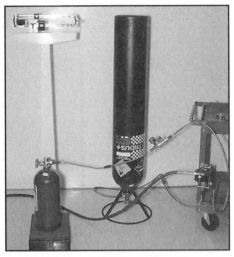

Never fill any NOS cylinder above the "FULL" weight as stated on the cylinder label as "Weight of Cylinder and Gas."

on and continue pumping.

9. Close the valve on the NOS cylinder.

10. Close the valve on the N_2O control valve assembly.

11. Carefully disconnect the 6AN transfer line from the NOS cylinder.

12. Close the valve on the nitrous oxide source bottle. Slowly open the valve on the N_2O control valve assembly.

BOTTLE WEIGHT CHART

The following is a list of the weights of NOS nitrous oxide cylinders.

Bottle Size	Weight Full (Pounds)	Empty (Pounds)
10 oz	2.0	2.6
2 lb	4.3 or 3.7	6.3 or 5.7
5 lb*	8.3 or 9.7	6.3 or 5.7
10 lb**	15.0, 14.7 or 13.6	25.0, 24.7 or 23.6
15 lb	23.9	38.9
20 lb	27.0	47.0

NOS has produced two different weight 5 lb bottles. Visually they appear the same. Regardless of what the bottle label says, always weigh the bottle completely empty to determine which unit you have before filling.

NOS has produced three different weight 10 lb bottles. The radiused neck bottle (6.2 inches in diameter) weighs 23.6 pounds full, The stepped neck bottle (6.2 inches in diameter) weighs 25.0 pounds full. The short, fat bottle (6.9 inches in diameter) weighs 24.7 pounds full.